THE ROAD TO
WOODSTOCK

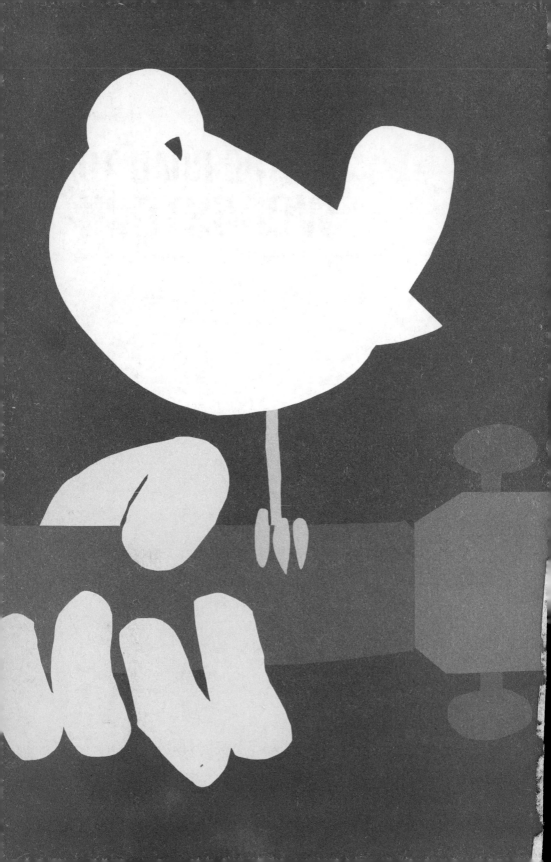

THE ROAD TO
WOODSTOCK

MICHAEL LANG

WITH

HOLLY GEORGE-WARREN

An Imprint of HarperCollinsPublishers

Grateful acknowledgment is made to reprint the following:

"Woodstock," words and music by Joni Mitchell. © 1968 (renewed) Crazy Crow Music. All rights administered by Sony / ATV Music Publishing, 8 Music Square West, Nashville, TN 37203. All rights reserved. Used by permission from Alfred Publishing Co., Inc.

HarperCollins books may be purchased for educational, business, or sales promotional use. For information, please write: Special Markets Department, HarperCollins Publishers, 10 East 53rd Street, New York, NY 10022.

FIRST EDITION

Designed by Suet Yee Chong

Library of Congress Cataloging-in-Publication Data is available upon request.

ISBN: 978-0-06-157655-3

09   10   11   12   13   WBC/RRD   10   9   8   7   6   5   4   3   2   1

For my wife Tamara and my children, LariAnn, Shala, Molly, Harry, and Laszlo, who fill my life with love.

And for my parents, Harry and Sylvia.

From a certain point onward there
is no longer any turning back.
That is the point that must be reached.

—KAFKA

CONTENTS

THE ROAD TO
WOODSTOCK

PROLOGUE

-- - -- --------------------------------

I t's 10 A.M., Monday, August 18, 1969: Jimi Hendrix is playing to a crowd of forty thousand. Another half million or so have left during the night. Many had to be at work; others had to return to worried families who'd heard conflicting reports about the chaos at Woodstock. As I watch from the stage, I see more and more people wandering away. Jimi notices too, and says, "You can leave if you want to. We're just jamming, that's all. You can leave, or you can clap." He looks up at the streaks of sun pouring through the clouds—some of the first rays we've seen in a while. "The sky church is still here, as you can see," he murmurs.

Those of us gathered around the perimeter of the stage are transfixed by Jimi and his band of gypsies. They've been up all night, or maybe longer—like many of us, who haven't slept more than a few hours in days. Jimi, dirt under his fingernails, still looking regal in his white fringed leather shirt. Teenaged percussionist Gerry Velez, dripping in sweat, thrashing the congas in a frenzy. Juma Sultan, shaking maracas and pounding out percussion with mallets, a dervish in purple. Jimi's old army buddies: guitarist Larry Lee, wearing a green fringed scarf as a headdress that covers his eyes, and Billy Cox, Jimi's steadfast anchor on bass, his head swathed in a multicolored turban. And the phenomenal Experience drummer Mitch Mitchell, in nearly constant motion.

Jimi apologizes for stopping to tune between songs: "Only cowboys stay in tune," he says with a laugh. One minute Jimi's joking with the audience, calling out to a "girl in yellow underpants" whom he tangled with the night before; next he's directing the band with a glance, an expression, a wave of the hand; then he's lost in the riff—his guitar taking him to places unknown. Back again, focusing on the small but enthusiastic crowd, Jimi addresses us with empathy and appreciation: "Y'all've got a lot of patience—three days' worth! You have proven to the world what can happen with a little bit of love and understanding and *sounds*!"

We are about to be "experienced" in something that will be unique in our lifetime: from "Voodoo Child" he veers into the melody of "The Star-Spangled Banner." Billy Cox and Larry Lee stand erect, as if at attention. As Jimi builds the song, adding feedback and distortion, I am carried away just as is everyone around me. I realize the national anthem will never be the same. Jimi has plugged into our collective experience: all the emotional turmoil and confusion we have felt as young Americans growing up in the sixties pours from the sound towers. His song takes us to the battlefield, where we feel the rockets and bombs exploding around us; to demonstrations and marches, confronting police and angry citizens. It's a powerful rebuke of the war, of racial and social inequity, and a wake-up call to fix the things that are broken in our society.

— — —

Listening to Jimi takes me back to a tiny nightclub in Manhattan's East Village where, as a sixteen-year-old Brooklyn kid, I watched John Coltrane play his horn. He took me on a trip, and like Hendrix, he was a revelation.

This whole journey—the festival and the road to it—has been marked by moments like these. What feels like a lifetime of near misses, small victories powered by an engine of committed and tireless individuals, serious optimism, and amazing ideas culminated in three days unlike any the world has seen before. I flash on Joan Baez standing in the rain, pregnant, just enjoying the moment; Jerry Garcia, hanging out at the free stage, sharing a joint with kids he's never met before; the lightning that split the skies at night; the Hog Farm passing out cups of granola to the folks entrenched at the foot of the stage, unwilling to leave their spots; Crosby, Stills and Nash harmonizing at 3:30 A.M. on "Suite: Judy Blue Eyes," the song that floored me months earlier and led me to book the then-unknown band; Pete Townshend knocking Abbie Hoffman in the head with his guitar; Sly Stone and his Family leading the entire congregation in an amazing call and response that left everyone higher.

Looking out at what's left of the audience, I see a lot of tired faces, the hard-core fans and those who just don't want to leave, ever.

I cross the stage and go over the footbridge to our trailer compound. I want a few minutes alone before dealing with the aftermath of this incredible weekend. I've slept a total of about six hours over the last four days and I'm starting to feel it.

My partners, John Roberts, Joel Rosenman, and Artie Kornfeld, have left for the city. I realize I have not seen and barely heard from Joel and John all weekend and wonder how things were for them. I know how things went for Artie. When he realized there was no way to keep an ocean of people from washing over the fences, that the tens of thousands coming to our little party were not going to buy tickets, Artie experienced a moment of panic. But he soon recovered, and between getting dosed with LSD, escorting artists onstage, and trying to convince them to be filmed, Artie had the time of his life.

It was the time of all our lives.

For me, Woodstock was a test of whether people of our generation really believed in one another and the world we were struggling to create. How would we do when we were in charge? Could we live as the peaceful community we envisioned? I'd hoped we could. From the beginning, I believed that if we did our job right and from the heart, prepared the ground and set the right tone, people would reveal their higher selves and create something amazing.

Woodstock came to symbolize our solidarity. That's what meant the most to me—the connection to one another felt by all of us who worked on the festival, all those who came to it, and the millions who couldn't be there but were touched by it. Over that August weekend, during a very tumultuous time in our country, we showed the best of ourselves, and in the process created the kind of society we all aspired to, even if only for a brief moment. The time was right, the place was right, the spirit was right, and we were right. What resulted was a celebration and confirmation of our humanity—one of the few instances in history, to my knowledge, when joy became big news.

On Max Yasgur's six hundred acres, everyone dropped their defenses and became a huge extended family. Joining together, getting into the music and each other, being part of so many people when calamity struck—the traffic jams, the rainstorms—was a life-changing experience. None of the problems damaged our spirit. In fact, they drew us closer. We recognized one another for what we were at the core, as brothers and sisters, and we embraced one another in that knowledge. We shared everything, we applauded everyone, we survived together.

Jimi finishes his set, and I leave my trailer and get on my bike to ride to the top of the bowl. It's a BSA Victor, notoriously difficult to start, but this morning it fires up on the first crank. As I ride through what has become a sea of mud, the smell of the recently deserted "city" rises up strong and fetid. When I crest the hill, I can see the crew clearing Jimi's gear and hundreds of people beginning to clean the devastated field of debris. The stage, where the beyond-exhausted crew is coiling cords and packing equipment, stands against a background of mottled brown. A huge expanse of white canvas flies above it in the wind, like some great sail ripped from its mast. It reminds me of the ship to never-never land. It has carried all of us through the greatest adventures and safely home again. Off in the distance, the lake that has been the source of most of our drinking water is visibly lower. Farther back on the surrounding hills, streams of people are leaving the campgrounds and moving toward their journey's end. Behind me, the concession stands are abandoned and stripped bare. Sanitation trucks and honeywagons are making their way up the now-passable roads, beginning to approach the site. The woods off to my left across Hurd Road still flash with colorful bits of cloth and paint from the markets that sprang up there.

I kill the engine and park myself in the remnants of a shredded lawn chair, surrounded by a muddied bedroll, a broken sandal, and a squashed canteen. Thinking back over the long weekend, I understand that we have all been tested, and we were not found wanting.

It was a strange, sometimes magical trip that led us here. Hundreds of people joined me on this odyssey and worked tirelessly, moving forward against what at times seemed like impossible odds.

I'm not sure where we will go from here. There will be financial problems and the fractured partnership of Woodstock Ventures needs attention—but for now, it's enough that Woodstock has happened.

Looking down the hill, I remember the moment on Friday when Richie Havens, a beacon of strength in his orange dashiki, hit the stage. He was the first act, simply because he and his band were there and ready. As we were coming over the bridge, there was a look of amazement and then a flash of fear in his eyes as he took in the unbelievably immense crowd—what looked like miles and miles of people.

"We're just coming home," I said.

Woodstock was an opportunity, a moment, a home we had all been waiting for and working toward. When Richie started singing, rhythmically attacking his acoustic guitar like it was a talking drum, I knew for the first time that we were going to be okay. The show was on and we were off and running. Everything we had been through for the past ten months had led to that moment, and I was overcome with joy.

Suddenly someone pulls up behind me in a pickup truck and I snap out of my reverie. "Michael! Artie just called and they need you down at Wall Street—*pronto!*"

one BROOKLYN

Sitting in the dark, smoky Five Spot club on the Bowery, in lower Manhattan, I watch John Coltrane travel out to the edge with his music. There is no net. He's trying to see where it all goes—letting it happen to him, his sax following what's inside him. He doesn't worry about where the music takes him or what's ahead. Knowing there's danger there, yet somehow it's going to be okay, that there's something incredibly exciting about being out there on that edge: It's the place to be. For me, as a sixteen-year-old kid from Brooklyn, this is a totally new concept. The idea of not having to stay within a form or follow the rules, but to improvise, work from internal inspiration, will serve as my own noninstruction instruction book.

Growing up in Bensonhurst in the late forties and fifties, I was surrounded by Jewish and Italian families. My parents, Harry and Sylvia Lang, were of Eastern European descent, and we lived modestly, like other middle-class families in the neighborhood. My father ran his own business, Lang Engineering, installing heating systems, and my mother kept the books. He was an inventor, and in his youth, my father designed a ballast system for navy submarines and a system to remove pollutants from smoke generated by coal-burning power plants. I always felt he would have led a really adventurous life if my older sister, Iris, and I hadn't come along.

My father always taught me to be self-reliant. That was his thing—just take care of it, no matter what. Early on, he gave me a strategy for getting out of tough situations: Take charge and keep moving; step back just enough to think clearly; and trust your instincts. That's how he dealt with things, and this would serve me well.

From the very beginning, my parents took on side ventures, with varying degrees of success, the coolest of which was a Latin nightclub on the Upper West Side called the Spotlight Club. In the 1950s, the mambo was king and musicians from Puerto Rico and Cuba drew big crowds. The Spotlight Club was a long, dark room with a bar spanning one wall, a large dance floor in the back, and a bandstand at the end of the bar. During the day, the interior looked pretty sad, but at night it was all sparkle and glamour. Downstairs, a huge basement ran the length of the place, and there the great bandleader Tito Puente stored some of his drums. Known as El Rey, he popularized the Latin music that would become known as salsa. I was only eleven or twelve and had just started playing drums myself when I met El Rey at the Spotlight Club. Handsome, with jet black hair, he encouraged me to play and even let me pound out a few rhythms on his set. In those years, one of his most popular numbers was "Oye Como Va"—which, a decade later, would become a hit for Santana after they performed at Woodstock.

The early rock and roll that emerged when I was a kid—Elvis Presley, Buddy Holly, Chuck Berry, Little Richard, Bill Haley and the Comets' "Rock Around the Clock"—made a big impression on me, as did the movie *Blackboard Jungle*, which introduced the song. Street-corner harmonizing was popular around my neighborhood, and I played stickball with a fantastic doo-wop singer who lived down the block.

The only one in my family to play an instrument, I was twelve when I joined a rock and roll band. It meant lugging my drum kit up endless flights of steps to perform at glamorous hot spots like the Jewish Community House on Bay Parkway. But it gave me a glimpse of the thrill that comes from connecting through music. I also played drums in the school band at Sethlow Junior High. Marching and uniforms were not for me, though. The first time I paraded with the school band on St. Patrick's Day, down Fifth Avenue, I took a quick left turn on Sixtieth Street and never looked back. That was my first *and* last parade.

Every summer, I'd go to camp in Sullivan County, ninety miles north of New York City, in the Catskill Mountains. I liked being out in nature, especially on horseback. My last year of camp, when I was eleven, I convinced a lazy stable hand to let me tend the horses and take campers on trail rides for him. He gave me a gorgeous paint named Bobby for the summer. Riding him bareback at a full gallop was the epitome of freedom. That summer, I also had my first-ever sexual encounter, in the barn with one of the counselors-in-training.

In the winter, our family would road-trip to Miami and in the fall head north to Canada, catching the changing of the leaves along the way. My parents loved taking Iris and me on these long drives. I shared my father's love of driving and he started showing me the ropes when I was ten or eleven. The day I got my learner's permit, he took me to Midtown Manhattan and made me drive home to Brooklyn through insane traffic. Soon after passing the driver's test, I bought a motorcycle. I was a little nuts. I'd lie down on the seat, which cuts the wind resistance, then open it up on the Belt Parkway. After a couple of years, I stopped riding on the street because I knew I'd kill myself, but the rush I got from racing was like an out-of-body experience, and it was a feeling I was always trying to recapture.

Not long after I turned fourteen, my friend Irwin Schloss and I tried pot for the first time. His older brother, Marty, who's now a radical rabbi in Israel (Marty bar-mitzvahed one of Bob Dylan's sons in the eighties), ran the Cauldron, a funky macrobiotic restaurant in the East Village that was way ahead of its time. Marty influenced us quite a bit. He was into Eastern philosophy, leading a very bohemian life, and one day he gave Irwin some pot. At that point, marijuana had already become associated with jazz musicians and the Beats but was not in the public eye. Irwin and I first lit up on a fall afternoon at Sethlow Park, just outside our junior high school. I actually remember my very first joint: It was rolled on yellow papers, and after the joint was lit, the marijuana seeds inside kept popping. This was long before hydroponics and the elimination of seeds.

At first I didn't get high. Marty had explained to Irwin how to inhale and hold it in. I don't recall how many tries before I finally did get high, but when it happened, I laughed for what seemed like hours. It was sort of *"Ah, now I get it!"* Irwin and I would get high and listen to music. We'd laugh and then we'd want to eat. Experimenting with pot, and later LSD, would take me further than any motorcycle or car I ever owned.

On weekends, I started buying nickel bags of marijuana, sold in little brown envelopes. I would hang out in my room, tune in to radio station WJZ on Friday nights, and listen to Symphony Sid, who turned me on to Charlie Parker, John Coltrane, Thelonious Monk, Miles Davis, Dizzy Gillespie, Max Roach, Celia Cruz. Sitting next to my open window, I'd light up a joint and exhale into the alley. I loved listening to jazz while stoned. Some nights, Symphony Sid would put out the word that he was getting sleepy and issue an invitation for listeners to stop by the station if they had something to keep him awake. He was eventually fired from WJZ after a marijuana bust.

I soon discovered that my friend Kenny, who had dropped out of school, was into pot. We'd go over to his house and get high. His parents were never around. One day I came home from Kenny's and my mother confronted me: While cleaning my closet, she'd discovered my stash, a couple of ounces. I didn't want to lose the pot, so I had to make my case quickly: I whipped out the *Encyclopaedia Britannica,* looked up *Cannabis sativa,* and stuck the scholarly article under her nose. I knew the description was pretty benign—I'd checked it out soon after I started smoking. In a matter-of-fact description, the encyclopedia stated very clearly that marijuana was nonaddictive. "I know what I'm doing," I told my mother. "It's a myth that pot leads to hard drugs. Smoking is fun and it helps me see things in a new way. And you know I don't drink any alcohol."

This conversation defused the situation enough so that when my father came home, we sat around the kitchen table and discussed it further. My parents turned out to be pretty reasonable. They weren't exactly thrilled with the idea but accepted that it wasn't harmful. After all, they'd lived through Prohibition—and my father had even briefly worked for bootleggers. In 1958–59, there was some antidrug propaganda at school like "Beware, marijuana is the first step down that road to drug addiction . . ." But the big antidrug campaigns hadn't started yet; authorities were still blaming comic books and rock and roll for juvenile delinquency.

When I was sixteen, I discovered LSD-25—the original pharmaceutical formula developed by Sandoz in Basel, Switzerland. In 1961, LSD was still pretty far off the radar. Timothy Leary hadn't yet started his "turn on, tune in, drop out" campaign, and the drug wouldn't become illegal for another five years. I really didn't know what to expect. I tripped for the first time at Kenny's house. He pulled out a little vial of a clear blue liquid. I can't remember how he got it or who gave him the instructions on how to take it. With a medicine dropper, I squirted a tiny amount onto a sugar cube, then popped it into my mouth, let it dissolve, and waited.

Everything became superclear, superreal. Every sense was heightened, and some senses went *beyond* being heightened. I'll never forget that feeling of everything coming into sharp focus. I loved listening to music on acid. You entered that world, whether it was jazz, classical, or Indian music, or, later on, psychedelic music like Hendrix or the Mothers of Invention—whatever the music was, it sort of ate you up. You *became* the music.

LSD opened my mind to a new way of thinking, and I started reading books like Hermann Hesse's *Siddhartha,* the writings of Kahlil Gibran, *The Doors of Perception* by Aldous Huxley (the book that would give Jim Morrison and Ray Manzarek's band their name). Suddenly, I was on a journey. Dropping acid meant putting yourself out on the edge, beyond your comfort zone and what you were used to. It seemed you gave up control of your mind to your spirit. From the first time I took acid, I felt I was opening a door between my subconscious and my conscious, between myself and the cosmos. I could look around at my whole person. I was connected to everything. When I was tripping, I was very comfortable being in that altered state. Sometimes people I was with would get a bit freaked out on acid, but I was always at ease with the sensations and could help bring them back to a good place. It was a learning experience—a revelation, never paranoia. I never had a bad trip.

The second or third time I dropped acid, my friends and I decided to ride the subway into Manhattan. Sitting by the train door, I watched the guy across from me turn into a rabbit. He began twitching his nose, then grew whiskers and ears. It didn't freak me out; I just took it all in. Arriving at Times Square about 4 A.M., we strolled through empty Manhattan canyons. I was so absorbed, the next thing I knew I looked around and was alone. My friends had vanished. After walking for what seemed like miles, I found myself in a deep forest. Sitting on a bench and communing with nature for hours and when I looked up the sun had risen. I noticed the Empire State Building looming overhead, jarring me back into the real world. It turned out I'd wandered into a small park by the Little Church Around the Corner, just off Fifth Avenue.

The summer after eleventh grade, I discovered Greenwich Village. I'd been there a few times with my family, going to *The Threepenny Opera* at a theater on Christopher Street, and just walking around. But in 1961, I met Kenny and his new girlfriend Kathy at a little place called the Village Corner and I was instantly taken with the neighborhood vibe, its culture, its people. With Kenny and Kathy was Pauline, a beautiful black woman in her mid-twenties. Kathy, a gorgeous red-head, shared an apartment with her at 500 West Broadway. Pauline and I hit it off. I ended up spending most of the summer with her, crashing at their apartment.

Pauline and Kathy were "working girls." Pauline didn't turn tricks, but operated as the madam. She did the booking, making appointments out of the West Broadway apartment. Pauline would drop the girls at various locations for their "dates." I really didn't think that much about what she did, it was just, this is her life and what she does to earn a living. I'd had a couple of other girlfriends, but being with Pauline was a very worldly experience. At night, she dressed elegantly, as the girls would then, in high heels and a tight-fitting cocktail dress, kind of high-class call-girl mode, quite elegant, never trashy. They had an upscale clientele of well-to-do businessmen, and their services were expensive, several hundred dollars. In those days, that was a lot of money.

The girls lived in a small square back building in the border area between the Village and what's now called SoHo, then still industrial, with warehouses just starting to be converted into artists' lofts. Pauline's apartment was quite bohemian: mattresses on the floor, candles burning, music always playing, dark scarves on the windows, scarves on lamps. We didn't hang out at the apartment very much except to sleep there. In the afternoons, Pauline, usually in a leotard and skirt and wearing a wig, would show me around the Village. At night, we'd start the evening at the Village Corner and then make the rounds, stopping in at the Village Gate or the Five Spot to hear some jazz. It was always fascinating to me how four or five musicians would lock into wherever they were going, improvising, with no map. Sometimes we'd end up in Harlem, checking out jazz and R & B clubs.

The whole world Pauline lived in fascinated me. The counterculture was developing out of what had been the Beat era, becoming the folk scene. It was inspiring being among photographers and painters, as well as fringe people and outsiders, pursuing their interests rather than marching in time with the status quo. People were starting little businesses that catered to the locals. In the East Village, on St. Mark's Place, A Different Drummer sold vintage clothes. People began to dress in a new way. I let my hair grow. The Village opened my eyes to a very appealing lifestyle, one completely different from what I knew in Bensonhurst.

After about two months, Pauline said she thought I was falling in love with her and that our thing wasn't meant to last. Pegging me for the innocent I was, she didn't want me to get too attached. It hurt, but she let me down with a lot of kindness. I never saw Pauline again, but the summer we spent together changed me. She opened doors that have never closed.

During my senior year of high school, thanks to Mr. Bonham, my student advisor, I was given the opportunity to start college early. New

York University accepted me to begin in January, as long as I finished high school at night. As 1962 started, I was heading back to the Village.

My parents were delighted about this series of events: College was always the objective for them, and in those days, NYU wasn't very expensive, and I could commute from Brooklyn. That summer I got a job at a funky boutique on Bleecker Street called the Village Cobbler. We sold oddball earrings, leather goods, crafts, and all kinds of other trappings. I liked being in the middle of the Village's unfolding folk scene. The music had really taken off, with a whole new generation of singer-songwriters testing the waters in Village clubs. Bob Dylan's first album had come out on Columbia, but he still sometimes performed around the neighborhood. I'd go to the coffeehouses and clubs that dotted Bleecker and MacDougal streets—the Café Wha?, the Bitter End, Gerde's Folk City, the Gaslight—and check out artists like Bob Gibson, Phil Ochs, Jack Elliott, Fred Neil, Dave Van Ronk. Washington Square Park was filled with pickers and bongo players, artists of all kinds and dealers galore. You could score grass around the clock.

In a tiny coffeehouse on MacDougal Street called Rienzi's, I would sit by the window and watch crazy, colorful characters walk by—not hippies yet, but some early freaks. I'd gotten a Super 8 camera and decided to make a documentary of Village street life. I started filming what was to be called *A View from Rienzi's* but never finished it.

Before turning eighteen in December, I got my notice to register for the draft. In 1962, Vietnam was still an undeclared war, but the situation there was escalating. In my opinion, the U.S. had no reason to get involved in a conflict that had been going on in Southeast Asia for forty years. I had nothing against the Vietnamese. I saw a psychiatrist for three weeks in the hopes of getting a medical note recommending a deferment. The doctor could see I had no respect for authority and that I would never fire on another human being simply because I was ordered to do so. He wrote a letter of assessment saying I was not a good candidate for the military. I thought everything was set for me to get a pass, but instead I received a notice to show up for my physical at Borough Hall, in Brooklyn.

Going through the whole process and undergoing tests and assorted examinations, I kept waiting for them to pull me out of line and say, "You're not what we're looking for." But that didn't happen. Finally, despite the uniformed officers trying to usher us along, I ducked out of formation. I ran downstairs to look for the psych's office. I walked in and blurted out, "Listen, I don't know if you looked at my paperwork, but you really don't want me in the army." I sat down with the shrink and we talked it through. I told him I was against the war on moral grounds, that I didn't believe in killing. This was still so early in the Vietnam conflict that the U.S. military wasn't desperate for troops. They would be in four or five years, when getting drafted was nearly inescapable. After a long discussion, the doctor gave me a deferment.

That was the last I heard from the selective service. I'd avoided being forced to fight in a war I didn't believe in. I had no idea that by the end of the decade, there would be millions of like-minded kids at Woodstock taking the same stand for peace.

MICHAEL LANG

two THE GROVE

As rain pelts the roofless stage, the crowd is turning ugly, with tempers rising as high as Miami's humidity. A few jerks start lobbing Coke bottles and rocks, and angry demands for music ring out. I can't put any of the electric acts onstage, though a madman British vocalist announces that his band, the Crazy World of Arthur Brown, would like to perform and hopefully experience electrocution. "It would be beautiful!" he insists. I'm thinking the sight of Arthur frying would not be beautiful.

What we need is a powerful acoustic act.

Just as the rain subsides and the crew starts clearing water from the stage—a pair of flatbed trailers—I spot John Lee Hooker, cool as ever, smoking a cigarette, sitting backstage waiting for his slot. He's my man.

Twenty minutes later, the fifty-year-old blues veteran has them eating out of his hand. He's probably performed under worse conditions. Porkpie hat pulled low, shades still on, he growls his signature "Boogie Chillun" and pounds out the beat on his guitar. He follows that with an improvised talking blues about playing in the rain. The audience is mesmerized. I'm

struck by the power of music to reach into people and change them. At the
end of the set, a girl climbs onstage and lays a bouquet of flowers at John
Lee's feet.

In the spring of 1964, I transferred to the University of Tampa, which turned out to be a town full of astronauts and not much else. I lasted only six months. It was just too straight, too uptight. I moved back to New York and returned to NYU, but continued to make trips to Florida. A friend from Bensonhurst, Bob West, and I would drive south to Miami. Traveling through the South with New York plates could be scary back then. Freedom Riders journeying from the North to help register black voters and fight for civil rights often ran into trouble. My sister was among the activists: When Iris got her law degree, she and her attorney husband, Paul Brest, spent nearly two years in Mississippi, working for the Legal Defense Fund to help enable school desegregation.

Down South, most Northerners—especially longhairs—were looked upon with suspicion. On one trip, when Bob and I were driving a Corvette to Florida, we stopped in South Carolina at a luncheonette. Our hair was pretty long at that point. We sat down at the counter, and while ordering coffee, we noticed a sign on the milk machine that read: THE EYES OF THE KU KLUX KLAN ARE UPON YOU. Not really thinking about where we were, we cracked up, which caught the attention of some of the customers. The place heated up quickly, and like in a movie, we ran to our car, a bunch of local boys at our heels. They jumped in a pickup and gave chase, but our Vette easily outran them.

During one of those trips, Bob and I ended up in Coconut Grove, a lazy tropical community just south of Miami. Close to the University of Miami campus, it had an artsy, laid-back vibe, the kind of place where dogs lie down and sleep in the middle of the road. Coconut

Grove was a great revelation to me—it seemed like the perfect place to live.

In late 1965, during my fall semester at NYU, I realized I was done with school. I decided to move to Miami and open a head shop. Having seen my parents take on new businesses, whether they knew that particular line or not, I thought, Why not? I could learn on my feet, like they had. "School is not happening for me," I told them. "I want to get out into the world." As usual, they were wary but supportive. I left NYU that semester and spent the spring developing ideas, making contacts, and figuring out just what the head shop was going to be. I sold a little pot to get by, and I had a bank account with four or five thousand dollars in it, mostly made up of my bar mitzvah money and earnings from odd jobs. That gave me enough to buy merchandise, rent a space, and set up a shop.

During my last semester at NYU, I'd reconnected with Ellen Lemisch; we'd originally met as kids at her father's optometrist shop. Ellen and her identical twin lived in a huge Upper West Side apartment. They rented out rooms, and the place became a crossroads of ideas, with interesting people constantly coming and going. A kind of countercultural salon, there the energy was nonstop. Ellen and I fell in love, and she decided to move to Florida with me. She knew lots of artisans and craftsmen who were creating little stash boxes and all sorts of beautiful things for heads. We started collecting them for the shop.

In the East Village, Jeff Glick, a very hip entrepreneur, had opened the Headshop. Located on East Ninth Street, it was the first of its kind, selling rolling papers, pipes, and other things for heads. Jeff stocked his store with Peter Max's early posters and other psychedelic art. Peter's art was famous as a pop phenomenon. A very generous guy, Jeff showed me the ropes of the business and also introduced me to Peter. When I told Peter my plans, he invited me to his Upper West Side apartment to pick out posters for my own store. I guess he was expecting a big order and rolled out dozens of posters. But, with my minuscule budget, I chose only six. It didn't faze him, thankfully, and we immediately became close friends—a friendship that's lasted to this day.

Ellen and I got a roomy drive-away car, packed everything up, and took off for Miami. In the fall of '66, after searching in vain for a space in Coconut Grove, we found a vacant store in South Miami near the University of Miami. The Head Shop South opened on Sunset Boulevard with rock and roll in the streets. I booked a local band to play and the place was mobbed. The kids in South Florida still looked pretty straight—not a lot of longhairs like in New York and San Francisco—but they were eager to check us out. Unfortunately, so were the chief of police and Wackenhut agents—a notorious private security force that operated like the DEA. On opening day, they showed up, looked around, and the next day shut us down for operating without a license. It was a very conservative right-wing community and we were not exactly their cup of tea.

I took my case to court. During the packed hearing, filled with hostile citizens and a few freaks, a professor from the University of Miami got up to speak in support of my rights. He got carried away and consequently completely buried me. My application for a license was turned down flat. Before I had a chance to appeal, the police chief— originally from the Bronx—called, and we had a very direct off-the-record conversation. "Look," he said, "this is not New York. This is the conservative South, and they'll never let you open in a place like this."

I took his advice and looked again in the Grove to see if a location had opened up. Ellen and I moved into a motel on Bayshore Drive and eventually rented an old wooden bungalow on Twenty-seventh Avenue from a saxophone player named Twig. The Grove was a fascinating mix of tycoons living on gorgeous estates in South Grove and outsiders—artists, craftsmen, musicians, fishermen, smugglers, and a sprinkling of hippies. Folk music could be heard at the Gaslight, opened by Sam Hood, son of the owner of New York's Gaslight. The reclusive genius Fred Neil, a native Floridian, had returned to the Grove after living in New York and making a stir in the Village. He was a magnet to singer-songwriters like David Crosby, who often traveled to the Grove to play the Gaslight and hang out with Fred.

Situated on Biscayne Bay, the Grove was as relaxed as South Miami was uptight. In the heart of the Grove, I found a large white-washed cottage with a porch surrounded by windows where we could display posters. Among my neighbors were Adam Turtle's woodworking shop, the Ludicios Leather Shop, the studios of sculptors Lester Sperling, Michael "Michelangelo" Alocca, David Dowes, and Grail Douglas and painter Tony Scornavacca. The Grove was also home to Dr. John Lilly's Dolphin Research Center, set up in an old bank building in the center of town. Lilly's early research on communicating with dolphins included giving them LSD. He eventually began tripping with them in a saltwater tank built into the main vault of the building.

Having lost my deposit and rent on the South Miami shop, I had expended all my funds. I called my parents and told them I needed a loan, and they agreed with no questions asked. My father arranged for my uncle Sam, my mother's brother who lived in Miami, to give me $3,500, which my father would reimburse. Sam was beside himself—he could not believe my father was doing this: "What are you, crazy? A *head shop*?"

This time, before opening, I applied for and received a license to operate a "gift shop." Bob West helped Ellen and me with the store in the beginning. The shop had five rooms, where we displayed our merchandise: glass cases filled with all kinds of smoking paraphernalia, including a variety of rolling papers, Turkish hookahs, and exotic pipes. The poster market had exploded in 1966 and we plastered the walls and ceilings with black-and-white posters of pop-culture icons like the Marx Brothers, Marlon Brando in *The Wild One,* Allen

Ginsberg, Bob Dylan, and Lenny Bruce. In addition to Peter Max's posters, we carried the San Francisco artists who created the fantastic handbills for the Fillmore and Family Dog shows. Beaded curtains hung in front of open doorways, and in some rooms strobe lights flickered and black lights glowed, adding a purple hue. We played records nonstop—the Beatles, the Stones, the Mothers of Invention, Dylan, the Byrds. On weekends we did great business. Friday nights were party time, and we'd stay open until midnight. The shop became the gathering place for a growing counterculture in Miami.

When the store was closed, we'd go sailing or hang out at various friends' places, cook, listen to music, and get high. I'd bought an old VW van, which was perfect for cruising around the Grove. The safari front windows would open out, and we'd take midnight mystical excursions. We would drop acid, get really stoned, and head out to the water or the electric power plant and watch the lights.

I continued to use acid as a tool to explore. An educational experience, it expanded my awareness, and I found a very clear spiritual path. I liked taking people on trips and guiding them. I'd play certain records to create a musical journey. In the beginning, it was jazz albums; then it became the great Indian sitar player Ravi Shankar and Frank Zappa and the Mothers of Invention.

Eventually, things fell apart between Ellen and me, and she moved back to New York. After a few months, I started seeing Sonya Michael, a local artist. She was a beautiful blonde and in her late twenties. Sonya shared a painting studio with another artist and musician named Don Keider. DK, who played vibes and drums, eventually would be the link between me and my future Woodstock partner Artie Kornfeld. Sonya, DK, and I started a poster company together called Sodo (short for Sonya and Don) Posters. They created gorgeous artwork for black-light posters with names like "Speed," "Lucy in the

Sky," "Mushroom Mountain," and "The Trip." They sold well and we began shipping them to other head shops around the country.

A real scene developed around the shop, and in 1967 an underground newspaper called the *Libertarian Watchdog* set up operations in the back of the store. It didn't take long for the cops to come around. The police had been hassling me for a while, giving my customers tickets for the slightest things, like jaywalking. It got even worse after the shop and I were featured on a local TV news special called "Marijuana in Miami." An exposé on youthful drug use in Dade County, it aired on June 13, 1967. They filmed at my shop, and, looking about sixteen on camera, I explained how some of our merchandise could help recreate a psychedelic experience. Some of the pot-smoking interviewees were darkly lit to protect their identities. But I felt we were spearheading a movement in the South, and I wanted to let people know about the shop and what we had to offer.

Soon the shop had a squad of motorcycle cops all its own. They would park on our corner every Friday and Saturday night, writing whatever tickets they could and, whenever possible, arresting me. This went on for several months and after a while I became pretty good friends with several of them. These were decent guys, about my age, and eventually their curiosity got the better of them and we began to talk. One of them, "Bob the Cop," would later show up to work at Woodstock.

The local politicos became intent on putting a stop to the use of grass, and they hatched a plan for a massive bust all over Coconut Grove. Thanks to a friend who worked in the attorney general's office, we found out about their plans well in advance, including a search-warrant list of about ninety names and addresses. My shop wasn't on it, but it included my house on Twenty-seventh Avenue, where I'd hosted the occasional party.

At the time, I had already made plans to move into a house in the lushly tropical South Grove, where the air is heavy with the scent of jasmine. I'd rented a beautiful Spanish-style adobe house there owned by an old Southern aristocrat named Mary Whitlock. By the time of the massive sweep, I'd moved everything into my new place, except for a few items I'd left behind to "entertain" the cops the night of the planned bust: When they arrived at my Twenty-seventh Avenue address, warrant in hand, they found a record player blasting music and strobe lights flashing nonstop.

We had gotten word to others on the warrant list too, so everyone's houses were free of contraband, and no one was around to be served with a warrant. While dozens of cop cars bivouacked in the Florida Pharmacy parking lot to head out for a night of arrests, we were all cycling along the streets of Coconut Grove. It was the Keystone Cops rather than *Dragnet*: As a line of police cars raced through the Grove in one direction, an equal number of long-haired cyclists would whiz past them, going the opposite way. They managed to arrest only the two or three people who didn't get the message.

With the Head Shop South becoming the hub of the Miami underground, I focused on bringing more music to the area. Everyone wanted to see the bands whose albums we were listening to. The first be-in, featuring the Grateful Dead, had taken place in January '67 at Golden Gate Park in San Francisco, and soon be-ins were occurring in New York's Central Park too. I organized a gathering of the tribes for our own little park in the Grove. Some local bands performed, and we got a good turnout. People with acoustic guitars sat around and played; incense and smoke filled the air.

Most of the touring bands from New York and California played a large rock club in Miami called Thee Image. The biggest acts performed at Dinner Key Auditorium, located in what was originally a Pan Am seaplane hangar on the waterfront in the Grove. That venue would later ban rock bands, after Jim Morrison was arrested for allegedly exposing himself onstage during a Doors concert there in March '69. In late 1967, I started promoting a few shows at an outdoor amphitheater on Key Biscayne. The acts included Ravi Shankar, who'd been a sensation at the Monterey Pop Festival in June. I looked for interesting places to hold concerts, including the Seminole Indian reservation in the Everglades, where you could smoke pot without being hassled by the police. I met with tribal elders to discuss the possibility. They liked the idea, but we couldn't work out the timing.

Anyone involved in the underground—from Timothy Leary to Jerry Garcia—would stop by my shop when in Miami. One December day, Paul Krassner, the publisher of *The Realist,* dropped in. I'd met him in New York a couple of years before when I took his class "From Mickey Mouse to the Green Berets" at the New School for Social Research. With him was Captain America himself, Abbie Hoffman. Abbie introduced himself and we connected right away. He had a great sense of humor and was committed to spreading the counterculture and infiltrating the mainstream. He and Paul dreamed up the Yippies, or Youth International Party, while they were hanging out in the Keys. Abbie and I would cross paths again in New York, and he'd eventually play an important role at Woodstock.

ABBIE HOFFMAN: I first met Michael Lang about a year before [Woodstock]. He was running a paraphernalia shop in Coconut Grove. After a speech down there, I hung around a few more days because it was warm and I was writing *Revolution for the Hell of It* . . . He told me that he had this idea—a floating, free idea—for a festival. It seemed like a little head-shop owner from Coconut Grove might be having a reverie but wouldn't have the actual vision to put together something like, well, what I think is the greatest cultural event of the century. But he did.

Another intriguing scene in Miami surrounded the Seaquarium, home to the various bottlenose dolphins that played Flipper on the weekly TV show. Their trainer, Richard O'Barry, would become a pioneer in animal rights. A sort of mystic when it came to dolphins, Ric had become aware of dolphins' intelligence and their desire to communicate. After Cathy, one of the dolphins that played Flipper, became depressed and "committed suicide," Ric had an epiphany. Realizing that it was inhumane to hold dolphins captive in tanks, he began a lifelong crusade to free them. Ric and Fred Neil became close friends, and Fred was convinced he could communicate with dolphins through music. Many of Fred's friends came to Coconut Grove to hang out with Fred and the dolphins.

RIC O'BARRY: I remember watching Fred with his head under the water with bubbles coming out all around, trying to sing to the dolphins underwater. He would also play his twelve-string guitar. The dolphins would come up and tap the guitar when he played certain chords. Fred always said it was the tone that attracted them. He would bring his friends to play music for the dolphins—Joni Mitchell, Ramblin' Jack Elliott, David Crosby, and several other far-out people. People were wondering what all these longhairs were doing, tripping around the grounds.

Ric and I were neighbors and became friends. Inspired by what had happened the year before at Monterey, we decided to put on Florida's first-ever music festival. We wanted to present a diverse lineup in an outdoor setting over the course of multiple days, much like Monterey. My kitchen became our office and we formed a partnership called Joint Productions, along with a drummer named James Baron and my friend and attorney Barry Taran. In April, after the Grateful Dead played three nights at Thee Image, the club's owner, a slightly shady character named Marshall Brevitz, called to say he wanted in on the festival too.

We looked for sites and chose Gulfstream Race Track, in neighboring Hallandale. Ringed with palm trees, it was one of South Florida's oldest horse-racing tracks, the site of the Florida Derby, and had a mile-long dirt track and a grass infield, as well as grandstands for seating. We came to an agreement with the Gulfstream management just as racing season ended in late April. Marshall Brevitz could put up his end of the money only if we held the concert within three weeks, so we picked May 18 and 19 as the dates. He suggested I see Hector Morales, a booking agent at William Morris in New York, so I flew north to meet him.

"You want to put on a show of that size in three weeks?" Hector repeated when I explained that I wanted to sign six or seven big-name artists to perform for an audience of twenty-five thousand. "You're nuts!" But as we talked a while longer, I convinced him to help. We managed to sign an impressive roster of talent: John Lee Hooker, Chuck Berry, the Mothers of Invention (led by Frank Zappa), Blue Cheer, the Crazy World of Arthur Brown, and the Jimi Hendrix Experience. Hendrix had been touring the United States that spring and this would be a last-minute final show. We rounded out the bill with some local groups: a Latin-tinged pop-rock band from Tampa, the Blues Image; a Miami free-jazz combo, the Charles Austin Group; and a garage band called the Evil.

We had to scramble for sound equipment and staging. Because of the time crunch, I decided on flatbed trucks that could be rolled onto the racetrack. The idea was to create a series of three separate stages lined up so we could rotate setting up and breaking down equipment. That way, one band could quickly follow the next.

For sound, we turned to Miami's venerable Criteria Studio, then known mainly for recording jazz and R & B artists but where the

Grateful Dead had just cut a few songs. It was the major recording studio in the South at the time and would later become famous as the studio responsible for Derek and the Dominos' *Layla* and the Allman Brothers' *Eat a Peach*. DK introduced me to Criteria's recording engineer Stanley Goldstein—who not only helped us pull this off but would become a major player in putting together the team for Woodstock. Ric and I met with Stan at Criteria to determine what we'd need for the festival.

We lucked out in that Mack Emerman, head of Criteria, trusted us with their equipment and gave Stan the green light to work on the festival. Stan's ability to improvise impressed me. A quick study, he was not afraid to try something new. I also met Bob Dacey, a filmmaker willing to shoot the festival on spec. With the lineup finalized just days before the festival, we didn't have much time for promotion. We quickly created a few versions of festival posters, some featuring a portrait of Hendrix, to distribute around town. Tickets cost $5, with an afternoon and evening show slated for both Saturday and Sunday. We also rented out booths to various vendors to sell assorted psychedelia.

My father came down the day before the festival opened, and I took him out to the track and explained what we were up to. He soon got to the bottom line: "How do you think you guys will do financially?" he asked. I answered by pointing over to the betting windows. We both laughed.

May 18 was magical. About twenty-five thousand people turned out and settled on blankets in the grass or perched on the stands, facing the stages set up on the western end of the track. The music started around noon. A handful of freaks, looking like they could have been from New York or San Francisco, were scattered among the crowd, but much of the audience looked like straight college kids. The *Fort Lauderdale News* had a field day, running an article entitled FLOWER CHILDREN STRANGELY MANNERLY: REPORTER RUBS ELBOWS WITH WEIRDOS: "Call them hippies, flower children or whatever, this generation has much to its credit. They are gentle people, likable, polite to strangers and to each other. I spoke briefly with the most sloppily dressed, with the longest hair, and with the weirdos. All were pleasant, well mannered, gentle spoken. And all agreed they were there to hear the music they like the most and to see others of their ilk."

The paper's basically positive stance was the opposite of the *Miami Herald*'s, which warned that hippies in the neighborhood could wreck an area's real estate value and was quick to report on the few thefts that occurred at the festival—eight-track players and tapes stolen from cars.

Most acts performed two sets, except for Hendrix. Jimi and the band had missed their pickup at the airport, and while the Mothers of Invention played, we realized that Hendrix was overdue. In a panic, we paged the Experience's tour manager Gerry Stickells at Miami International Airport and found out that they'd missed their pickup. So we chartered a helicopter to ferry them to the show. Soon we heard the whir of blades overhead. Jimi, Noel Redding, and Mitch Mitchell landed in spectacular fashion just beyond the stage. I don't know who was more ecstatic—me or the crowd. Dressed in a white ruffled shirt and a black fedora, Hendrix played a blistering set. As I watched from the scaffolding that evening, everyone in the audience looked totally engrossed and amazed by what was coming off the stage. I found out later that the Experience was *experiencing* STP:

MITCH MITCHELL: This guy comes along to give us some extra energy, but it turned out to be some sort of hallucinogen. I looked up and saw the guy who gave us the powder in a lighting tower about twenty feet above the stage. Suddenly I was on the same level as him, looking down at this empty shell, playing the drums. Obviously, the powder wasn't what we thought. I looked across and there's Jimi up here with me and we kind of look at each other and nod . . . it was straight out of *The Twilight Zone*.

As with most of the performances, Jimi's was recorded: For years, "Foxey Lady," "Fire," "Hear My Train a Comin'," and "Purple Haze" have floated around on bootleg recordings. On the Internet, fans still rave about the show: "the most mysterious and fascinating JHE gig," "the greatest set I ever saw from anyone ever." In addition to the documentary footage, ABC had been following Hendrix around and shot some of the performance. Linda Eastman (later McCartney), a good friend of Jimi's, took some great photographs of the Experience, and Hendrix's sound engineer Eddie Kramer (who would later record the Woodstock performances in '69) shot some of the festival too. Decades later, the Petersen Museum in L.A. exhibited the Stratocaster Jimi played, which ended up with Frank Zappa that day. He got it, he said, after Hendrix broke its neck, doused it with lighter fluid, set it ablaze, and threw it off the stage. Frank replaced the guitar's melted pick guard and broken neck and played it for years.

The show on Saturday ended with a fantastic fireworks display—the finale was a spectacular peace sign lighting up the sky. Things seemed too good to be true. They were. Because South Florida had been suffering through a lengthy drought, with no sign of precipitation, we decided to forgo expensive rain insurance. Unbeknownst to us, on Saturday, officials had ordered the clouds seeded over the Everglades. The result was a monsoon on Sunday—torrential downpours, hail, lightning, and fifty-mile-an-hour winds. Four inches of rain fell through the day and night, which cut attendance way down. Adding to our problems, it turned out that counterfeiting of tickets took a chunk out of our gate both days. On Sunday, we got two or three acts on early and then it just went completely to shit. Dark clouds threatened the Mothers of Invention's set, and Zappa recommended the covered grandstand to the audience, in case it poured, but—"Of course, if sitting in the rain is your thing, well then, just groove."

No grooving for us. We had to stop the music while waiting for a break in the downpour. Hours passed, and a guy climbed up on the empty stage and tried to incite the drenched audience to riot. Before putting John Lee Hooker onstage, I had to get $750 in cash from the box office to pay him. When I opened the door, I discovered a nasty standoff in progress. John Ek, our head of security, was threatening the Brink's driver who'd arrived to pick up the gate proceeds. A heavy-handed character, Ek was famous for having invented the Ek Commando Knife, which he would describe at the drop of a hat. It's a long, thin knife, very narrow at the hilt, so when you stick it into someone, you can break off the blade. Ek figured we were in financial trouble because of the rain and demanded to be paid before any cash left the premises. The Brink's guard, whose mission was to collect the box office receipts and transport the cash box to the bank, was not about to back down. They were yelling at each other, with me in the middle; then both sides went for their guns. I was petrified, but I knew there was a possibly more dangerous situation brewing outside. I instinctively tried to change the energy in the room.

"Hold it right there!" I shouted as I put my hands up. "This is still our money and nobody is taking anything anywhere until I get some music on. I'll be back and we'll work this out." While they were absorbing this new information, I grabbed the cash and rushed to find John Lee. He took the stage and played that remarkable set, and I returned to the box office to work out a compromise.

STAN GOLDSTEIN: Michael cooled that scene down. It was close to the O.K. Corral. On that day when everything was falling apart, Michael simply shone, and that was the beginning of my respect for Michael in those kinds of difficult circumstances. He kept his head. He continued to function. He did the best he could, which was often quite spectacular. When everyone around him in his organization was failing, Michael dealt with situations as they arose and as they had to be addressed, whereas everyone else was running, hiding, disappearing, panicking, and so forth.

Though there was a respite during John Lee's set, the rain never really let up. The last act of the day, the (very) Crazy World of Arthur Brown, finally got to go on. They more than lived up to their name, and at the end of their big psychedelic hit "Fire," Arthur kicked the organ off the stage. I later found out that, in the wee hours of the morning, he set out for Fort Lauderdale on foot. After the concert, several of the bands went back to their hotel to party at the bar.

NOEL REDDING: The Miami Pop Festival gig we did was excellent, and when the second day's show was rained out, Jimi and I headed to the hotel for a jam and general craziness with Arthur Brown, [club owner and artist manager] Steve Paul, the Mothers of Invention, and Blue Cheer.

EDDIE KRAMER: "Rainy Day, Dream Away" was written [by Jimi] in Miami, I'll never forget. It was in the back of a car. We were pulling away from Gulfstream Park . . . It was a torrential rainstorm, and then he started to write it right there.

Our headaches continued after the show, since Joint Productions owed a lot of people money that we didn't have. Stan probably knew we weren't going to be able to pay Criteria what we owed, but he continued to work his ass off.

STAN GOLDSTEIN: We had set up all of the catering in one of the trucks, which was also the truck in which I had placed my personal tools. When the Hendrix people decided he couldn't play because of the rains, they threw all of Jimi's equipment into that truck and took off—disappeared. I had no idea that that had happened. After the show, I began looking for the truck with my tools, because I needed them to disassemble all the equipment, and it had simply disappeared. We didn't find it until a couple of days later—at the

Miami International Airport, sealed up. I opened the back door of the truck, and there was this horrific stench. The truck had sat in the sun containing all the deli platters that we'd purchased to feed everyone—coleslaw, potato salad, corned beef and pastrami. That was all there was in the truck. My tools vanished with Jimi.

In the wake of the festival, we had to deal with numerous unpaid bills. We never got to take possession of the festival recordings and footage. They were held by the parties who made them until we could pay for them—which we couldn't. They gradually disappeared over the years. Part of the Mothers of Invention set turned up on their 1969 album, *Uncle Meat*. Zappa helped the Blues Image get a record deal, and they hit with "Ride Captain Ride." Lead guitarist Mike Pinera went on to join Iron Butterfly, and percussionist Joe Lala became a top L.A. session guy, playing with Crosby, Stills, Nash and Young and others. The Jimi Hendrix Experience flew to New York, where they recorded the gorgeous "Rainy Day, Dream Away" for *Electric Lady-land*, released later in the year. As for us, our attorney advised us to declare bankruptcy. We met at Criteria with Mack, Stan, and other creditors and gave them the bad news.

STAN GOLDSTEIN: Michael showed up and there was unhappiness, disgruntlement on the creditors' part. Michael said that they were going to do the very, very best they could to honor all the debts and obligations and pointed out that the recordings might have some value. He was cool, and so that was yet another moment at which a relationship was forged between Michael and me, because I was, by default, the lead player for the debtors' group. And Michael was the lead player for the promoters' group. After the Miami Pop Festival, Michael promoted some additional concerts. One of them was at Miami Marine Stadium, for which Criteria provided sound. But I wouldn't turn the sound on until I got money.

RIC O'BARRY: We tried to make it up by putting on a show with the Byrds and Steppenwolf later on at the Miami Marine Stadium. It started raining again, and it rained for forty days. I lost a fortune—all the money I had saved from the *Flipper* TV series. Michael packed up without a dime and went back to New York.

All around us, the Grove was changing: Police continued to hassle hippies, rents and condos were going up, the old wooden houses were being torn down, and head shops were proliferating. Broke and a bit burned out on South Florida, I thought it was time to head back to New York. Ninety miles north of the city, Woodstock had become a magnet for musicians. I remembered its small-town, artsy vibe from when we used to visit there in the fifties. The town had a history of attracting artists and bohemians. My girlfriend Sonya and I decided to check it out for ourselves.

three WOODSTOCK, NEW YORK

Lying on a blanket under the stars and listening to loud rock and roll, I feel like I'm in paradise. A woman with long red hair belts out the blues with a voice that's bigger than she is. "Who's that?" I ask the guy sitting next to me.

"Ellen McElwaine," he says, while handing me a hefty joint. "Jimi Hendrix used to back her up at the Café Wha. She moved to Woodstock from the city with her new band, Fear Itself. She's got the best voice in town and plays killer slide guitar."

Several hundred people sprawl in the grass—some have bedrolls and lean-tos set up next to VW vans. Aromatic smoke wafts through the breeze. I've heard about how cool the weekly Saturday Soundouts are, and now I see why everyone in Woodstock raves about them. The best-kept secret on the East Coast, the rural setting is key: a grassy meadow off a winding country road ten minutes outside town. The Soundout embodies the kind of laid-back feeling we tried to create in Miami. This is the way to

hear music, I think, surrounded by rolling hills and farmlands, under a
big sky.

On the surface, Woodstock, in the late summer of '68, hadn't changed much since I'd visited there as a kid: a quaint village nestled in the arms of lush green and blue mountains. Sonya and I checked into the Millstream Motel—the only one in town—and started exploring. By the next day, a Realtor had found us a beautiful red converted barn on a quiet lane called Chestnut Hill Road. The same sparkling stream that meandered by the motel ran alongside our new home. The serenity was awe inspiring.

Along Tinker Street, Woodstock's picturesque "downtown," stood a hardware store, art galleries, cafés, and eclectic shops. Our favorite was the Juggler, an emporium of art supplies, books, guitar strings, and records. The owners, Jim and Jean Young, had moved to the East Coast from Berkeley. About fifteen years older than me, they were open-minded music fans who took us under their wings.

At night, a goodly number of Woodstock's three thousand residents ventured out for a bit of music making and partying at Café Espresso, Deanie's, the Elephant, and the Sled Hill Café. The towns-folk were a combination of "descendants of Dutch settlers and successive waves of artists, craftspeople, dancers, musicians, urban dropouts, and rebels looking for a green alternative to Greenwich Village," as described by Dylan biographer Robert Shelton. The village had long been populated by this blend of workaday, rural folk and free-spirited bohemians. Originally farmed by the Dutch in the mid-1700s, the eastern Catskills area had been nurturing artists for more than sixty years. In 1903, a trio of utopians—wealthy Englishman Ralph White-head, writer Hervey White, and artist Bolton Brown—settled in Woodstock to pursue philosopher John Ruskin's stance against rampant industrialization. On 1,200 acres, in the shelter of Overlook Mountain, they created the Byrdcliffe Arts Colony to pursue the ideals of the arts-and-crafts movement. White moved to nearby Glenford and founded the Maverick Colony, where performing arts and music were the focus. In 1912, a branch of New York City's Art Students League set up a summer program, and some painters and sculptors stayed on in town.

By the 1920s, there were bacchanalian fêtes, with eccentric celebrants wearing handmade costumes for all-night revelry. A flyer for the first annual Maverick Festival, held in August 1915, promised: "wild sports going on" and the dancer Lada, who "illumines beautiful music like poems, and makes you feel its religion . . . you cry, it is so exquisite to see . . . All this in the wild stone-quarry theater, in the moonlight, with the orchestra wailing in rapture, and the jealous torches flaring in the wind! In the afternoon, there is also a concert, with a pageant, and strange doings on the stage . . . There will be a village that will stand for but a day, which mad artists have hung with glorious banners and blazoned in the entrance through the woods."

Though folk-music collectors and classical musicians including Aaron Copland had lived in the area since the forties, the music scene really picked up after Albert Grossman arrived in the early sixties. Several of the artists he managed, including Bob Dylan, fell in love with the place. By the time I arrived, Dylan had settled outside town with his family and was lying low. More visible locally, his backup musicians, who called themselves the Band, had just released their first album, *Music from Big Pink*. Its namesake was a house in nearby West Saugerties, where some of the Band lived in '67—ground zero for the soon-to-be-legendary, bootlegged *Basement Tapes*, recorded there with Dylan. By the summer of '68, the Band—Rick Danko, Levon Helm, Garth Hudson, Richard Manuel, and Robbie Robertson—who'd been on the road for years, had dispersed into the Woodstock community.

GARTH HUDSON: We got to like this lifestyle, chopping wood and hitting our thumb with a hammer, fixing the tape recorder or the screen door, wandering into the woods . . . It was relaxed and low key. Which was something we had not enjoyed since we were children.

At the Elephant Café, impromptu jams would break out with the likes of Paul Butterfield, a great blues vocalist and harmonica player, and Tim Hardin, a brilliant singer-songwriter. You would often see Rick Danko playing checkers at Café Espresso or Richard Manuel sipping red wine at Deanies. (All of them would be part of the festival a year later.) The Café Espresso, which had been a haunt of Dylan's in the early sixties, was run by a kind of paternal Frenchman named Bernard Paturel.

BERNARD PATUREL: There's a magic here—an emanation. Lots of musicians, artists, and writers. A gifted person would feel the vibrations and get support from people like that living there. There is something in the air. You can visit someone who might have the same spirit, the same attitude.

LEVON HELM: The people here are like the people down in the Ozark Mountains. They're just as country in that good kind of solid citizen way as they are back home [in Arkansas] . . . Anyone who lives here is blessed.

The town did seem like a shelter from the storm (as Dylan would later sing) in September '68. As the Vietnam War escalated, America had gone haywire that year, with one horrible event after another: the murders of Martin Luther King Jr. and Bobby Kennedy; race riots in cities everywhere; antiwar demonstrators beaten up and jailed; students arrested for protesting on campus. In August, the cops clobbered and gassed protesters at the Democratic National Convention in Chicago. Abbie Hoffman, the Yippies, the Black Panthers, and other activists known as the Chicago Eight were indicted on trumped-up charges; Abbie, by then, seemed to get busted every other week.

In Woodstock, the Soundouts were in direct contrast to the national climate. They had a joyous, healing feel to them—a result of that bucolic setting—with little kids running around, people sharing joints and lazing around on blankets as the sun set. Since 1967, the concerts took place every summer weekend at Peter Pan Farm, a property on the winding Glasco Turnpike between Woodstock and Saugerties. It was owned by Pan Copeland, a feisty woman who ran the Corner Deli in town. Three or four artists would perform on a makeshift stage, about six inches off the ground, in what had been a cornfield. There were local acts like Ellen McElwaine and Fear Itself, Chrysalis, Cat Mother, and the Caldwell Winfeld Blues Band, and later national artists who'd moved to town, such as Van Morrison and Tim Hardin. Between sets, we were serenaded by cicadas and birds. People pitched tents or parked campers in the adjoining cow pasture. "Wouldn't it be cool to put on a big concert where people could camp out like this and make a weekend of it?" I asked Sonya. The Soundouts reignited the idea that had first struck me in Miami. But here I began to see the pieces of something even larger coming together.

On a trip into the city, I reconnected with Don Keider, who'd moved up from the Grove to New York to play vibes with a band called Mandor Beekman. Don and some guys from his Miami jazz quartet—drummer Abby Rader and keyboardist Bob Lenox—hooked up with some Brooklyn rockers and changed their name to Train. DK asked me to manage the band, and though I'd not yet heard the music, I said, "Sure, I'll check it out." He needed the help, and I would get to learn something new.

Train was transitioning from straight-ahead jazz to a more rock-fusion sound. I introduced them to Garland Jeffreys, a talented singer and guitarist. Garland owned a lighting company in the East Village called Intergalactic. I'd gotten to know him when I bought his strobe lights for the Head Shop South. Garland was writing some great songs and performing in the Village, and DK and the guys liked his poetic lyrics. Once Garland joined, the band's sound started to jell.

DON KEIDER: We were staying in this bombed-out building over by the railroad tracks on the West Side. Up over a sweatshop, it was also our rehearsal space. It was sick! I don't know how we survived that. But I had a lot of faith in Michael that he could help us get somewhere. He'd proved his business prowess in Miami with our poster company. We'd started out with a couple posters, and then all of a sudden we were having them printed by the thousands. He distributed them all around the country. Quite a bit of money was made from those posters.

I'd take the Trailways bus from Woodstock to Port Authority to work with Train. On one of those rides I thought: Wouldn't it be great if there were a studio in Woodstock where artists could record in the country? Just like Miami had Criteria, which was an outreach for Atlantic Records, Woodstock needed a recording studio. More and more musicians were spending time upstate—Van Morrison, Jimi Hendrix, Janis Joplin. Fred Neil moved up from Coconut Grove.

I started looking around and found a dilapidated Victorian house and some outbuildings on a secluded wooded property just outside town. Originally, it had been the Tapooz Country Inn, a vacation spot operated by an Armenian family, with cabins, a dance hall, a swimming pool shaped like a grand piano, and a gazebo. Alexander Tapooz, a colorful character who was a rug dealer, said the thirty acres and buildings could be had for around $50,000. Down a rutted, tree-lined drive off Yerry Hill Road, the place was in serious disrepair, but

I could envision converting the dance hall into a studio. With financial backing, I thought, I could build a state-of-the-art recording facility, a retreat for musicians who wanted to get away from it all while recording.

Meanwhile, on a late October day when I was in the city with Train, Abby Rader told me about a label guy he knew. "He's a bigshot at Capitol Records," Abby said. "Artie Kornfeld. He's originally from Bensonhurst, same as you." We were standing on the sidewalk and I spotted a phone booth. "Got a dime?" I asked. I called Capitol and reached Artie's office.

ARTIE KORNFELD: I was vice president of A & R at Capitol. I had been a musician and a songwriter originally, working with [Gerry] Goffin and [Carole] King and [Neil] Sedaka and Leiber and Stoller at the Brill Building. Then I'd been at Mercury, where I wrote and produced some big hits for the Cowsills. I was only twenty-four when I got to Capitol. One day my secretary told me, "There's a guy named Michael Lang to see you." I said, "Who's Michael Lang?" and she said, "He said, 'Tell him I'm from the neighborhood,'" so right away I knew—Bensonhurst. That's why I said, "Okay, send him in."

Michael was my second hippie. I had signed Debbie Harry—later of Blondie—and her band the Wind in the Willows, so they were the first hippies I'd met. Michael and I had an immediate affinity for each other. We talked about the neighborhood—we smoked a J and it was better than anything I'd ever smoked. I sort of fell in love with Michael because intellectually we were very close—and we were both nuts. We connected on a very high level.

When I first walked into Artie's office, with gold records on the wall, I was expecting someone much more corporate. Instead, there's

Artie sitting cross-legged on his desk—it was a little bit of that square attempt at being cool. But he was very sweet and really welcoming. The son of a cop, he definitely had the "neighborhood" kind of personality—someone I immediately understood. We talked about people we both knew in Bensonhurst and hit it off immediately.

Artie and I got together very soon thereafter, and I brought the band up to see him. Train didn't have all their songs worked out. A chaotic kind of band, they were pulling from what Coltrane was doing, a lot of improvisation and jamming on keyboards. Bob Lenox, in particular, was a very interesting jazz player. Though it took them a while to lock in, there were moments when they were on—and when it was all working, it sounded great.

ARTIE KORNFELD: Train was terrible. But I liked Michael, so I gave him a $10,000 budget. I said I'd take them into the Capitol studios and do some demos and see if we could sign them.

Though Train's trippy sound and political lyrics weren't Artie's thing, he trusted me. I thought their music could fit the new, free-form FM radio stations, which favored heavier rock albums, unlike AM radio's pop-singles fare—which had been Artie's world. Train, needless to say, was overjoyed by this turn of events.

DON KEIDER: Michael really came through for us with the Capitol deal. Right after that, we showed up at our place to rehearse one night and it was completely empty. Someone had broken in. They took a B-3, my vibes, two sets of drums, all the guitars and amps. All of our personal stuff—clothes and everything—was gone. The place was even swept out! But the money had just come through from Capitol, and Artie and Michael gave us the okay to go ahead and buy what we needed. So I got a dynamite set of drums and another set of vibes, and all of our stuff was replaced, and Capitol gave us a real dynamite sound system.

Artie arranged for Train to cut demos in Capitol's studio to see if the label would sign the band. Train gigged around town—eventually at Bill Graham's Fillmore East, which had opened in March on Second Avenue, and at the Electric Circus on St. Mark's Place. They got booked on some amazing jazz bills with John Cage, Cecil Taylor, Charlie Mingus, Ornette Coleman, Don Cherry, and Jack DeJohnette. (Capitol ultimately rejected the demos the band recorded, and Train signed with Vanguard, which released the group's sole album, *Costumed Cuties*, in 1970.)

I spent more and more time in the city with Artie and his wife, Linda, hanging out at their apartment on Fifty-sixth Street, off Sutton Place, shooting pool, smoking pot, and talking into the wee hours. It seemed as if Artie and I had known each other all our lives. He and Linda were soul mates—they lived in one of the newer, very posh high-rises with their little girl, Jamie. Eventually he would lend me his company car, a Buick, to more easily make trips back and forth to Woodstock. Sonya didn't like the city, so I always came down by myself and returned home every night. Later, as I became completely wrapped up in the festival planning and production, Sonya and I gradually drifted apart.

ARTIE KORNFELD: Michael, Linda, and I became like Butch Cassidy, Etta Place, and the Sundance Kid. He was my first hippie friend. We used to smoke a J and we'd look out over the city from the thirty-sixth floor. We'd sit up until three or four in the morning shooting pool. He called me Krombine and I called him Clang. One night he said, "Artie, you've already been doing this for years—and you're jaded." I said, "What do you mean I'm jaded?" and he said, "Well, you sign acts, you go in the studio, and do that kind of stuff, but you don't go to clubs anymore like you used to—you don't go and hear the new acts unless you have to."

I told Artie about the Soundouts in Woodstock and my festival in Miami. For weeks we talked about creating a version of the Sound-outs as a summer concert series. Then during one of our midnight musings, the concept of a Woodstock festival evolved: "Let's really do something big! Let's invite everyone and put it all together out in the country where people can camp!" Artie's excitement propelled the idea forward. We also discussed the possibility of a studio/retreat at the Tapooz property on Yerry Hill Road, and he loved the idea. We decided to pursue both projects.

My friend who ran the Juggler, Jim Young, was involved in real estate, so in December we started looking together for possible festival sites. I paid him a small retainer to help me find a spot, and we visited several properties in Ulster County. There was a seventy-acre open field down on Route 212, east of Woodstock, which at one time was going to become a golf course. In an area called Krumville we found an old racetrack for midget cars and go-carts, which was pretty cool. But I realized these sites were too small and inaccessible for a festival.

Then, soon after New Year's, close to Saugerties, we chanced upon the Winston Farm. It was perfect—over seven hundred acres, rolling hills, and right off the New York State Thruway. It was owned by a Mr. Schaller, the kingpin of Schaller & Weber meats, famous for their German sausages. Schaller used the land only for hunting and the occasional weekend retreat. After we spoke several times to his caretaker, it seemed Schaller might be open to renting the property. When I told Artie about it, he agreed that it sounded ideal. All we needed now was an investor. Artie put out feelers to various record-company execs.

I'd recently met an entertainment attorney, Miles Lourie, and told him our ideas. He was intrigued by the festival and studio, and he knew a couple of young venture capitalists, John Roberts and Joel Rosenman, who were financing a new recording studio in Manhattan. Maybe they'd back the studio in Woodstock. He set up a meeting for an early February afternoon at the guys' apartment on the Upper East Side. About our age, they were roommates, and their East Eighty-fifth Street bachelor pad doubled as their office.

Upon meeting them, we realized we were from completely different worlds. A trust-fund kid, John Roberts, at twenty-one, had inherited a million dollars from his late mother's estate, part of a pharmaceutical empire, and would be collecting more. Joel, the son of a Long Island orthodontist, was a recent Yale Law School graduate. They had formed an entrepreneurial partnership called Challenge International Ltd. Their first big project, Media Sound, was under construction on Fifty-seventh Street. With an open and relaxed demeanor, John had me from hello. He was a forthright, down-to-earth guy, completely without guile. Joel seemed more what I expected from suits. He was somehow less accessible, while at the same time trying very hard to be charming. I wasn't at all sure about him, but both he and John had great senses of humor, and Joel had a good and open laugh. That put me at ease.

In their 1979 book, *Young Men with Unlimited Capital,* Joel and John recalled their impressions of us at our first meeting:

> Kornfeld has longish brown hair and is wearing an embroidered leather vest over a T shirt . . . Lang, however, cannot be placed on the spectrum. An enormous halo of dark curls frames a face that is, by turns, evil, wanton, fey, impish, and innocent. Beneath this disturbingly protean countenance: a frayed work shirt, an Indian leather belt, faded Levi's, cracked and filthy cowboy boots.
>
> There isn't time to register astonishment. On introducing himself and Lang, Kornfeld grasps first John's, then

Joel's, hand in both of his and smiles a smile of fraternal commiseration, as though he and they share some painful secret or are about to embark on a dangerous mission behind enemy lines. Lang is cheerfully acquiescent, all-accepting, attuned to unknowable vibrations.

I didn't say much. My father once told me: "If you're talking, you're not learning." Artie expertly handled the meeting, enthusiastically articulating our concept of the Woodstock studio. We hadn't intended to discuss the festival in detail, but Artie mentioned it in passing. Once in a while, John and Joel would glance over at me, and I'd smile while Artie made the presentation. Our future partners did not seem too interested in the idea of a studio in the country.

JOEL ROSENMAN: The tale they unfolded was an essentially uninteresting tale about the need for a recording studio in Woodstock, New York. They impressed us with the superstars who lived in Woodstock, but they failed to make a case for spending the money to construct a huge facility for these stars. Even though we hadn't opened our doors at Media Sound, we knew enough already from talking to the experts about what it takes to make a recording studio profitable, and it takes more than a few albums by a few superstars, no matter how great they are, because the fact that they're going to sell a million albums does not increase your rates, and does not increase the amount of time they'll book at the studio to produce that album.

Of course Joel's experts didn't know that a studio where successful albums are recorded will garner a steady flow of business among artists who hope to capture their own lightning in a bottle—as we later saw at the Bearsville Studio. In late 1970, Albert Grossman would open that facility less than a mile from the Tapooz property. One of the country's most sought-out independent studios for thirty years, Bearsville Studio was the origin of albums by the Rolling Stones, Foreigner, Bonnie Raitt, R.E.M., Patti Smith, Jeff Buckley, Van Morrison, the Band, Dave Matthews, Phish, and dozens of other major artists.

But on this day in February 1969, John and Joel primarily wanted to know more about the festival—though I thought that the studio idea had begun to grow on John. They asked about the festival's size and location, ticket prices, and the overall budget. We said we were not prepared to discuss the festival. John and Joel seemed an unlikely pairing as festival partners, but more suited for the studio project. They were smart and had a great staff in place to design and set up a studio operation. Artie and I could provide the right aesthetic and ambience. Artie told them, "We're already pretty far along with some other people on the festival, but okay, we'll come back and bring the budget."

Artie and I had been discussing a possible festival partnership with both Alan Livingston, who brought him to Capitol Records, and Larry Uttall, head of Bell Records. A couple of days after our meeting at Challenge, Larry called Artie to say he wanted to meet to discuss Bell's involvement in the festival. We were thrilled by the news, and Artie contacted John and Joel to let them know what was up. "We're already set with the festival," he told them, "but we'd still like to follow up on the studio."

John and Joel were bitterly disappointed—from our brief description, they'd been bitten by the whole idea. I believe they were viewing it as a somewhat unconventional but lucrative investment possibility— and one that might be fun. "Every time we find a project we like, some big corporation comes along and grabs it out from under us," Joel told Artie. Artie and I talked it over and decided to go back and see them again before making a final decision. We both liked them, and the thought of working with a couple of guys our age appealed to us. If they would agree to both projects, we'd consider going with them.

As we were still in the early stages of planning, I had not put together final numbers for a festival. Extrapolating from the Miami budget, I had figured a total cost of about $500,000. I drew up a rough plan requiring a cash investment of $250,000. The balance would come from advance ticket sales. I figured $100,000 for talent deposits and $150,000 for pre-event staff, legal, office, site leasing, site prep, and production. I hoped to rent the Winston Farm for $5,000, but that was still up in the air. As a model, we figured 100,000 people attending a two-day festival at $5 or $6 a ticket per day. We could have our dream and make a profit. (Of course, this would all change as the concept evolved and the festival went to three days with an estimated audience of 200,000 per day.) After a few additional meetings, John agreed to finance the festival and the studio. We would become partners, and because the projects were based in Woodstock, we decided to call our company Woodstock Ventures.

The contract was drawn up, and it began:

> Whereas, Rosenman and Roberts are sole shareholders, officers, and directors of Challenge, which is in the business of investing funds in new business ventures.

> Whereas Lang has presented to Rosenman and Roberts two business ventures, one calling for the establishment of a music festival in Saugerties, New York, and the other calling for the creation of a sound studio in Woodstock, New York.

The contract called for an investment of $200,000 plus a 10 percent contingency fee for the production of the festival and $275,000 plus 10 percent for the creation of the studio. The company would issue 200 shares. As it was his money, John would receive 60 shares, Joel 40, and Artie and I would receive 50 each. I was to provide a life insurance policy on myself worth $500,000 with Woodstock Ventures the beneficiary, and it was my responsibility to acquire any additional funds if the agreed-upon cash commitment was not sufficient to finance either the festival or the studio. Based on the Winston Farm property that Jim Young and I had found, I had to warrant that the festival would be located in upstate New York. I would be personally responsible for any loss or expenditure by Woodstock Ventures or Challenge if the site or permits could not be obtained. Up through the festival, I would receive a salary of $400 per week.

Because he was under an exclusive two-year contract with Capitol, Artie couldn't sign a partnership agreement, but we agreed I'd hold his share until he could legally participate. On February 28, 1969, the contract was signed.

Joel worried that since Artie and I had clear-cut roles and the expertise to put on the festival, that John wouldn't need him as a partner.

JOEL ROSENMAN: I remember saying, "You're well on your way, Jock. You've got a good project and good partners. You don't need me. You've got Michael and Artie."

John took me aside and asked if I could find a role for Joel. I was impressed by his concern and more than happy to have Joel's involvement. There was certainly going to be enough work to go around. With the paperwork signed, we divided up the responsibilities. Artie was in charge of publicity and advertising. John and Joel would be handling the business administration and ticket distribution. My job was to be the hands-on producer of the festival, book the talent, design and prepare the site, and put together the production team. My first thought for the studio was Stan Goldstein. It occurred to me that he could also be of help in fleshing out plans for the festival.

Our number one priority: Nail down the festival location and get it ready in six months' time. That seemed like a piece of cake. We were off and running.

four WALLKILL

– –

"Is that 'Miss Lang' or 'Mr. Lang,' a girl or a boy?" I hear people snickering as I walk toward the dais. Amid catcalls and whistles, I focus on the task at hand: convincing the people of Wallkill to let us keep our festival in their township and show them there is nothing to worry about. The Wallkill Town Hall meeting room is packed, standing room only. Emotions run high. Middle-aged housewives, small-town businessmen, and weather-beaten farmers are trading horror stories about hippies. There's a real fear that they're going to be overrun and molested by hordes of long-haired freaks. Wallkill town supervisor Jack Schlosser raps his gavel on the table, where he sits among six town board members. "Let Mr. Lang have his say."

On this balmy night in mid-June, I'm here to present our festival plans, accompanied by my ace production team. While I'm prepared for a bit of push-back, I'm surprised by the depth of their concern.

"Look," I tell them, "we're here to bring something to Wallkill that will be good for everyone. We're not aliens and we're not drug addicts and we

do know what we're doing. We are professionals in our fields." They act a
bit surprised that I can speak an English they understand, and begrudg-
ingly they begin to lose some of the hostility.

It quiets down in the room as I explain our plans in a down-to-earth
way. "We're going to have music and art, food and fun. We're going to
camp out in the country—the kind of thing you did when you were kids.
We've hired the best professionals in the business to make sure the event is
safe and that the community is inconvenienced as little as possible. It will
be no more intrusive than the Orange County Fair that comes to town
every year."

While I continue my talk, the temperature in the room lowers. Calm is
overtaking agitation, and I figure I'd better quit while I'm ahead. I wrap it
up. "Are there any questions?"

"Yeah!" says a guy who looks like he could be a high school football
coach. "You've told us about these famous musicians who are going to be
performing up here. But what about all those people who are coming to see
these musicians? What kind of people are they?"

"They're like your own kids," I answer without hesitation. "They're
music lovers." The younger members of the audience applaud and even
some of the suits laugh.

Our intention is to stay here—no matter what—and put on the festi-
val in two months' time. I'm optimistic that the opposition can be over-
come.

As for Woodstock Ventures, during the early weeks of our partnership, Joel, John, Artie, and I developed an uneasy rapport. One
night we all met at Artie's apartment. We sat on the floor, passing a
joint and discussing our plans. I couldn't help thinking how interesting this partnership was—what they wanted from us and what we
wanted from them. John and I got into a discussion about "vibes." I
could tell he was out of his comfort zone, but the joint softened the

edges and we had a good laugh. They seemed intrigued by this world we were opening up to them, yet our experiences and approaches to life were entirely different. I relied on intuition and instinct, and they relied on experts, surveys, and marketing tools—proven business techniques in their world. Artie was talented in songwriting and music promotion and fit somewhere in between.

I knew if Woodstock was to succeed it had to be authentic from top to bottom. We were setting out to create a new paradigm in festival events, while attempting to bring together various factions of the counterculture community. Overall, I envisioned the festival as a gathering of the tribes, a haven for like-minded people, where experimental new lifestyles would be respected and accommodated. I knew flexibility and adaptability were key to creating this never-before-seen commingling of art and commerce. John and Joel were too conservative to make my idea into a reality.

Since the Woodstock concept was proving to be a developing blueprint in my head, I found it difficult to collaborate. I could close my eyes and see the festival's components, then keep them juggling in the air until they were formulated to the extent that I could assign their execution to team members. Other than an initial organizational chart I had drawn up showing various functions and positions to fill, we made it up as we went along.

We settled on calling our creation "An Aquarian Exposition: The Woodstock Music and Art Fair." That name "Woodstock" symbolized the rural, natural setting I envisioned. I suggested "Aquarian Exposition" to encompass all the arts, not only music but crafts, painting, sculpture, dance, theater—like a 1969 version of the old Maverick festivals. And I wanted to reference the Aquarian age, an era of great harmony predicted by astrologers to coincide with the late twentieth century, a time when stars and planets would align to allow for more understanding, sympathy, and trust in the world. Our festival would be that place for people to come together to celebrate the coming of a new age.

There had been so much conflict over the past year, with violent confrontations occurring on college campuses, in urban ghettos, and at demonstrations across the country. At Woodstock we would focus our energy on peace, setting aside the onstage discussion of political issues to just groove on what might be possible. It was a chance to see if we could create the kind of world for which we'd been striving throughout the sixties: That would be our political statement—proving that peace and understanding were possible and creating a testament to the value of the counterculture.

It would be three days of peace and music.

To determine the possible size of the audience, we started researching the major population centers of the northeastern corridor—New York, New Jersey, Connecticut, Massachusetts. When we did the math, we realized we could have as many as two hundred thousand people. The number seemed almost inconceivable for a concert: Attendance records had been broken at Shea Stadium when the Beatles played there in 1965 and '66 to some fifty-five thousand people. In '67, between twenty-five thousand and thirty thousand attended Monterey Pop for each of its three days—but no one stayed overnight at the Monterey Fairgrounds where it was held.

In early March, I contacted a real estate agent about the Winston Farm property. He spoke to Schaller, the owner, and seemed encouraging about our leasing it for a music-and-art festival. He quoted $40,000 for a twelve-week rental—much more than we'd budgeted—and passed along the contact info for Schaller's Manhattan attorney. In the meantime, word got out in Woodstock that I was thinking of having a festival in the area. Soon, I was hearing from the town supervisor, Bill Ward, and an official from the county health department, who made it clear they did not want a large outdoor event to occur in the town of

Woodstock. Suddenly, Schaller's real estate agent stopped returning my calls. John and Joel contacted Schaller's attorney and set up a meeting for the last week in March.

At least we had the location for the Woodstock recording studio. On April 17, we'd put down $4,500 as a deposit on the Tapooz property, which we'd negotiated to purchase for $55,000. We determined the scope of the facility, the description of which would run in an article in *Billboard*: "A recording center is being established [in Woodstock] by Woodstock Ventures, which has just purchased a 30-acre site near the Woodstock Music and Art Fair—a 16-track studio and hotel complex . . . Joel Rosenman said the Woodstock Sound Studios will allow producers and artists to create in a pleasant atmosphere where adequate recording time is easy to secure. The studio will provide housing, rehearsal studios, a 24-hour kitchen, and recreational facilities, including a swimming pool and tennis court. Stan Goldstein, formerly of Criteria Studio in Miami, is consulting on construction of the studio and will be an engineer there."

Though the festival site wasn't nailed down, we chose the weekend of August 15 as the festival date. I needed to get things moving and sign bands before they were booked elsewhere. From the concerts I'd promoted and organized in Miami, I'd learned a lot about staging, what worked for audiences and what didn't. At Miami Pop, we experimented with different kinds of music—blues, classic rock and roll, acid rock, pop, folk—and I found that the audience got into all of it. The kids of the counterculture were not pigeonholed in their musical tastes. So I decided on an eclectic group of artists and made up a wish list that ran the gamut from Jimi Hendrix to Johnny Cash.

I started spending time with Hector Morales, at William Morris, again. When he'd helped me with the Miami festival, we'd become good friends. He let me hang out in his office from morning until night learning to book talent. Hector's assistance would be invaluable throughout the project. I soon realized that to create credibility for our show, I had to immediately sign a few of the bigger acts by offering them a fee that would ensure their acceptance. For example, if an act was getting $7,500, I'd offer $10,000. Once two or three big names were signed up, I'd find myself being taken seriously by artists' agents and managers, and fees would become more reasonable. Jefferson Airplane, Creedence Clearwater Revival, and Canned Heat were the first artists to accept. We got the Airplane and Creedence for $10,000 each. Canned Heat had scored two major hits since appearing at Monterey, "On the Road Again" and "Going Up the Country," so their fee was $12,500.

I booked Crosby, Stills and Nash before their debut album was released. Their manager, David Geffen, came into Hector's office one day, clutching a test pressing of their just-completed recording. "Wait till you hear this!" he gloated. We were knocked out. The Buffalo Springfield and the Byrds had been two of my all-time favorite groups, and CSN took their music to a new level. The vocal harmonies were fantastic on "Helplessly Hoping" and "Suite: Judy Blue Eyes." And I loved the guitar and organ interplay on "Wooden Ships," which I later discovered was inspired by Crosby's adventures in the Grove. I knew "Marrakesh Express" would be a hit.

Geffen was looking for the right venue to kick off the band's first tour, and we all agreed Woodstock should be it. I booked them on the spot, paying his asking price of $10,000. We did a lot of interesting booking that way—signing new acts like Joe Cocker and Mountain to be introduced to our peers at Woodstock.

Even by late March, buzz began circulating about the festival. One night Garland Jeffreys and I went to see Van Morrison perform in New York at Steve Paul's Scene, a very cool club owned by Johnny Winter's manager. We chatted about the festival to Steve and others, and by the next day, I heard from someone in Los Angeles who called to say he wanted his band to play. Artie began calling his friends at radio stations and got them to mention Woodstock on air.

My philosophy in all areas of festival staffing was to get the very best people available on our team. I looked for those with the most expertise in their field and, whenever possible, people who understood what we were trying to do. When I contacted Stan Goldstein in Miami to see if he was available, I learned he'd left Criteria and happened to be in New York. He was working as a sound engineer (his first love) at the Hit Factory but was about to leave for a job in Los Angeles. I met with him in New York and I hired him for a salary of $500 a week, $100 more than I was making.

STAN GOLDSTEIN: Michael offered me the opportunity to be in charge of physical arrangements for the festival. I told him I really wasn't interested in doing a festival. My interest was in pursuing my recording career. Michael disclosed that a recording studio was being built, simultaneous with the development of the festival, on the Tapooz property. Eventually we came to an agreement that I would help him design and staff the festival, and once the major players were in place and the design complete, I would be released and begin building the studio in association with the chief engineer of Media Sound, John and Joel's studio. We would be cochiefs of this new studio to be constructed.

Within a fairly short period of time after I joined, the decision was made that it would be a three-day event and the outline of what each of the days would be was established. The Friday concert would start late in the day—gentle music without major, major headliners, so that we could stage arrivals, with some people arriving on Friday, late in the day, after work. Saturday and Sunday would be headliners. The slogan "Three Days of Peace and Music" was determined, and Michael came up with the idea of having a guitar and a dove as the logo—which was later developed into a brilliant poster by Arnold Skolnick.

Unlike the enclosed location at Gulfstream Race Track, for this festival we needed to build a city, a place where people didn't depart at day's end, where they would want to camp overnight and have a longer experience. Stan and I immediately started researching the logistics for accommodating two hundred thousand people spending three days at the site. As there was no precedent for what we were planning—outside the military—we began to develop strategies to determine what we'd need on-site and how much it would cost. For example, to estimate how many Porta-Potties we would need, we'd time people going in and out of bathrooms at public facilities.

STAN GOLDSTEIN: I would get to Yankee Stadium early and go into a bathroom and count the stalls. I had a watch and a clipboard and would count how many people went through the doors in what period of time. Then I would divide that by the number of available seats to figure out how many people would use how many toilets over a period of time.

We thought that the U.S. Army would have information on setting up temporary "cities," for troop deployments overseas or in rural locations. Stan made arrangements to go to the Pentagon, but his appointments were canceled. The army was unwilling to divulge information about field sanitation.

When John and Joel met with Schaller's attorney in late March, the meeting did not go well. They were informed that Schaller had decided not to rent the property to us after all. We started to get concerned. We had booked talent, we were hiring staff, and we had no place for the festival. We began searching areas farther afield from Woodstock, surveying properties via helicopter, and driving to check out possible sites. There was still snow on the ground, so an accurate assessment of potential sites meant a lot of walking. It was on one of these site walks that I became acquainted with Tom Rounds, Tom Driscoll, and Mel Lawrence, from Arena Associates, based in L.A. Taking advantage of my groundwork, they had produced the second Miami Pop Festival at Gulfstream Race Track in December '68, after I'd moved to Woodstock. I'd heard good things about the festival from Stan, who'd recorded some of the acts. I invited them east to meet and discuss our Aquarian Exposition. Rounds's background was radio, Driscoll controlled a strawberry empire in California, and Mel was the operations guy. Lacking experience running a huge operation, I was considering hiring a line producer, someone skilled in production as well as in conducting a business with hundreds of employees. Arena Associates wanted $50,000 for each partner, plus a percentage of the gate, for the physical production. That was too much money. "Thanks for coming out," I told them, "but I think I'll do it myself."

But during our meetings and site surveys, Mel and I had quickly clicked. He was a very practical, "get it done" guy, and he understood what I was trying to do. I needed someone to be site manager, and he seemed to have the right skill set and my kind of vision. When the three were leaving, I asked Mel to stay on. He agreed to join my staff for a flat fee of $8,000.

MEL LAWRENCE: I was hooked on being a general and said, "I want to do this." I liked Michael. He had an air of confidence—and he made *you* feel confident. This quality gave you faith in him.

Mel had entered the concert business through radio and had been involved with some big concerts in Hawaii. He worked on the country's first pop festival, the Magic Mountain Festival in Northern California, and handled staging, fencing, and traffic operations at Monterey Pop the following week. As our site manager, he could help in all these areas and more.

MEL LAWRENCE: Our first planning meeting for Woodstock took place in a luncheonette on Sixth Avenue. Michael, Stan, and I started one of my patented outlines, which can run fifteen or twenty pages. We sort of laid out the festival on napkins.

On the last Sunday in March, John and Joel went for a drive upstate to look around, increasingly desperate to find a site. Heading back to the city in John's Porsche, they saw a sign on Route 17 that read: MILLS INDUSTRIAL PARK FOR RENT. It was two hundred acres in the township of Wallkill, in Orange County, about a ninety-minute drive from New York City. The asking price for a four-month lease was $10,000, pending approval from the local zoning board. Joel and John paid $1,500 as a deposit for a two-way, thirty-day option on the land. They appeared before the Wallkill Zoning Board on April 18 and told them we'd be having an arts fair at the Mills Industrial Park with a possible forty to fifty thousand people attending over a couple of days. They downplayed the rock and roll component, perhaps a bit too much, and promised to take out liability insurance for the event. The Wallkill Zoning Board members seemed a bit dubious but told them they had no objections to our plans.

When I checked out the Mills Industrial Park, my first reaction was horror. The flat, bulldozed property looked as if it had been raped. Buzzards were flying around. It was as far as you could get from the feeling I was looking for. I had pictured walking into an open, pastoral scene of beauty and calm that could make you feel comfortable and at peace. This was ugly, cold, hard, and dirty and felt as if someone had taken what they wanted from the land and left the debris.

John, not unreasonably, was getting anxious, and after talking to Mills and showing the site to Mel, I was persuaded that we could transform it into an acceptable landscape. It would never be idyllic, but it did have electricity, water, and access from major roads. Our festival's name would remain Woodstock, no matter where it was held. I was not going to give that up. The name Woodstock had come to represent the heart of what I hoped to accomplish.

We rapidly started filling staff positions. Most of the technical people came through Bill Graham's Fillmore organization. The top lighting director in rock and roll, Chip Monck, had worked at Monterey and at Mel's Miami Pop Festival. He'd started his career at the Village Gate, had run the lights at the Newport festivals since their inception in 1959, and had designed the lighting for the Fillmore East. He rang me up about the festival after he heard about it from Hector Morales.

CHIP MONCK: I went to see Hector Morales and Hector said, "Hey, this curly-headed kid has been in here and he's booking every bit of talent in the world." I wasn't working at the moment and thought, It sounds like it's going to be something pretty big! So I called up Michael and said, "Gee, let's have a cup of coffee and put our heads together." I contacted Annie Weldon, who was John Morris's wife at that time, and said, "Can I bring this kid over and introduce him to you and John? Will you please just politely host the evening so we can get this thing moving?" So we met at their place on Thirteenth Street and Sixth Avenue.

"Hector explained to me what you're booking," I said to Michael, "and I really want to know more about it and if we can be of help." Michael laid out his vision—without revealing too much but giving just enough. It was up to us to lock in and agree. That's what you do with a promoter or a skilled entrepreneur. You take orders. Michael was understated, and when he got into a hole or into a corner, he did his famous mumble.

He was looking at having maybe two hundred and fifty thousand people. My feeling was we were looking at between one hundred thousand and two hundred thousand. It was going to be huge and it was going to be everybody, and it had to be done correctly.

Any time anybody saw Michael and realized what he was doing and what the accomplishment could be, they immediately signed themselves on.

Chip came on board for a $7,000 salary. A charming and unflappable guy, he had a good grasp of what we were trying to put together. Chip's friend John Morris sort of talked his way into a job. He had been concert promoter Bill Graham's right-hand man at the Fillmore, and he knew numerous artists and their managers. I hired him to do artist relations—he would help with some of the booking and then work with the agents and managers on fulfilling the individual riders listing the technical requirements for each artist. During the festival he would be the artist liaison.

Chip and John both recommended Chris Langhart as our technical director. An acknowledged genius by everyone who worked with him, Chris taught theater design at NYU and had set up the plumbing and engineering plans for the Fillmore East. He would do the same for us.

CHRIS LANGHART: There came to be salary negotiations, and Michael [was] very street wise. We finally settled on a figure—a low and a high—having argued it back and forth. He announced he would flip a coin, and as far as I was concerned, the low and the high were a little far apart. I said, "We're not having that flipping of the coin routine, because I have a student in my class who can flip a coin reliably twelve times out of thirteen." And this wide, Cheshire cat smile [came] onto his face, so we settled on [a] figure, and from then on we got on pretty straight ahead.

I hired Bill Hanley to build our sound system. I say *build* because a system that could provide sound for the size crowd we expected did not exist. Originally for the job, I'd considered Owsley Stanley, who designed the Grateful Dead's massive system and was their sound engineer (as well as the country's leading manufacturer of LSD). But Hanley was the best live soundman in the business and that's what I needed. I met with him and explained the size of the project, and he seemed interested and eager to tackle it. "I know how to do it," he said. "I can build you a system that will work."

A company called Concert Hall Publications, operated by Bert Cohen and Michael Foreman in Philadelphia, had worked on Mel's Miami festival, primarily in staging and promotion. Artie knew Michael, who sometimes wrote for the underground press. We hired them to develop our advertising campaign and to create the festival program book. They wanted to do more, though, and Bert somehow convinced John and Joel into commissioning him to design the interior of the Woodstock Ventures offices on West Fifty-seventh Street. Though all four of us realized the absurdity very early on, Bert turned the new office space into an over-the-top psychedelic casbah. Meant to evoke an environment like the black-light poster rooms in my head shop, or the interior of the Electric Circus, the offices consisted of platforms arranged at various heights and were carpeted in chartreuse. This misguided attempt at hipness shot right past cool and landed on ridiculous.

I hated the design, but there were other reasons I wanted a separate office. The advertising, ticketing, and business operations would be located uptown, and I needed to work without interference. Because of the nature of John and Joel's complete unfamiliarity with the milieu, let alone the technical side of putting together a show or anything to do with production, I couldn't see a way to bring them into the specifics of my plan. I didn't think they'd get it or go along with it. From the start, I thought we would each focus on our individual roles. I would produce, Artie would promote, and they would deal with finance and ticketing. If I took time to explain my work to John and Joel, the festival would never happen. So I opened a separate office for production on Sixth Avenue, in the Village. That's where we would put it all together.

Stan Goldstein had an uncanny ability to come up with just the right person for many of the positions we needed to fill. One of the most indispensable was Joyce Mitchell, who became the administrator of the downtown production office. A striking brunette, she was in her thirties and had hung out with the Beats and writers like Terry Southern and James Baldwin. She'd been the media coordinator for Bobby Kennedy's presidential campaign, and before that, she'd produced programming for armed forces radio shows hosted by Merv Griffin and Eddy Arnold. She'd moved to New York in 1957, after graduating from the University of Miami and then living in Paris.

JOYCE MITCHELL: I met with Michael and Stan somewhere near Lincoln Center for hamburgers. This curly-haired kid said to me, "What would you do about toilet facilities if you had a hundred thousand people in a field?" And I said something to the effect of, "Well, I'd have two backhoes—one for digging and the second for covering the other trench." And either he or Stanley said, "Well, that's a better answer than we got from the U.S. Army—you're hired." And I said, "What for? To dig latrines?" That's how it all began. I don't think I walked away from that meeting knowing what I was getting into. Michael did tell me that they wanted to throw the biggest rock and roll party ever.

The first thing they wanted me to do was to set up the production office. All of the various production managers—Mel Lawrence, Chip Monck, John Morris—were arguing about who got what space. John wanted more space. But the ones who needed the space were Mel and Chip because they were doing broad design work. Mel created this big three-dimensional mock-up of the Wallkill site. I worked right outside of Michael's office. Things started pretty professionally.

Very smart, Michael had all the department heads meet to-gether regularly. Michael's method of management was that we should all totally understand what others were doing—so that we could shift into each other's place if we had to. Michael's managerial ability really impressed me. We did an awful lot of wrangling, we made up budgets, we were really playing it by ear. Michael just said, "Find me the money." Fortunately, I had taken a college class in accounting, at my father's insistence, so I was able to create budgets and keep production reports running. It was all so fast and furious.

Through Chris Langhart, we found Jim Mitchell, who'd been a the-ater professor at NYU. He became our purchasing agent and helped take some of the work off Joyce's plate. Jim set up accounts with various companies to obtain equipment and supplies. Slowly losing his sight, he was not in the best of health but was a hard worker nonetheless.

Our production office was very proletarian, just two floors in a brownstone, filled with desks and filing cabinets. Chip scavenged all the furniture, building some of it himself, and set up the office in less than forty-eight hours. We hired a receptionist who was a free spirit, but everyone else was grinding out the work. People could smoke pot whenever they felt like it, and we were having a good time, but no-body was goofing off. It was not a party. We had work to do and not a lot of time to do it and we had a budget, but it was sort of created from smoke. We didn't have any money to waste. Joyce dealt with John and Joel's bookkeeper uptown, a formidable redhead named Renee Levine.

JOHN ROBERTS: [Renee] became an indispensable part of our organi-zation. To the staff in general, she was a mother figure. To Mi-chael and Artie, she was the barricade that stood between them and reimbursements for their bizarre expense vouchers. To Joel and me, she became a loyal and trusted friend, the keeper of the checkbook, the ear-splitting voice of sanity, and the shrewd Jewish kvetch who always knew a bum when she saw one—and she saw plenty . . . She stood up to lawyers, accountants, agents, rock stars, and even armed policemen. All of them, like us, got a lot more than they bargained for.

Artie worked in the uptown office with John and Joel, and the relationship soon became strained. Artie was expressive with his ideas, some realistic, some not. John and Joel were focused on making money, and they wanted to see practical matters handled efficiently. Artie was starting to get a little too high and at times would lose focus, and they were becoming exasperated with him. Artie, on the other hand, would complain about John and Joel being too square and not appreciating his contributions. I'd tell him not to worry about it— "just keep them on track so I don't have to deal with this." Increasingly, they called me to complain about Artie being irrational or high or just not present, and I'd say, "Okay, I'll talk to him." But I couldn't constantly run uptown to deal with their conflicts. Had I been older, maybe I could have figured out a way to bridge the growing gap between them. But I didn't have the time or the belief that, given the personalities, it could be done. I was working twenty hours a day and just didn't have the answers to these questions.

I was spending so much time in New York, I'd rented rooms at the Chelsea Hotel, where Mel and I—and whoever else needed a bed— would crash. Meanwhile, Stan had relocated to Wallkill in April to troubleshoot any problems there before we set up our base of operations.

STAN GOLDSTEIN: I was the advance man into Wallkill, so I was the first person to actually go up there and move in. I began to introduce myself and us to the local folks. I went to the newspaper, the

Middletown *Times Herald-Record*, met the editor Al Romm and his staff, and told them about our plans. Up till that time, there had been no public notice. I went to see Jack Schlosser, the supervisor of the Wallkill township, and we had what seemed at the time to be a cordial meeting. I visited with the mayor of Middletown, who was not so cordial, but it was okay. And then I began to connect with local businesspeople.

In April and into May, Stan made the rounds in Wallkill, quietly setting up accounts with utility companies and investigating local businesses and contractors. As long as we were under the radar, all was well in Wallkill. But, by late May, once word hit the local papers, anti-Woodstock forces began to coalesce.

STAN GOLDSTEIN: There were incipient rumblings; there were all these questions about what our intentions were, and it seemed the best way to deal with that was to make myself available at a town hall meeting [in the first week of June]—to answer questions.

Preparing to relocate to the Wallkill site, Mel hired an assistant. He contacted an old friend from Bensonhurst, Barry Secunda, who managed the East Village nightclub the Electric Circus. Barry recommended his girlfriend, Penny Stallings, a Texan who'd just moved to New York after graduating from Southern Methodist University.

PENNY STALLINGS: I was very much adrift. I had a college education and nothing to do with it. I was totally at a loss in New York. I was a pure Texas girl with lots of makeup on and extra-blond hair— very *not* natural—and at the office I landed right in the middle of hippie town. Except for Mel, who was very preppy and a businessman, everybody else was funky and long-haired, and the women wore no makeup. They looked great, and I wanted to do that, but

I couldn't. Life in the office was fabulous—just hilarious. I was always laughing at the ongoing craziness—a total circus all the time.

Stan was like Allen Ginsberg. He was verbose and really smart. He had Michael's ear. Joyce vetted everything before any interaction with Michael. You had to go through her, and quite often she decided that it was not necessary for you to talk to him after all. She was the protective person who ran interference for Michael. She was in the "grown-up" group. She looked completely opposite from me. She wore no makeup and had that great bohemian fuzzy hair, salt and pepper. She was a very good-looking woman, and that added to her power.

I called Chip "Manners the Butler," a character on a TV commercial at the time, because he was so very British without being British. He was funny, gorgeous, and very cool. He and John Morris were really nice and awfully indulgent with me, because I knew less than nothing about what we were doing.

The first week in June, Mel took Penny and a small staff to Wallkill to start preparing the site, which needed extensive work to restore the land from industrial damage. On the property, we discovered old farm machinery and talked about how to deal with that. Mel's idea was to create characters out of them, which I thought was great. When Mel worked on the Miami festival, he had hired Bill Ward, a sculptor and art professor at the university there, to engage his students to create artworks at the Gulfstream Race Track. We wanted something like that for the Wallkill site, and Bill agreed to bring a crew to New York.

Mel and I mapped out everything. We wanted the place to be conducive to people feeling comfortable, safe, and close to nature. Based on crowd flow, we started locating the placement of the various elements: the stage, the camping area, the toilets, the kitchens, the concessions. Mel began with the landscaping and site development; we saved the stage construction, piping, and plumbing for last; I had a feeling that we should avoid putting down anything permanent, just in case we ran into insurmountable problems there. Confident that Mel and I were clear on the plan, I left him to do his part—the same went for Chip and the other senior department heads. Once I knew they understood exactly what I expected, I didn't try to tell them how to do their jobs. Mel and his team stayed in Wallkill, while I drove back and forth to the city, where Chip, John Morris, and Joyce still worked out of our production office in the Village.

MEL LAWRENCE: We set up an office in a big red barn on the site with Stan, Penny, the purchasing agent Jim Mitchell, and some others, and started solving the logistical problems. People would hear there was going to be a festival, and show up and say, "I'm a carpenter," "I'm a gardener," and I'd say, "Okay, you're hired!"

The Miami crew arrived during early June too and started brainstorming ideas. There was poison ivy and oak all over the Mills property, and spraying herbicide took up a lot of man-hours. We put everybody up at a Catskills resort that Mel remembered going to as a kid.

PENNY STALLINGS: We all stayed at a kosher bungalow colony in Bullville called Rosenberg's. Rosenberg's was suspended in time, in the 1950s. It was a place where you ate three meals and sat around in between, and the people looked it too—they were *quite* large. The food was overcooked brisket and potatoes, and the only thing any of us could eat was the apple pie, which was out of this world. We had our meals at the same time as the other guests, and it was hilarious.

Bill Ward came from Florida with his wife, Jean, who could

weld. I learned "the macho" from her—she'd grown up with brothers in Pennsylvania, so she had all these talents that no other woman I'd ever known had. Bill and Jean drove around looking for ancient farm equipment to make organic grown-from-the-ground art.

BILL WARD: When we first showed up, we had all these hippie kids working with us, and we rented three or four pickup trucks and a station wagon, and we'd go into town and buy supplies like shovels, rakes, and hammers. The people were glad to see us at first, because we were spending money. But then I started running into trouble. I realized when I showed up with a truck full of funny-looking kids, they were the focus of negative attention. I didn't look much better—I wore blue jeans, a denim jacket, and a baseball cap. Since I was the oldest one there, I was unofficially left in charge at the motel, and the Rosenbergs came to me and said, "Can't you get these kids to wear shirts and shoes at dinner?" They were very happy to see us when we got there, because the season hadn't started, and they were making money off of us. But when other people started to arrive, they began to get picky and wanted us out of there.

Back in New York, swamped with meetings, I needed an assistant. Through a musician friend of Stan's, we found Ticia Bernuth (now Agri), a fascinating woman about my age who'd spent the past few years traveling around the globe.

TICIA BERNUTH AGRI: When I heard about the job, something just came over my body and I said, "It's got to be me—get me the interview!" I had come back to New York after being in seventy-two countries and traveling all around the Middle East. In 1965, I'd had this desire for exploration and seeing the world. I lived in Italy, and from there I started traveling—Afghanistan, Pakistan, India,

North Africa, all over Europe. I had a sleeping bag and lived on a dollar a day—it was very free and easy in those days. During my interview with Michael, he asked me about myself, and I started talking about being in Saudi Arabia and driving through the desert, and coming across Arabs with bejeweled sabers who took us to a guest palace. I told Michael a lot of good stories like this, and that's probably why I got hired.

JOYCE MITCHELL: I was one of those who interviewed Ticia. When I heard her stories about the Sahara, I thought, "This is somebody who will keep Michael on time." She was wonderful.

PENNY STALLINGS: Ticia had red hair almost down to her waist. She was tall and skinny with very long legs and a teeny little skirt. She was very good looking—the perfect glamorous hippie secretary.

TICIA BERNUTH AGRI: Everybody was really friendly—like you already knew them. I remember one of Michael's staff, Peter Goodrich, talking about hot dogs—miles and miles of hot dogs. He said we needed enough hot dogs that if we lined them up, they'd go all across the United States.

The day Ticia came in, I was interviewing candidates for probably the most important job on our staff, head of security. She sat in while I met with a former deputy from Florida who was talking about barbed wire and attack dogs. Ticia and I gave each other a look that said, No way. It was nice to see we were in sync. After the man left, I told Ticia, "There's another security guy flying in tomorrow from Washington—Wes Pomeroy. Why don't you go pick him up at the airport?" I could tell when I met her that Ticia would not be intimidated by meeting and talking to anyone. I needed that ability, because I was dealing with a world that went beyond my own experiences and travels. To interact with all kinds of people, she needed to be comfortable in her own skin, smart enough to handle whatever came up, and conversant with everyone from politicians to rock stars to sanitation engineers. I thought, Let me see what she does with Wes—see if my reading of her is correct. She handled it really well and I knew she'd be a great personal liaison for me.

Wes Pomeroy was recommended to us by the Association of the Chiefs of Police. He was described to us as "not your typical law enforcement officer." He had never been a chief of police but was well known in the field. During the Johnson administration, he served as deputy director of the Law Enforcement Assistance Administration (LEAA), reporting directly to Attorney General Ramsey Clark. When Nixon was elected, replacing Clark with John Mitchell, Wes was asked to stay on. But Mitchell and the Nixon administration changed the LEAA's role from being a department that taught police and administrators how to deal peacefully with civil unrest, to primarily being a supplier of weapons (shotguns, tear gas, nightsticks) for local police departments. Wes had served as the Justice Department representative in Chicago during the '68 Democratic National Convention, where he had tried in vain to negotiate with Mayor Daley to avert the riots. He had just resigned from the Nixon administration to set up a security consulting firm. His Nixon credentials, I thought, would give us credibility with state and local police.

TICIA BERNUTH AGRI: Michael interviewed Wes and they had an immediate rapport. Wes wasn't into doing anything but peace and love. We had come through hard times in this country and Wes was trying to heal hippies' negative view of the police.

I asked Wes how he would handle the possibility of people arriving at Woodstock with the intention of crashing the gates. I knew that the traditional law enforcement approach of confrontation and force would bring nothing but grief and bad vibes. (And later in the summer, I'd see my theory come true at pop festivals in Newport, Atlanta, and Denver.) Other candidates I had interviewed for the job had suggested everything from double rows of barbed-wire fencing with dogs roaming in between, to armed guards every fifty feet, to walls like those at Attica. Wes, on the other hand, asked what *my* thinking was on the matter—a good sign.

I told him that Woodstock would be open to everyone. If you could not afford a ticket, there would be a free stage, as well as a sound system to allow you to hear the band on the main stage. There would be free camping and free kitchens. We would have fences and gates to the main concert area, but I believed that if we offered a fair admission price for all that the festival offered, most people would respect the gates and buy a ticket.

Wes thought this was not only the smart thing to do, but the right thing to do. We both knew there was really no way to police and control a crowd of the size we were expecting. What you had to do, then, was set the right mood and create the right atmosphere and the audience will do the rest.

We also discussed drugs: "If people are smoking marijuana," Wes said, "then let them. I've never seen pot make anyone hostile." If there were hard drugs being sold, we decided, we would try to root out the dealers and hand them over to the authorities. We agreed that enforcement inside the festival grounds should be handled by us. Wes had the clout to make that stick with the local cops. He was an enlightened person in the unenlightened world of law enforcement. Unconcerned with stereotypes and rhetoric, Wes approached his job with wisdom and an insight into human behavior.

After being hassled nonstop by the cops in Miami, I was so relieved to find someone whose idea of law enforcement was to help, not harass. Wes seemed less concerned with being judgmental and more concerned with being prudent. That was the key for me—not so much that he agreed with our politics. I knew we had found our man.

WES POMEROY: I liked what I saw. These were really interesting, idealistic guys. They were smart. They had a lot of big ideas that didn't scare them. They thought they could do something, and I thought, Yeah, maybe they can. You don't see people like that very often— they had a lot of bucks they were willing to put behind it, and Michael seemed to be someone who they all respected. I was very comfortable in my role, and they were comfortable in who I was, and it was a very exciting thing to do.

Wes recommended we hire Don Ganoung, who had been both an Episcopal priest and a colleague of Wes's in law enforcement at the LEAA. He would handle community relations and become Stan's ally in dealing with the increasingly hostile Wallkill townspeople. Don was a very friendly and freewheeling type. He was in his thirties and wore his collar with grace and humor. The first week in June, Stan and Don went together to a Wallkill Town Board meeting to answer questions and try to allay concerns about the festival (this would pave the way for the town hall meeting I'd attend two weeks later).

STAN GOLDSTEIN: The opposition coalesced very, very rapidly, and I got beaten up pretty bad. I had been informed that we had a permit, but in fact, we didn't. There was simply a nonbinding ruling that we didn't need one. I further learned that John and Joel had misrepresented the festival to the town: There wasn't going to be any loud music, there were going to be fifty thousand people or less, and it was going to be a nice quiet country and folk festival without a lot of noise and tumult. There was no discussion of camping. It became clear to me almost immediately that we were headed for trouble. I reported back to Woodstock Ventures: "We have a real potential problem here. We do not have a permit. We do not have the authority to proceed, and this is going to get messy, and what do you mean you don't have an attorney?"

To help deal with the brewing crisis, we hired a local attorney, Sam Eager. Since we had a signed lease with Howard Mills and the zoning board had given John and Joel the green light in April, we thought we were in the clear legally. We didn't realize that in places like Wallkill, new ordinances could materialize on demand and that our rights, as well as our hold on the site, were much more tenuous than we thought.

In the meantime, Don Ganoung ran into trouble at the place where he'd chosen to reside. He rented a room above the local brothel (which was disguised as a bar), where he met the daughter of the mayor of Middletown. The police raided the place in a drug bust and found Don with the mayor's daughter in his room. That put yet another strain on our relations in the Wallkill township, where things were moving from bad to worse. It was all too similar to my experience in Miami.

The phone line at our field office was getting bombarded with death threats from hippie-hating residents, and one night someone fired a shotgun into the walls of the barn. Mills and his wife were being terrorized by callers who threatened to burn down their house if they didn't pull the plug on the festival. With the headline WALLKILL FACTION GIRDS TO BLOCK FOLK FESTIVAL, the Middletown paper reported that a Concerned Citizens Committee had formed to stop us from proceeding. The Wallkill town attorney sent us a certified letter demanding that we submit for the board's review an extensive array of documents detailing all aspects of the festival, from security to water and sewage to parking and traffic—most of which was still up in the air.

My experiences in Miami had taught me about dealing with conservative people and small-town officials. That was good training for what was coming in Wallkill. Having spent time in the Catskills with my family in the fifties, I had an idea of what we were up against. But I thought we could overcome the prejudices against us—and the counterculture we represented. I've always felt common ground could be found among all people. When it came time to attend the Wallkill Town Board meeting with my core production crew in June, I thought that by hearing us out and seeing us face-to-face, the local residents would come to understand our point of view. I'd never had problems communicating with people. No matter what, I could reach most people. It didn't hurt that everyone on my team of experts was a good talker.

That June night after the Wallkill Town Board meeting, we were both exhilarated and worried. I thought we had been convincing, but we knew we had a long road ahead if we wanted to stay in Wallkill.

five NEW YORK CITY

- -

"I'm going to pull your acts! YOU'RE OUT OF BUSINESS!"

I'm sitting across the table from the most powerful promoter in the industry—the guy who invented it all. Bill Graham is glowering at me and talking real loud. "I'm going to buy them out from under you," he promises. He looks eight feet tall. It's only the pickled herring he's eating that brings him into focus for me.

A few days earlier, he'd called John Morris and started threatening him. John had worked for Graham at the Fillmore and was totally intimidated. A nervous wreck, John burst into my office: "We've had it! Bill's going to pull the plug!"

"What Bill? What plug? There's no plug here," I tell John. "Calm down."

"You don't understand!" he says. "It's Graham—he's got the power and he can do this! He can shut us down!"

I realize that John firmly believes we're completely fucked. "Call him back and set up a meeting. I'll take care of this. Trust me, John. Don't worry."

It's early June and I know my bookings are solid, the contracts are signed, deposits have been paid, and the festival is being discussed all over the country. For the first time ever, we are creating a national event. Graham's important, he's the most influential rock promoter in the country, but he's not God, I tell myself. I also know that Graham generally tries to get exclusive deals for engagements within a fifty-mile radius of the Fillmore East. Our festival is nearly twice that distance from the city.

In Bill's world, he has me at a huge disadvantage. I need to bring him into my world. So John and I meet Bill at Ratner's, the Jewish dairy restaurant next door to the Fillmore, on Second Avenue. "This is my business!" Graham pounds his fist on the flimsy table. "Where do you come off, trying to screw with me, kid?"

I breathe a silent sigh of relief. I see there's a real problem here—not just some irrational, ego-driven thing. This, I think, I can deal with. I flash on an incident back in Bensonhurst: Some of the neighborhood hitters, who owned the schoolyard, picking on my cousin, who was sort of geeky. It was always up to me to get him away from them without getting punched out myself. It was about gaining respect by not showing fear, and being able to alter the dynamics through a sort of empathetic insight into what's driving things.

"First of all—we are doing this. Nobody is going to stop this thing, not even you," I said to Bill, looking him in the eye. "What's your problem with us? We're not competing with you. We're almost a hundred miles away."

"You have booked almost my entire spring season," he says. "Audiences are not going to buy tickets to see these acts individually at the Fillmore when they can wait and see them all at once at Woodstock," he explained in a slightly softer voice.

The solution pops into my head. "Okay, I got it," I say. "I had no idea we would be affecting your box office. I think we have a way for this to work out for both of us. I'm planning on adding acts to the bill up until the week of the festival," I tell him. "Send me your schedule from now through August and I won't announce an act that's playing the Fillmore until after they've appeared there."

There's silence for a few moments and I can tell he's shifting gears and coming to terms with this new situation. He may not like the idea that we exist, but he really has no grounds to keep up the assault. "Okay," he says. "That works."

Graham announces most of his shows and loves to introduce the acts, so I invite him to the festival to emcee one of the days. I can tell he's flattered, yet he declines. He'll come up but won't announce, he says: "You're the producer—it's your show. We both can't be God on the same day."

By the third week in May, things were crazy busy in New York; the office was buzzing and expanding rapidly. I'd hired more people, including Peter Goodrich, an old friend from Miami. A raconteur and streetwise guy, Peter had been a fixture in the Grove. One of those guys who knew a little bit about everything and a lot about art, Peter was forty-one and specialized in pre-Columbian art *and* Colombian gold. I later found out that he and Joyce Mitchell were acquainted in Miami in the fifties. He seemed to know everyone who was cool, from Miami to L.A.

I needed a confidant like Peter, someone who could think on his feet and someone I could completely trust. I put him in charge of concessions, everything from crafts to Coca-Cola. We were creating a bazaar in the woods for purveyors of clothing, candles, ceramics, pipes, painting, and sculpture—all manner of countercultural items from outfits like Earthcrafts, the Sorcerer's Apprentice, Fur Balloons, and Xanadu. Vendors would pay a $300 fee to rent a booth, which we would build, and hip boutiques like A Different Drummer and Limbo signed up.

We would also construct concession stands at various locations around the site for food and drink. The most difficult task for Peter was to find a company to handle the food. We originally thought locating a food vendor would be a no-brainer and that this would be a big profit center for us. As it turned out, the large food-vending companies like Restaurant Associates, which handled ball parks and arenas, didn't want to take on Woodstock. No one had ever handled food services for an event this size. They didn't want to put in the investment capital necessary to supply such a huge amount of food, on-site kitchens, and personnel, plus transport everything upstate. And what if we didn't draw the crowds we projected? I hoped Peter could convince Nathan's—a favorite from Coney Island—to work with us.

MEL LAWRENCE: The oldest member of the crew, Peter had done almost everything a person could do, and we all respected him a great deal. He was very close to Michael and I became very close to him. He was having meetings with all the big catering outfits like Nathan's, the guy who later owned Windows on the World, and Greyhound—to no avail.

Another crucial person in our office was Kimberly Bright, whom I hired for $100 a week to light incense and place flowers around. She added a certain tranquility to the space and would lead yoga classes some afternoons. We'd list her as "spiritual advisor" in the Woodstock program book.

JOYCE MITCHELL: Kimberly opened the office every day and made sure things were neat and tidy. I called her "the incense gal," and she was this very beautiful spirit who would float around for a few hours a day making people smile.

My vision for the festival had evolved into a complex, three-dimensional picture encompassing multiple elements: physical and emotional, spiritual and practical, artistic and commercial. The interplay between them all was hard for some to grasp. Except for a core group, staff members didn't have to understand the big picture, as long as they accomplished their individual assignments. I hoped John and Joel would come to see, beyond the money, what the festival could be. Artie got it completely but didn't really know how to attain it. So I devoted myself to the task of staying true to the ideals Artie and I had developed at the beginning of this adventure. I made sure senior staff like Mel, Chip, John, Chris, and Joyce were all on the same page as far as production and design. But in terms of the big picture, I knew that everyone would get it when it all came together in the end.

JOHN MORRIS: Michael was the one with the vision and the idea and waving the fantasy. If it was anyone's dream or intention that we were aimed at, it was Michael's—and Michael's energy, no question.

I saw and appreciated the different qualities among our production staff: With John, it was his swagger balanced by his knowledge of the business. Joyce was worldly and had a background in management. With Chip and Chris, it was seeing the quality of their work and the depth of their experience. The fact that they were not intimidated by the project gave me a lot of confidence in them and the people they recommended for certain jobs.

My contract with Chip provided him with an additional $6,000 to hire a stage manager, designer, and construction foreman. Chip chose Steve Cohen, a Carnegie Tech graduate and draftsman who'd worked on production at the Fillmore and the Philadelphia Folk Festival. Chris, Chip, and Steve became the nucleus of the production crew. All three, along with John Morris and Bert Cohen, had strong opinions about the stage design, so I ran a "competition" where anyone on our team could present a design.

I had a few requirements: I didn't want the stage to be jarring or fancy; I wanted it to feel familiar and very organic. I wanted something substantial that would give everyone confidence. As at Miami Pop, I wanted a design in which the crew could set up the next band while an act was onstage so there'd be no long gaps between acts.

I got about a dozen submissions—including models constructed from Good Humor sticks—of different types of stages, some pretty wacky. One looked like a birthday cake, with spiral decking rising into the sky. Those outrageous designs didn't fit what I was trying to do. I wanted something more rustic, as if it was growing out of the ground. Like the Soundouts but on a huge scale.

It finally boiled down to three finalists: Bert Cohen, Chris Langhart (John Morris's choice), and Steve Cohen (Chip's pick). Bert had designed the stage for Mel's Miami festival and devised a similar idea for Woodstock featuring a pair of large turntable-style platforms connected by a kind of trolley system so band setups could be alternated on each stage. A giant umbrella-shaped structure formed a roof, connected to the stages by tall shafts shooting up from between the platforms. The top twirled around and was decorated with two dozen flags. I decided it was too fancy for a pastoral landscape.

Chris's stage focused on a single circular platform, flanked by a pair of eighty-foot-tall telephone poles supporting a crossbar shaped like a peace sign. A canopy, with lights mounted underneath, sat on top, attached to the poles by a series of cables. Chris said he was going for a "modern, whiz-bang thing" and had been inspired by some Japanese ice-rink drawings he'd seen. It was an interesting idea but provided no quick means for switching from one band to the next. I passed, but Chris took on another assignment: a beautiful, rough-hewn concept for the artists' pavilion, where musicians would hang out when not onstage: an open, airy, sculptural structure made from thirty-four telephone poles—looking like Lincoln Logs—with a white fabric "roof" hung over the crossbeams.

Chip was pushing for Steve's stage design, and after making a few suggestions, I agreed. A pair of seventy-foot telephone poles anchored in blocks of concrete would secure the stage to the ground. On top of the poles would be a massive mushroom-cap-shaped roof, where more than 250 lights would be affixed. It featured a massive turntable system consisting of three half circles on wheels, for quick band transitions. Planned to be the largest stage constructed at that time, it would cost an estimated $20,000.

In late spring another really energetic and bright woman joined our staff. Lee Mackler (now Blumer) was hired to work for Wes in security and community relations. Like me, she grew up in a Jewish neighborhood in Brooklyn, Sheepshead Bay. Very worldly, she'd lived in Africa for a while, then had come back and worked for Dick Clark, handling the Monkees tours with the then-unknown Jimi Hendrix as the opening act. She put in a stint at Albert Grossman's office, followed by Bill Graham's, where she met John Morris, who recommended her to us.

> **LEE MACKLER BLUMER:** Bill Graham had great taste, and his skills were just beyond anything anyone could imagine. The Fillmore East had this incredible group of people. He motivated the crew—it was *not* just a job. The attitude there was that it was more than work—you knew you were part of something much bigger than yourself. And that same idea was translated for those of us working together on Woodstock.

By early June, I was focused on wrapping up as much of the booking as I could. I planned to ease into the festival weekend by making Friday the folk day, with Saturday primarily presenting artists from the West Coast, and Sunday featuring the bigger international rock bands. Bookings for August 15 were nearly complete, at a reasonable expense: Tim Hardin, who had become a friend ($2,000); the Incredible String Band, a psychedelic folk-rock group from England ($4,500); Ravi Shankar, whose music had been part of the soundtrack at my head shop ($4,500); Richie Havens, an incredible performer, then as well as now ($6,000); Arlo Guthrie, whose "Alice's Restaurant" epic had become a part of the fabric of the sixties ($5,000); and Joan Baez, one of the keepers of the flame ($10,000). We had hoped to persuade Donovan and Johnny Cash to perform, but each declined. The brilliant songwriter Laura Nyro was a possibility, but her stage fright prevented her from accepting our offer.

Simon and Garfunkel would have been great for Saturday's lineup, but after touring earlier in the year, they'd had enough of each other and didn't want to perform that summer. The Doors were also at the top of our list, but since Jim Morrison's arrest in Miami in March, he'd become really paranoid. He told his booking agent he didn't want to play Woodstock for fear of being assassinated onstage.

There were still slots yet to fill for Saturday. We had some great Bay Area bands lined up: In addition to Creedence Clearwater Revival, Canned Heat, and Jefferson Airplane, Bill Graham had confirmed the Grateful Dead ($7,500). I'd booked Janis Joplin ($15,000) through Albert Grossman, who also gave us the Band ($15,000). Albert liked the policy of "favored nations," as long as his nations were the ones favored.

The Band was to be part of the festival since the beginning. *Music from Big Pink* had broadened the musical landscape and made a deep impact on me. I had gotten to know Rick Danko and Richard Manuel, and I was hoping Dylan might show up with them. He had not toured since 1966, and I didn't want to push it with him. Bob felt put upon by so many people in the counterculture laying claim to him. I didn't want to add to that burden—so I didn't make an offer.

Of course, I would have wanted the Beatles too, but they would have overpowered the bill, and anyway, they had stopped touring and were about to break up. John Lennon was a big influence on me, and I reached out to him through Chris O'Dell, who worked at Apple, the Beatles' new management company/label. Chris was working with me to make it happen, but in May immigration officials denied Lennon entrance into the United States because of drug charges the previous year. The Nixon administration wanted to keep him out because of his antiwar work, his bed-ins with Yoko, and other protests.

I was a huge Stones fan, but as with the Beatles, they would dominate the festival and change the focus of our message. Woodstock was not intended to be about any one band or group of bands. It was about the people—and the ideas and music interwoven through their lives.

Blood, Sweat and Tears was booked for Sunday night. They were a hot group with a killer horn section that harkened back to the big bands of the forties ($15,000). I also made an offer for Iron Butterfly, known best for their "In-A-Gadda-Da-Vida" jam and drum solo ($10,000).

For what I thought would be the midnight close of Sunday night, it had to be Hendrix. Jimi had played my Miami festival for $5,000. Now, a year later, Hendrix had become the highest-paid rock musician in the world. He'd just earned $150,000 at Madison Square Garden. My favored-nations policy for booking the bigger acts had a cap of $15,000. This was not going to fly with Jimi's manager, Michael Jeffrey. Michael lived in Woodstock, and Jimi was renting a house in nearby West Shokan. So far I'd gotten Jeffrey down to $50,000—but that was still more than I could pay. I knew from Jimi that he wanted to play; he'd occasionally drop by and jam unannounced at Steve Paul's Scene and other clubs. So I went to see his agent Ron Terry. With a very deep tan and wearing white patent-leather shoes, Ron seemed like he could not wait to get back to the beach. I explained to him our favored-nations cap of $15,000, but he wouldn't go for it—he'd been instructed by Michael Jeffrey to make a deal, but for more. (Michael, it turned out, was fixated on Jimi being the highest-paid performer at the festival.)

There was another problem with the Hendrix booking. Jeffrey

and Terry required headline billing for Jimi, which meant he would be listed first on all radio and print ads, with his name bigger than any other act, and that he had to close the show. This headliner system had been sacred ground in the industry up until then, but for Woodstock I developed a different approach. I had decided that all artists would be treated equally—on ads and posters, they would be listed alphabetically and would share the same typeface. This was important, I thought, because of the large number of big-name acts, as well as the tone it would set in general.

I really wanted Jimi, but I could not breach the favored-nations clause or change the billing policy. So I offered Terry a solution: $30,000 to play two sets. Jimi would open the festival with an acoustic set and close with his band. (Little did I know that the Experience would play their last gig together at the Denver Pop Festival on June 28.) We could draw up two contracts for $15,000 per set. Terry wasn't sure if this would work, so I asked him to get Jeffrey on the phone. Michael and I talked, and after I threw in $2,000 for expenses, he agreed.

I had my heart set on having Roy Rogers end the festival with his theme song "Happy Trails." We had all grown up watching Roy, Dale Evans, and Trigger on Saturday mornings and I thought this would be the perfect good night to three days of peace and music. But their manager Art Rush turned me down.

To help finance the bookings and our ever-increasing budget, we needed to get ticket sales under way. We hired Keith O'Connor, who'd worked at the Fillmore box office, to run ticketing for John and Joel. He set up a network of ticket outlets at boutiques and head shops, as well as a mail-order operation from the Woodstock Ventures offices uptown. We sold our very first advance tickets for $6 each. Then we repriced them for $7 for one day, $13 for two days, and $18 for three; we had coded tickets printed that would be difficult to counterfeit. Several young women were hired to start filling the orders. In the first two weeks, we'd sell $169,338 worth of tickets.

When Artie left Capitol in May, he moved full-time into the offices with John and Joel. He brought with him his secretary Gisella Bitros. John became smitten with the lovely "Gizzy," and before long, thanks to her influence, he began to change—growing his hair, wearing love beads, and getting into acid rock.

Though John was loosening up, Joel would remain very reserved. Their relationship with Artie continued to disintegrate, creating more pressure for me. They would call me to report that Artie would disappear for days at a time, and John and Joel increasingly questioned his role in our enterprise and whether he should remain an equal partner.

Word continued to spread about the festival. Early on, Artie and I met with a big-time publicity firm run by Michael Goldstein, whose clients included Jimi Hendrix, but I didn't like his old-school strategies and attitude. A trio of young publicists there understood much better where we were coming from. I asked Jane Friedman, Pat Costello, and Rod Jacobson if they could personally handle our publicity, and they became so impassioned with the idea that they decided to leave Goldstein Associates and start their own company, which they named the Wartoke Concern.

JANE FRIEDMAN: We desperately wanted to do the festival, not only because it was a PR account, but we were really involved in the antiwar movement in those days. There was so much going on politically and sociologically in the world, and we realized Woodstock was going to be special. If you were into the whole politic of the era, it was the most exciting account to have at the time. Michael and Artie really built it that way—and that's how we built the festival in our campaign. We were desperately looking for a project on which to hang our hope for *change,* and this festival stood for a new way of thinking and living.

We put an awful lot of work and energy into making it happen. We had a three-month contract, and we spent every single day in the office, from about ten in the morning till three in the morning, and we sent out about three thousand pieces of mail nearly every single day of those months. We had developed an incredible list of underground press. In those days, there was very little daily coverage of pop music, very few music magazines. We kept pummeling them and sending out the same kind of information day after day, always with something new but the same old stuff included, so that it would start to resonate. And we covered radio too, all over the world.

Our first press releases stated that there would be two days of concerts—a ploy to gain additional coverage in publications when we later announced an added third day of the festival. (At the end of the year, thanks to Woodstock, Wartoke would be cited in a trade publication as being the most effective publicity company in the country.)

JANE FRIEDMAN: People started to call from all over the country, and back then, talking to someone even eight hundred miles away about a New York event just wasn't in the cards. Who cared, if it wasn't in your own neighborhood? Suddenly we had people from across the nation wanting to come: college newspaper editors, student body presidents, student activities organizers, daily newspaper columnists, music writers, people interested in rock and roll, underground newspaper writers and editors, politically involved people. Woodstock was a political event in the sense of its very existence, as a demonstration of the countercultural lifestyle.

Wartoke's approach included making me the main "face" of Woodstock. Though I was pretty shy about the limelight and felt uncomfortable being the voice of the festival, Artie encouraged me to take on this role and he shared in it to an extent. I've always been reluctant to talk about plans. My thinking is, let me do it and it will speak for itself. For a period of time, John and Joel were absent from festival publicity. Apparently, some at Wartoke thought their image as capitalists would derail our credibility with the counterculture—an element critical to our success. Artie also felt their image as straight businessmen would run counter to our underground credibility. Excluded from some press releases and interview opportunities during the period when we were solidifying our relations with the underground, Joel became outraged and confronted us about it. This took me by surprise. At the time, I did not imagine that personal publicity would be important to him. The whole thing blew over, and in mid-August, Joel and John probably wished they'd never insisted on being included in the press.

One of the last bands booked was Santana—and that turned out to be one of the most positive events in an increasingly difficult month. After making peace with Bill Graham at Ratner's in early June, he returned threatening to cancel the Dead's appearance if I didn't book the Bay Area bands he'd started managing, It's a Beautiful Day and Santana. Neither had released records and I hadn't heard their music. I wasn't about to book anyone without hearing the music first. "Send me tapes," I requested. He did and I liked them both, but Santana really knocked me out: Carlos Santana's distinctive Latin-rock guitar style, Gregg Rolie's soulful vocals and B-3, and a fantastic rhythm section. It reminded me of the music Tito Puente had played at my parents' nightclub all those years ago, but with a heavy rock and roll edge.

"Tell Bill I'll take Santana," I told John Morris. "They can open Saturday's show. They sound amazing." Bill let us have the group for $1,500—the best bargain of the festival and one of its highlights.

With an incredible array of talent already booked and the best team in the business in place, I was momentarily on top of the world. Yet, by mid-June, despite two meetings at the Wallkill Town Hall with the locals and our best efforts to keep positive channels of communication open, things in Wallkill were boiling over. And just when it looked like things couldn't get any worse, new conflicts were rapidly developing in New York.

six **DOWNTOWN**

"I don't give a rat's ass about your festival! We'll bring this motherfucking festival down around your motherfucking ears unless you meet our demands!" Abbie Hoffman is yelling in Joel's face. At Yippie headquarters, the stark room on the second floor of the squat brick building reverberates with the sound of Abbie's voice. When Joel tries to negotiate with him, Abbie lets him have it. Joel blanches and I feel his fear.

If I didn't know him, I might have been afraid too. But I know Abbie— and a bit about his theatrics. Right now he's playing Jesse James. Instead of robbing a train, he wants a piece of our festival. I need to be Billy the Kid.

For weeks, we'd been hearing shots from the underground. While working in the Village office late one night, I was listening to WBAI-FM, the "people's station." DJ/commentator Bob Fass, a great friend of the Left, started trashing Woodstock:

"Word on the street says this festival is a rip-off! These promoters don't care about the people. They just want to make a buck. The music is for the people. It should be free!"

Angry, I dialed the station number and got Fass on the phone. Fass had emceed some of the Soundouts, so I was surprised by his attitude.

"Listen, do you think we're here working at three in the morning because we don't care about people?" I challenged him. "Do you think something this big can be put together without money? How would you pay for stages and doctors and bands and water and toilets and food and power and the million other things it's taking to make this happen? *And* do it in a way that gives better than it gets?

"I'm talking about *fair exchange*!" I went on. "I firmly believe if we're looking for more than that, the movement is not going anywhere!

"This festival could be the opportunity for people to really come together," I continued, "to be ourselves on our own. For once we are in a position to do it right and do it righteous. You're not doing anybody any favors by trashing us, because if you succeed, it will mean the festival *doesn't* happen. And once again, all we'll be left with is a lot of talk!"

He was pretty cool with my rant, and when we hung up after nearly an hour, I hoped I'd left him with some things to think about.

The next day, Abbie Hoffman dropped by our Village office. He wanted to talk about Woodstock. He'd heard about the festival at a Yippie meeting in Ann Arbor.

ABBIE HOFFMAN: I said [to Michael], "This culture belongs to the people in the streets—we're trying to build a counterculture. I'm putting together a coalition of Lower East Side groups and we want a meeting." We came up with about eight or ten groups—the Yippies; the Medical Committee on Human Rights; the Up Against the Wall

Motherfuckers; antiwar people; the East Side Service Organization, which took care of bad trips and runaways on the Lower East Side. Michael agreed to meet with us.

ROZ PAYNE, ACTIVIST FILMMAKER: I was with a film group called Newsreel and hung out with the Yippies. They were so much fun compared to the other movement people. Abbie and I just went into Michael's office one day and said to him, "All right, this is a stickup, we've come to get what's ours!" We were really cocky in those days. Michael was so cute and had this pretty hair. He wasn't a threat or anything—he was very friendly. He said, "Okay!" I think Abbie thought that we'll get in there and we'll do our thing, but at the same time, these guys aren't our enemies. Michael was smiling, he was nice, he just agreed to everything.

TICIA BERNUTH AGRI: Michael had the ability to allow everything, to not resist it and even give it a little space, which would defuse the situation.

I couldn't reach John, so I called Joel and gave him a brief overview of the Abbie Show. It was hard to convey its nuances to Joel because there was no common frame of reference. I did what I could and set up a meeting for Joel and me to sit down with Abbie at Yippie headquarters. With all the pressure and negativity coming from Wallkill, I was buoyed by the thought that at least we were finally going to get some support from our brothers and sisters in the underground.

The Lower East Side community of activists, radicals, and politicos thought we were trying to rip off the counterculture—at least that's the position they chose to take. They seemed to worry that their ideals were being co-opted by corporate America in the guise of Woodstock Ventures. All along I tried to make it clear that we were part of the counterculture. That I was trying to marry our common principles with just enough commerce to actually manifest something of the better world we envisioned, that Woodstock was of and for the people, that it was okay for someone willing to bankroll this thing of ours to make a fair profit.

At our meeting, we discovered that the solution for now, ironically, was money. Abbie was asking for a twenty-grand donation to the cause.

"You're taking from the culture, so you should give back to the culture!" he argued.

"What about *our* cause?" I asked. "What exactly is it you think we should pay for?"

"Listen," he answered, "you're gonna get all these city kids up there in the country with their smoke and their acid and no services and no survival abilities. We want to come up there and put out a daily survival sheet and distribute our leaflets—information on the political and social movements we're involved in. And we wanna take care of our people. All you guys are interested in is making money."

His words seemed aimed for the benefit of the other movement people in the room, the thrown-together "coalition" for which he was the spokesman. Abbie and I had already had at least one conversation about our preparations. But his words made sense to me. "Joel and I need a minute to discuss this," I told the gathering, and we headed to the hall.

Joel asked me if they could really cause problems and I said yes. He asked me if there was some other way out of this that wouldn't cost us money and I said no: "But if they'll really do what they say they will—and I believe they will—it would be a big help to us on the ground and also add to the credibility of our message."

Joel was not happy. He didn't like these people, he didn't like their politics, and he didn't like being extorted. But this was a street thing and the rules were different, and I believed we could turn the situation into something positive for all of us.

We went back inside and I said, "I'll tell you what—if your concern is really about helping people cope, we'll give you enough money to put out your survival guide, for your printing press, and space to set up your tables. You've told us that you don't think we're doing enough to prepare, so you can help us help the kids when they arrive."

Abbie seemed to like this idea and asked for a few moments to converse with his posse. Afterward, Abbie—no stranger to negotiation—asked what we were willing to offer. We proposed $5,000 but settled at $10,000. Though Joel was still reluctant to fork over $10,000, I took the deal back to John to get his approval to release the cash.

ABBIE HOFFMAN: With half of the $10,000, we bought a printing press, which ultimately was a lifesaver. I'm sure it saved several lives. We handed out survival-type information, as well as political information. The money also went for a truck rental, for paper supplies, and a certain vitamin that we used for bad acid trips. We got one or two hundred free tickets. Many of them we gave to WBAI-FM, to help raise money for the station, and we gave them away to people on the street who couldn't afford to go.

There was a revolutionary community that felt the music had grown out of its bowels and that it was in conflict with mainstream society—with the police, who were working for mainstream society; with the war in Vietnam; with racism being practiced by society. It would seem quite natural, if we're going to have this kind of event, to try in some way to inject some kind of political content into it. It's not that we were against the festival—we wanted the festival to be seen within the context of what I later termed "the Woodstock Nation," to be seen in a context not removed from the politics.

Our meeting at Yippie headquarters happened to fall on the same day, June 19, that we ran a "Public Notice and Statement of Intent" in the Middletown *Times Herald-Record*:

> Certain persons in this area have started rumors with the
> express intent of creating such an emotion-laden atmo-
> sphere that reason and common sense cannot prevail . . .
> They are attempting for some unknown reason to make it
> impossible for officials to do anything other than present
> a solid block of opposition to our presentation, regardless
> of what their investigations & consultations reveal . . . It
> is our intention to remain in your community . . .
>
> —Woodstock Ventures

What had started as a skirmish of mistrust and confusion in Wallkill had turned into an all-out war. Our half-page ad was our attempt at defending ourselves against attacks coming from the Concerned Citizens Committee (CCC) and the moves made by town officials to stop the festival with a new ordinance prohibiting crowds of five thousand and more from gathering. We'd been served with a pair of summonses to appear in state supreme court on July 7 to face actions filed by the owners of property adjoining the Mills property, who claimed our festival would be a public nuisance and should be banned.

The *Times Herald-Record* later reported that, according to the town attorney, a preliminary injunction stopping our festival might be issued in three weeks. CCC spokesman Frank Jennings told the paper that his group had gathered two hundred signatures on a petition to stop the festival because "citizens fear for the health, welfare, and moral well-being of the community and festival visitors as well."

Mel, Chris, Stan, Wes, and their crews were working around the clock to finalize our plans for sanitation, sewage disposal, water distribution, medical personnel, traffic routes, parking, food preparation, and security to present in detail to the Wallkill officials. These plans would determine whether or not we'd met the criteria necessary for a permit enabling a large assembly of people. Officials threatened: no permit, no festival.

In the Wallkill community, we were trying to convince the opposition that we knew what we were doing and that we could bring something positive to the county. Mel asked the Hallandale, Florida, chief of police, George Emmerich, to issue a statement about how well run the Miami Pop Festival had been: "It was orderly and the problems were minimal considering the number of people involved," Emmerich reported. "The crowd was polite and well behaved. The producer complied with any requests made for security precautions."

To improve community relations, we hired Mel's then-girlfriend Rona Elliot to help with local PR. Rona, though only twenty-two, already had experience doing promotion and publicity in radio (which is how she met Mel) and for a couple of festivals. She made friendly overtures to newspapers, local radio and TV stations, and various organizations like the Kiwanis, where she gave a talk on how the festival would benefit the community. She even helped to organize a community square dance. We enlisted a soft-rock band out of Boston, Quill, to perform gratis in the area. Because they played rather benign rock and roll, we thought they would make a good impression on the locals.

LEE MACKLER BLUMER: I organized a "goodwill" tour for Quill. We went to the Warwick School for Boys, a juvenile delinquency home, to some prisons, and to a mental hospital. But it didn't really help to elevate our stature in the community. They only wanted to know that we were a danger. They didn't want to know any of the good we were doing. Don [Ganoung] would put on his priest garb and try to convince them that we weren't going to put acid in the water, but I don't think he changed many minds.

We also tried to prove our sincerity to the underground community. To that end, Wartoke organized a public meeting at the Village Gate in New York to bring together various factions for a discussion.

Wartoke's invitation read: YOU ARE URGED TO PARTICIPATE IN A SEMINAR TO DEVELOP AND SET GROUND RULES FOR OUTDOOR PEACE AND MUSIC PROGRAMS.

> **JANE FRIEDMAN:** We decided that we should do something to give people ownership of the festival, because there had been a threat from various political factions of an insurgency at the festival, like, if we didn't do this, they would cause riots. We invited college kids from all over to come to our seminar and make a decision: Should this be three days of peace and music where we can take a well-earned vacation from spending the year working for the revolution—is it okay to drop the politics and have a good time? Or should we turn it into a political event?

Artie and I wanted Woodstock to be a cultural event, not devoid of politics but a chance for the culture to stand on its own and simply be about itself. If Woodstock worked, that would be the strongest political statement possible.

On June 26, to a packed house at the Village Gate, an activist named Jim Fouratt served as moderator. Extremely articulate, Jim led the discussion in the direction of peace and love. Wes Pomeroy and I both gave talks about how we could prevent conflicts with police— another violent riot had just gone down at a festival in Northridge, California. We wanted to explain in a public forum how ours would be different from those where problems had arisen. I'd already planned to go to other festivals to see how they handled crowds—and learn from what they might do, both right and wrong.

"We plan to create a community among all the people who attend the festival," Wes told them. "What happens then will be the responsibility of the audience as much as the promoters. If you give people enough to do, and give them what they pay for, there won't be any trouble."

"Publicity for the festival will be geared to letting kids who come know the kind of facilities and the kind of community we are creating," I said. "The idea is to get the audience almost as involved as the performers. If the crowd participates in the festival, people will want to respect the rights of others."

I also wanted to let the audience know that this wasn't all about money. As far as money goes, we all do what we can to get by. But if you can get by and also do some good, that's where it's at. I was single, had simple material needs at the time, and was living my dream. But I knew that John should make a return for the investment and his and Joel's hard work, and that Artie and I deserved something for all our work.

After about four hours of discussion, the two hundred or so people at the seminar voted that Woodstock should remain as we envisioned it: three days of peace and music. Politics, while represented in booths and in distributed literature in an area called Movement City, would not be part of the onstage proceedings.

Being hammered from the right and the left, I clearly saw the road we had to travel: It was the place where art and commerce could coexist, where opposing ideas could coexist, where our humanity would come first and our differences would just add color. Elements of the festival were deeply grounded in the underground movement but without the overt politics—the focus would remain peace and music.

Around the same time, Stan had contacted a group with experience setting up and running the campgrounds and free kitchens. The Hog Farm was—and still is—an entertainment/activist commune that formed in Los Angeles in 1965. By 1969, they were living in New Mexico when not presenting their free "Hog Farm and Friends" road show. (They got their name babysitting a pig farm in Sunland, California.) One of the founders, Hugh Romney, had been a Beat poet in the fifties and, backed by jazz players, used to give readings in the Village. He opened shows for John Coltrane and Thelonious Monk, and in the early sixties was poetry director of the Gaslight. His wit and subversive one-liners impressed Lenny Bruce, who became his manager for a while.

The Hog Farm included Hugh's wife, Bonnie Jean (the subject of Dylan's "Girl from the North Country"), and several members of the Merry Pranksters, who cooked up the Acid Tests with Ken Kesey and the Grateful Dead in the Bay Area. The Pranksters' psychedelic bus further inspired the Hog Farm's own bus, Road Hog. Stan first contacted the Hog Farm back in April when they were marooned in New York following an incident in Pennsylvania. They'd been driving through in their bus and were pulled over by the cops. One Hog Farmer had been busted when the cops found a pipe with cannabis ash in it in his sleeping bag. The others were doing odd jobs in New York to raise money to pay his bail. Stan met with them in a loft on Houston Street that belonged to Calico (aka Elizabeth Zandermee), a friend of the Hog Farm and the Grateful Dead. Stan told them about the festival and that we'd like them to participate. They seemed dubious but agreed to meet me.

HUGH ROMNEY: Stan Goldstein walks up to our kitchen table and looks like Allen Ginsberg on a Dick Gregory diet. He says, "How would you guys like to do this music festival in New York State?" He was one toke over the line, so we dismissed him.

A couple of days later, Stan and I met Hugh and Bonnie Jean and some of the others at the Cauldron. An unforgettable character, Hugh was missing most of his teeth and was wearing a straw cowboy hat with a big feather in it. He struck me as some sort of cosmic clown/word slinger. Today, everyone knows him as Wavy Gravy—B. B. King gave him that name at a Texas festival a short time after Woodstock.

That day at the Cauldron, over bowls of brown rice and steamed vegetables, we talked about what Woodstock was going to be and the role I envisioned for them: mainly to run the campgrounds, free stage, and free kitchens. The conversation turned to their experiences dealing with people having bad acid trips and OD'ing on drugs, and I realized how important they could be in helping us accomplish our goals. "How would you deal with a fight breaking out in the campgrounds?" I asked. When Hugh answered, "With pies in faces!" I was totally sold.

We agreed that a small group of Hog Farmers would drive the Road Hog to New York in July to help Mel and his team build a children's playground and clear trails around the camping areas. When Hugh asked how the rest of the eighty or so Hog Farmers would get to New York, I said, "There won't be time for you to drive, so we'll bring you in by plane." They were blown away by that, but I had the feeling they didn't believe I was really serious. For their services, we came to a fee of $8,000, plus all the leftover supplies and equipment bought for the kitchens and campgrounds.

STAN GOLDSTEIN: After they returned to New Mexico, Bonnie Jean would walk from the Hog Farm's property, some many miles, to the nearest telephone, and each time we would have a conversation regarding plans for their involvement in the festival. Then we would arrange for our next conversation, as we continued to pursue matters.

Stan and I sat down with Wes Pomeroy and discussed the role we had mapped out for the Hog Farm. He was a bit skeptical, thinking they might cause more problems than they would solve. He wanted the Hog Farm to be checked out. That made good sense to me, so I sent Stan to New Mexico on June 21. He arrived as the Hog Farm, the

Pranksters, and others were having a summer solstice celebration in Aspen Meadows, outside Santa Fe.

STAN GOLDSTEIN: I made it my business to wear a white business shirt, formal slacks, and carry a briefcase. There I met with Jim Grant, a friend of Wes's who was the head of the New Mexico Governor's Crime Commission, who was going to come along and be the outside observer reporting back to Wes. He wrote to us in a preliminary report, "The Hog Farm can be recommended, not necessarily for its artistic merit (no judgment), but for its responsible attitudes and conduct." But after the Solstice, he followed up with a "supplemental report": "The entire affair appeared to be completely without organization or management . . . There was a certain amount of mammarial exposure . . . It may be that when these people do their 'thing' for themselves, the circumstances are completely different than when they stage a production strictly for profit."

HUGH ROMNEY: Stan shows up with one of those classy aluminum attaché cases like the high-rolling rock and rollers tend to sport. He announces that we'll have our own American Airlines astro jet to fly us to New York. We were blown away, and we got the cream of everybody in the commune scene to be part of our team.

STAN GOLDSTEIN: The Hog Farm seemed to have their scene pretty much together, so we didn't see anything wrong with it. Fortunately, Jim Grant left before the bus races: Ken Kesey came down for the event and showed up with the usual accouterments—pot and friends—and he had a lot of beer with him. This was the first time most of us had ever seen screw-top beer bottles, and Kesey had dosed the beer. Psychedelic beer! In the throes of that beer, everyone decided to have a bus race through the meadow. All these buses raced across, swerving to avoid sinkholes at the very last instant, with people riding on the tops of buses and hanging on, and riding on the fenders and hoods, all psychedelicized. It was one remarkable sight.

Soon after Stan got back from New Mexico, I traveled to Denver to check out the three-day pop festival at Mile High Stadium, June 27 to 29. There I ran head-on into everything I wanted to avoid at Woodstock.

From the outset, there was tension between the police and a large group of dissidents called the American Liberation Front, who were in town for a big Fourth of July protest. They were agitating the kids, saying that the festival should be free. By the time I arrived on Saturday, there were several squads of police—maybe 150 men in full riot gear—placed in the stands to the left of the stage. I guess they thought a show of force would serve as a deterrent to the gate-crashers and protesters, but I had the feeling it would do just the opposite.

A few hundred people started rushing the gates, and to stop them, more squads of cops in riot gear showed up. A melee between rock-and-bottle-throwing kids and billy-club-wielding cops resulted in lots of injuries on both sides. Then, during the middle of Johnny Winter's set, the cops started spraying tear gas to clear the area by the entrance gates. The wind came up and blew it as far as the stage, affecting everyone. Finally, the police had the promoter open the gates, and thousands flocked inside the stadium in time for Creedence Clearwater Revival's closing set.

I thought I should get back to New York Sunday night, but I really wanted to check out Joe Cocker and the Grease Band. As it turned out, Sunday saw more violence than the day before. Thousands showed up without tickets, expecting another free concert, and were greeted by vicious police dogs, mace-spraying machines, and hundreds of cops suited up for battle. It seemed obvious to me that the confrontational approach taken by the police provoked the violence. I had a lot to think about. I decided we would not have a uniformed police presence within our event. I'd do whatever it took to prevent something like Denver happening at Woodstock.

As for the music, Joe Cocker and the Grease Band were amazing. I'd signed Cocker after Artie gave me a tape he'd gotten from Denny Cordell, Joe's producer. He was virtually unknown then. When we first heard him, everyone assumed he was a black soul singer, but he turned out to be a skinny English guy who hopped around the stage like he had Saint Vitus's dance. He could wail!

By the time I flew to Denver, the relationship between Joel and John and Artie had completely deteriorated. Since Artie had left Capitol, he was no longer prevented contractually from being signed into the company. I had been holding his shares and we needed to legally transfer them. I had been getting increasing pressure from John and Joel not to sign him in because they thought he was getting further out of it. Almost daily they would call and report some new travesty they said Artie had committed or complain about a responsibility he was ducking. My offhanded attempts to keep the lid on both sides had not helped matters much.

"Look, we'll make this right," they said, "but we just can't see bringing him into the company the way things are. We'll split his shares among the three of us."

As far as I was concerned, Artie's shares were his from day one and I was certainly not in a position to take them back. I had enough on my plate, and I did not have the time or the skills to change the dynamic of their relationship. I told them that they were putting too much pressure on me, that I was going to Denver, and then signing Artie's papers when I got back. I said, "It's up to you guys. Work it out!" I later heard that after I left, Joel panicked, thinking I had flipped out and split for good. All I wanted was for them to take care of what they had to do, and let me take care of what I had to do. Joel went to see Artie that weekend and they started a dialogue. They resolved things enough so that our partnership remained intact.

Late June found John Morris spending an intense evening at booking agent Frank Barsalona's apartment in Manhattan with Pete Townshend. John had asked Frank, who ran Premier Talent, to help us book the Who. The band had been performing their brilliant rock opera *Tommy* all spring, touring the United States and playing mostly theaters and halls. John and I agreed that the Who was what we needed for Saturday night. But Pete Townshend was dead set against doing Woodstock, even though Frank tried to convince him that it would be a huge boost for the band's career. Apparently, the band was exhausted and wanted to return to England as soon as the tour ended.

So Frank invited both Pete and John to his home for dinner. He figured, if necessary, they could spend all night talking Townshend into playing Woodstock. That evening, John and Frank kept bringing up the subject, even though Townshend refused to be swayed. When the Who's road manager John Wolff showed up around 1 A.M., Frank reminded them that the band had to return to the States the same week as Woodstock for an August 12 concert at Tanglewood promoted by Bill Graham. Still, Townshend and Wolff said no. Frank and John Morris stayed up all night, refusing to give up, and outlasting Pete, who by 4 or 5 A.M. was dozing off. They kept waking him up until finally, at 8 A.M., Townshend couldn't take it anymore: "Okay, we'll do it!" he said. "Just let me go to fucking bed!" After a bit of a negotiation, John Wolff agreed to a $12,500 fee, half of which was paid upon signing the contract. The contract also spelled out our "no star billing" policy: "Artists are billed in alphabetical order. This is a festival concept therefore placement of act is at the discretion of promoter." (The

Who would later include a facsimile of our contract inside the album cover for *Live at Leeds*.)

Now that most of the booking was complete, we needed to create a visual that would carry our message in ads, posters, and billboards. Early on, we had announced the Aquarian Exposition with a poster by David Byrd, but it was not the image we were looking for. John Morris suggested we give graphic artist Arnold Skolnick a shot. I gave Arnold the copy and told him the main message was "three days of peace and music," and that I wanted a dove perched on a guitar as our image. The bands' names would all be the same size and in alphabetical order, and there would be a description of the site. Many people thought that not emphasizing the acts in our advertising was counterintuitive. Every other concert event before (and after) Woodstock had focused on the acts—but that was just the point. Woodstock was not to be like any other event. Woodstock was to be advertised as an event that was about us: our culture, our music, our art, and our values.

A few days later, Arnold returned to my office with a mockup of the poster. It was perfect: inspired by some cutouts made by his young daughter, he had crafted the simple image in primary colors of a white bird perched on the neck of a blue-and-green guitar set against a red background.

ARNOLD SKOLNICK: I was staying on Shelter Island, and I was drawing catbirds all the time. I just took a razor blade and cut that catbird out of the sketchpad I was using and turned it into a dove.

Artie continued running ads on FM radio stations and in underground newspapers, from Atlanta's *Great Speckled Bird* to Kalamazoo's *Western Activist,* Minneapolis's *Hair* to San Diego's *Door,* nearly forty in all. After the confrontation with Joel and John, Artie focused more in this area.

ARTIE KORNFELD: I ran an ad with a coupon in it, for people to buy tickets in advance. We were running out of money and that ad took in over a million dollars.

The coupon ad listed the same description of the festival site that appeared on the Skolnick poster:

ART SHOW
Paintings and sculptures on trees, on grass, surrounded by the Hudson Valley, will be displayed. Accomplished artists, "Ghetto" artists, and would-be artists will be glad to discuss their work, or the unspoiled splendor of the surroundings or anything else that might be on your mind. If you're an artist and you want to display, write for information.

CRAFTS BAZAAR
If you like creative knickknacks and old junk, you'll love roaming around our bazaar. You'll see imaginative leather, ceramic, bead and silver creations, as well as Zodiac Charts, camp clothes, and worn out shoes.

WORKSHOPS
If you like playing with beads, or improvising on a guitar, or writing poetry, or modeling clay, stop by one of our workshops and see what you can give and take.

FOOD
There will be cokes and hotdogs and dozens of curious food and fruit combinations to experiment with.

Walk around for three days without seeing a sky-
scraper or a traffic light. Fly a kite, sun yourself. Cook
your own food and breathe unspoiled air. Camp out:
Water and restrooms will be supplied. Tents and
camping equipment will be available at the Camp
Store.

By the end of June, daily newspapers across the nation were running articles on the festival, including a lengthy syndicated feature
with the headline ROCK RUMBLING INTO RIP VAN WINKLE COUNTRY. This
one detailed the problems we were having in Wallkill and the local
efforts to stop the festival.

Surrender was not part of our vocabulary, and our crews had been
working steadily on-site. Our numbers there had grown to about
seventy-five. We moved into a larger motel called Round Top and
hired a couple of women to prepare meals for all the workers.

Wallkill's proposed ordinance—with its list of insurmountable
obstacles—loomed over us. In addition to all the paperwork we had to
submit to the town board, we had to obtain approvals from the county
health department, the town sanitary inspector, the town health officer, the State Water Resources Commission, the town building inspector, the county highway department, the state department of
transportation, the sheriff's office, the state police, the chief engineer,
the local fire commissioners, the town fire advisory board, the zoning
board of appeals, the town police, and the county fire coordinator.
The conditions would be impossible for anyone to meet. An editorial
saying as much ran in the Middletown *Times Herald-Record*:

So severe are the "regulations" that it is inconceivable to us
that they would survive even casual court scrutiny. Plainly
town officials hope that the prospect of litigation will

discourage promoters of the massive art-music festival . . . We regard the proposed ordinance as an example of flagrant misuse of governmental power. It is proper for a township to protect its citizenry from excesses that might arise when thousands congregate; it is, in our opinion, highly improper to prohibit one event in the guise of regulating it.

The draft ordinance, for instance, stipulates that "no light shall be permitted to shine beyond the property line" . . . that no music "shall be audible beyond the property line," and that no noise or disagreeable odor "shall be permitted to emanate from the property" . . .

In their haste to stymie the festival, in mid-August, the architects of this ordinance may not have pondered all its implications. For one, the traditional Orange County Fair scheduled for late July could not possibly meet the light-noise-odor test Supervisor Jack Schlosser and his associates devised. For another, the privately operated stock car races at the fairgrounds, which spread their noise pollution 10 miles away, would be out of business . . .

We suggest that the town board discard its monstrous plan and direct its energies to a fair—repeat fair—set of regulations.

A vote on the ordinance by the town board—which we knew would pass—was to take place on July 2. Stan told the *Poughkeepsie Journal,* "Those areas of the ordinance that are just and righteous will be complied with in the fullest, just as we have always intended. But those areas of the ordinance that are unreasonable and impossible, we are going to fight."

Unlike the battles I'd been through over the past month, I had a bad feeling about this one.

seven YASGUR'S FARM

"I hesitate to think what will happen if the forty thousand people who've already bought tickets to our festival come to Wallkill and there is no event!"

"Is that a veiled threat?" comes a loud voice from the back of the packed room.

"There's nothing veiled about it!" I answer. "That's a problem that concerns all of us!"

Once again, I'm addressing a group of hostile Wallkillers. It's July 14, and I want them to know that there might be consequences for them, as well as for us, if the festival is canceled. The anger in the room is so palpable I can't help but think back to what happened last month at the Denver Pop Festival when the cops and kids clashed. Like Denver, communications have broken down completely. I try to understand how we got here—how does fear become so entrenched that it squeezes out all possibility of discourse, logic, and fair play?

Two weeks earlier, on July 2, after five hours of debate, the town board approved the new ten-page law regulating assemblies of more than five thousand by a vote of 5–0. Slight modifications have been made, including lowering our newly required insurance bond from one million dollars to half a million dollars—and exempting the Orange County Fairgrounds (with its county fair and drag racing) from complying with the regulations.

We're appearing before the town Zoning Board of Appeals (ZBA) and making our case for the festival, after having been denied a building permit for the site. This is the same room where exactly three months earlier John and Joel got the green light from the ZBA when they first proposed holding a music-and-arts fair at the Mills Industrial Park.

I've choreographed the presentation to impress the community with our competence and comprehensive planning. Mel, Stan, and Don make articulate and convincing arguments. Stan reads a statement characterizing our festival as "a cultural event of major magnitude involving artists of all kinds, including painters, sculptors, filmmakers, and theatrical groups as well as musicians." He also states that we are committed "to preserve and enhance the pastoral atmosphere of the festival site."

Mel, armed with detailed maps, diagrams, and charts, explains that the site will be enclosed by chain-link and concrete-reinforced fencing, that an intricate system of roads and pathways is being prepared, and that in addition to the music, fine-arts exhibits, and crafts booths, there will be food concessions, medical facilities, campgrounds, portable toilets, and many of the things you might find at the county fair.

Don Ganoung goes into more detail about our security and traffic plans. He says that we're hiring more than four hundred security personnel, sixty mobile radio units, and parking lot and stage security guards. Parking facilities, he explains, will be located throughout adjoining areas where we've rented more land, and two hundred buses will transport concertgoers to the festival from the lots. "There will also be a screening process for troublemakers since no one will be allowed to drive to the festival grounds," Mel adds. "Some of our people will be stationed at the bus pickup stations to screen those who may be looking for trouble."

Then it's my turn. "We've already put more than five hundred thousand into this project," I tell them. "We cannot get that money back. We are moving forward with this festival. Our work has been slowed by the circumstances of the past few weeks, but that's about to change. We are totally committed to the event, to the plans, and to the site."

My words are met with a loud and angry uproar. Being caught between two drawn pistols at Miami Pop comes to mind. I think to myself, It's definitely time to ramp up the effort to find another site.

The mood lightens in the room when the ZBA makes an announcement: Our field office—the barn next to the Mills property—is in violation of town zoning laws because we are operating a business in an area zoned residential. We have to shut down the office immediately. Following a big round of applause from the townspeople, the next announcement is just as bad. The ZBA will make its decision on our permit within forty-eight hours.

We're one month away from the festival, and we've ridden our horses into an ambush from which there is no escape. It's time to get the hell out of Dodge.

The next day, the Middletown *Times Herald-Record*, continuing its detailed coverage of the whole saga, reports:

> For the first time, conscientiously polite relations between residents and festival organizers broke down, as the ZBA hearing wore on for hours in a stuffy room at the town hall. Residents, seemingly annoyed at the length of the Woodstock Ventures presentation to the ZBA, hurled taunts and insults at festival officials. Long-haired Lang, 24, was

greeted with a barrage of stock long-hair comments ("Isn't he pretty?") when he stood up to address the audience. But he unsettled the audience with his prediction of 40,000 "disappointed" ticket holders appearing in Wallkill.

We really didn't hold out much hope that we'd get the building permit, especially considering the string of setbacks that had occurred since July 2. On July 8, the Middletown Fire Department had unanimously turned down a proposal to supply personnel to run Nathan's food concessions. The fire companies' membership objected to the long hours Nathan's had required (6:30 P.M. to 4:30 A.M.) of their workers and the low wages they offered ($1.75 per hour). Nathan's needed three hundred workers to staff their concessions, and talks between the hot-dog company and Peter Goodrich were beginning to break down. With our location now in jeopardy, Nathan's was threatening to pull out of the deal.

On July 11, the same day Mel and Rona conducted a press tour of the festival site, a hearing was held regarding the injunction brought against us by the CCC. Acting state supreme court justice Edward M. O'Gorman of Monroe refused to issue a decision in the case, stating that the injunction was premature since the zoning board at that point had not yet accepted or denied our construction permit. In other words, if the ZBA didn't stop us, then he'd look at the case.

Two days later, Ulster County assemblyman Clark Bell, a Republican from Woodstock, released a statement to the press about a letter he'd just sent to Governor Rockefeller requesting the appointment of a coordinator to oversee the festival. Bell's statement said, "The National Guard should be alerted," and he went on to say that state police and the Ulster County Sheriff's Department had been making preparations to handle masses of people mistakenly arriving in Woodstock looking for the festival. He accused us of "romanticizing

Woodstock. They made it known that Bobby Dylan lives in Woodstock and that the Beatles vacationed in Woodstock a few years ago." (In reality, during the weekend of August 15–17, the town of Woodstock would be a ghost town.) We also received complaints from the Ulster County hamlet of Wallkill, which prospective concertgoers were confusing with the township of Wallkill—in Orange County—our site's location. Apparently, the wrong Wallkill was getting overwhelmed with queries about the festival.

D-day arrived on Tuesday, July 15: With none of us present, the ZBA released a four-page decision, REJECTING our application for a permit. The ruling stated: "Generally the plans submitted are indefinite, vague, and uncertain. Furthermore, the estimated number of persons attending has been too indefinite and uncertain, and based upon the amount and type of advertising, the venture would be contrary to the intent of the Zoning Ordinance. Problems of fire, police protection, and health would be contrary to the health and safety of the public."

Disbelief, shock, anger, frustration. From our field office, where he was packing boxes, Stan told a journalist: "There's a field out there, and come August fifteen, sixteen, and seventeen, there are going to be people out there listening to some boss sounds. If you ask me how we're going to do it, I don't know. But we're going to do it."

I too knew we were going to do it, but *not* in Wallkill, and I was strangely relieved. Wallkill had not felt right to me from the beginning and things had only gotten worse. I spoke to John and could sense he and Joel were crushed. They also knew that we would not recover in Wallkill. I tried to reassure them we'd find a new site, but they had grown weary of my saying, "It's *covered*!" and felt that this was the final blow.

Calling Artie next, I had a similar conversation except that—as always—he was energized by my optimism and I was energized by his belief in me. I had a talk with the rest of the team and told them, "Don't worry, I've got this covered. This *is* going to happen. Just get ready to move."

We could appeal the ZBA decision, but we knew that would take longer than the month until the festival date. John immediately issued a press release stating that we had been unjustly kicked off the site and that we were going to sue those responsible:

> The statements . . . that have been made by the Wallkill town zoning board of appeals and other individuals are entirely false. Accordingly, we have instructed legal counsel in New York City and in Wallkill to institute damage proceedings and to provide relief from this offensive harassment and the totally dishonest statements of certain individuals. Never in the history of an outdoor event of this kind have such massive and thorough preparations been made for the security and well-being of everyone in attendance. There will be a Woodstock festival—make no mistake about it!

MEL LAWRENCE: You can't evaluate in money terms the sweat and love we put into that land during that month and a half. We built rock walls and rock structures with our own hands. We turned those acres into a work of art before we were turned out by pettiness and jealousy.

We had already dug postholes, and utility companies from Orange and Rockland counties were installing power lines. I had ordered telephone poles that were going to be the supporting structure for the stage. They were coming from far away on a big truck. When you unload giant telephone poles off a flatbed, they just roll off, and it's not so easy to retrieve them. Just as the office phone was ringing with the zoning board decision, these guys drove up with the poles, saying, "Can we unload?" "*Hold it!*" I stopped them just as we got word that it was over.

STAN GOLDSTEIN: Michael's demeanor remained, ostensibly, unflappable through just about everything. You could rant and rave at Michael, as I did from time to time, and he just absorbed it like a sponge, and stayed cool. Which of course, if you were crazy, only infuriated you more! Michael remained very Michael, his usual, sometimes-enigmatic self through that.

We had to find a new location for the festival—and fast. I knew morale would go down the tubes if I didn't refocus everyone into action immediately. I put anyone who was not packing up the site or office onto the phones to talk to press, local radio stations, Realtors, and others who might help us find a new home.

PENNY STALLINGS: Michael just went into overdrive to get the next space. Once it was determined it wasn't going to work in Wallkill, he was extremely reassuring that somehow this was going to happen.

All the ensuing radio coverage resulted in several phone calls coming in from people suggesting locations. Some were crackpots, but we checked out everything. The day after the verdict, on July 15, Ticia got a call in our Village office from a guy who said he had a place in Sullivan County that would be perfect for the festival.

TICIA BERNUTH AGRI: When we lost the site, Michael told everybody, "Don't worry, we've got it under control!" He told me, "Ticia, you stay by the phones while I'm at the lawyer's office." He, John, Joel, and Artie were meeting with their attorney, Paul Marshall, to discuss their options. While he was gone, this guy called and said, "My name is Elliot Tiber and I've got land, and we want you in White

Lake!" I said, "Oh yeah? We'll be right there!" I immediately called Michael, and in a few minutes he picked me up to head upstate.

As soon as I heard from Ticia, I called Mel and Stanley and told them to meet me at the address Ticia had been given for the El Monaco Motel in White Lake. My one perk from Woodstock Ventures—a '69 Porsche 912 I'd rented for the duration of the project—could make it to the location in about ninety minutes. Ticia and I zipped up the New York State Thruway to Route 17, followed it to Route 17B and County Road 52. Our Catskills destination—the Sullivan County township of Bethel—brought back memories of family vacations there when I was a kid.

Following Elliot's directions, we pulled up to one of the sorriest-looking motels I've ever seen. The sagging sign said EL MONACO, so we knew we were at the right place. A chubby guy in his early thirties bounded out to greet us, introducing himself as Elliot Tiber. I discovered that his real name is actually Eliyahu Teichberg and he grew up in Bensonhurst, right around the corner from me. He told us the motel belonged to his parents and that only a couple of its eighty rooms were occupied.

At one point, a seemingly crazed Jewish lady with a thick Russian accent rushed outside, and she and Elliot started screaming at each other. She turned out to be his mother. Despite her bossing him around, Elliot remained cheery and upbeat. It was obvious that this kind of thing went on all the time between them. Elliot seemed overjoyed to see us and determined to somehow involve himself in our festival. He started talking about a theater he'd built in a barn on the property. "I put on a theater festival every summer," Elliot told us, "and I already have a permit for this year's production—so you've got your permit!" An off-off-off-Broadway troupe, the Earthlight Theatre, was there for two months, crashing in a dilapidated rooming house on

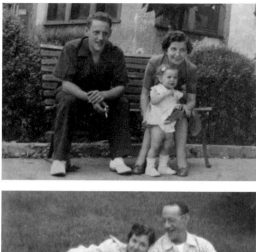

Clockwise from top right
My parents, Harry and Sylvia Lang, and my
sister, Iris, circa 1941; my parents and me,
circa 1949; Iris and me in Bensonhurst, circa
1949; Elvis is king—me at about age twelve

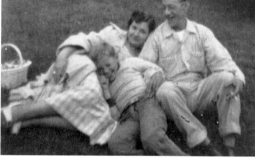

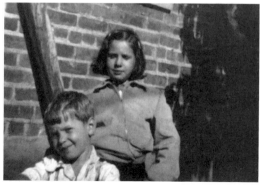

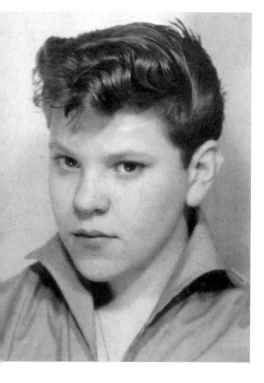

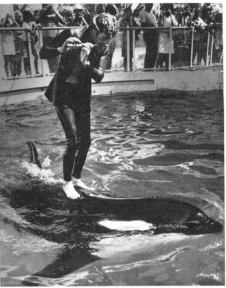

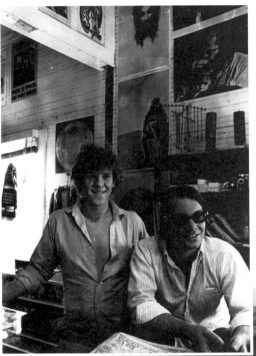

Left
Behind the head shop counter with
employee Howard Zaitcheck, 1967

Below
Me, Howard (standing), and a customer
in front of the Head Shop South, Coconut
Grove, 1967

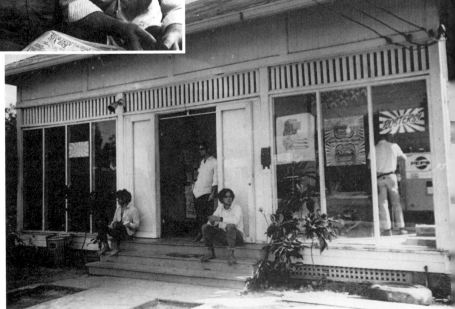

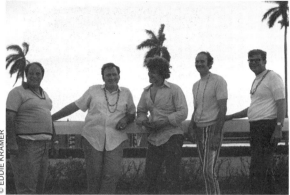

Joint Productions partners
(*from left*): Marshall Brevitz,
head of security John Ek, me,
Barry Taran, unknown

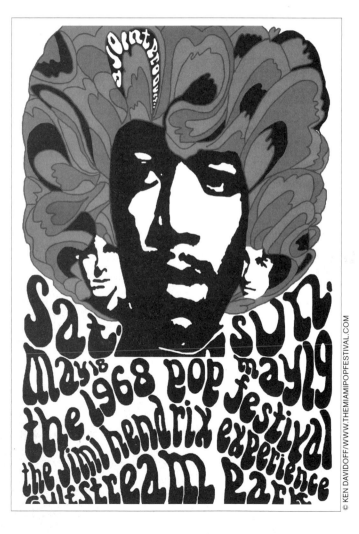

One of the Hendrix
Miami Pop Festival
posters, 1968

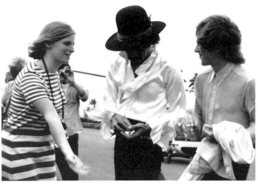

Hendrix lands: Linda Eastman (later McCartney), Jimi Hendrix, and Mitch Mitchell at Miami Pop, May 18, 1968

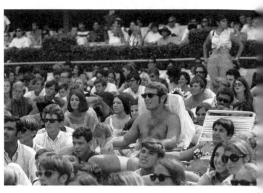

Miami Pop audience on our sunny day, May 18

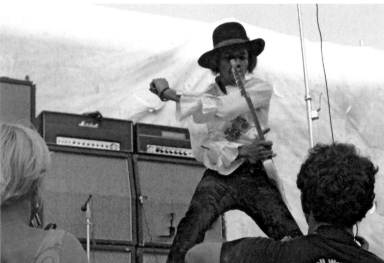

Jimi Hendrix Experience onstage at Miami Pop, May 18

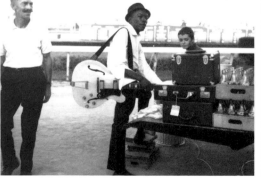

John Lee Hooker waiting to go onstage, May 19

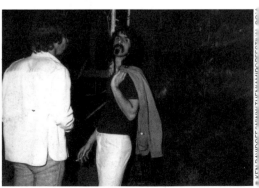

Frank Zappa backstage at Miami Pop, May 19

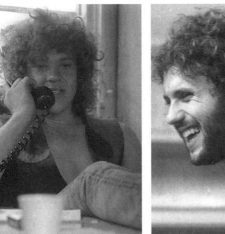

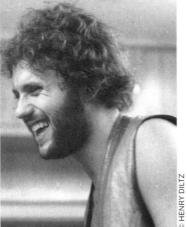

Far left
Me in the Woodstock
production office

Left
Artie Kornfeld

© HENRY DILTZ

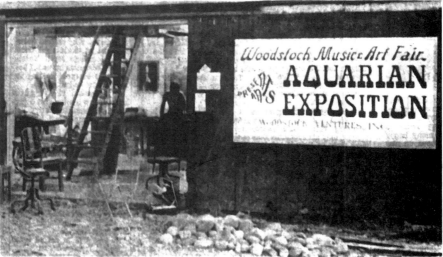

© ALBERT/TIMES-HERALD RECORD

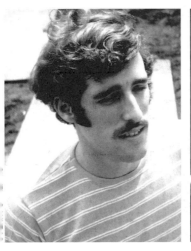

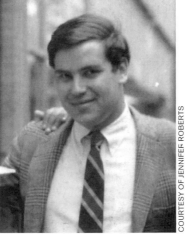

Above
Our barn office at the
Wallkill festival site

Far left
Joel Rosenman

Left
John Roberts

COURTESY OF JENNIFER ROBERTS

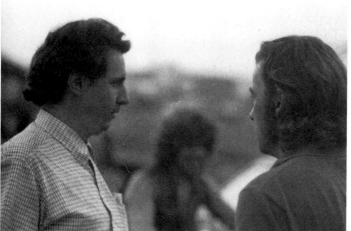

Left
Sound engineer Bill
Hanley and artist
liaison John Morris

Right
Artist Tom Edmunston (wearing hat)
and Mel Lawrence

Below
Peter Goodrich

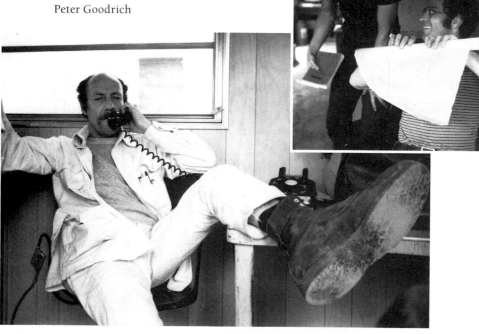

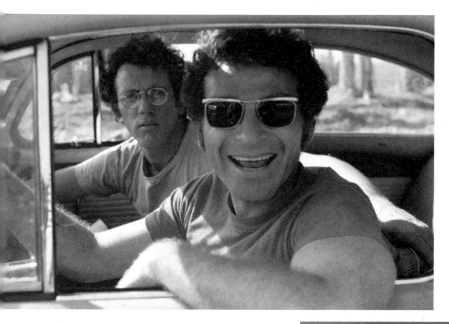

Above
Mel Lawrence and Dale from the art crew

Right
Lee Mackler Blumer, assistant to Wes Pomeroy

Below
Cameraman Michael Margetts and Don
Ganoung, who handled community relations

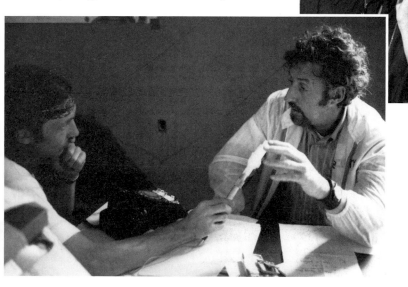

Right
Mel's assistant Penny Stallings

Below
Chip Monck and I reviewing site plans

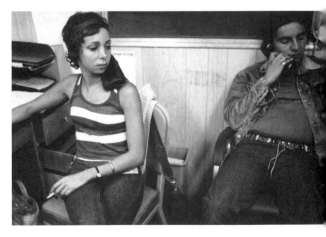

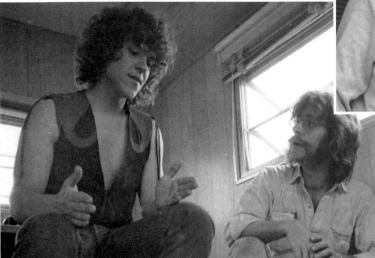

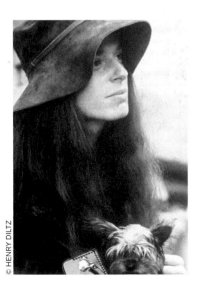

Above
Wartoke publicist Sunny Schneer and Billy Soza, one of the Native American artists invited to Woodstock by John Morris

Left
My assistant, Ticia Bernuth

the property. We decided to wait for Mel and Stan, who were driving the thirty-five miles from Wallkill to meet us, before seeing the site.

Finally they arrived and it's, "Okay, Elliot, let's go see what you've got!"

"Follow me! It's a natural bowl and perfect for the festival!" Elliot promised with a big grin.

On the way around the back of the motel, we passed all kinds of handmade signs on different run-down buildings named for various celebrities like Jerry Lewis and Elvis Presley. Scattered bungalows were caving in, and there was an empty swimming pool filled with debris. As we walked toward a sloping meadow, the ground felt soggy and springy under my boots. This did not bode well.

We started descending a gradual incline—straight down into a large swamp filled with nubby growth and amputated saplings. As we trudged through, I asked, dreading the answer, "So how much farther to the site?"

"You're *in* it!" Elliot answered, with a grand sweep of the arm. "Of course, we can bulldoze and drain all of this."

"This is the place we've been waiting to see?" Mel exploded at Elliot. "What an idiot! What do you think you're doing? You really think we could use this?"

I agreed, as diplomatically as I could. "This isn't going to work at all." When we got back to the motel office, I asked Elliot, "Maybe there's someone who could show us around?"

"I'll call a friend of mine," Elliot offered, perking up after having looked pretty crestfallen. "He's in real estate." Stan departed, but Mel decided to go with Ticia and me. About a half hour later, a sleazy-looking guy named Morris Abraham arrived in a big Buick. He was happy to take us to check out some properties.

A few miles from Elliot's, we drove along 17B through magnificent farmlands—it's absolutely beautiful farm country with open fields everywhere. We took a right turn off 17B onto Hurd Road. About a quarter mile up, we broached the top of a hill and there it was.

"STOP THE CAR!" I shouted, barely able to believe my eyes. It was the field of my dreams—what I had hoped for from the first. It was not lost on me that we had left *Wallkill* to arrive in *Bethel*—"the House of God." I left the car and walked into this perfect green bowl. There at its base was a rise just waiting for our stage. The others joined me. Mel, Ticia, and I exchanged looks of wonder. "Who does all this land belong to?" I asked Abraham.

"Max Yasgur," he replied. "He's the biggest dairy farmer in the county. He owns ten farms and two thousand acres. I can call him and see if he's interested in renting to you."

"Yes, let's do that," I said. I had to work hard at staying calm. I didn't want to appear too excited to this guy. We passed a sign that said HAPPY AVENUE, and drove until we got to a pay phone and Abraham reached Max. We drove on to his home—a simple white farmhouse—and met Miriam and Max Yasgur, a handsome couple in their late forties.

"These people are interested in renting some of your land, Max, to put on a music festival," Abraham explained.

Max had a sharply intelligent face and looked me in the eye. "You're the people who lost your site in Wallkill, aren't you?" I was preparing for the worst when he added, "I think that you young folks were done a grave injustice over there. Yes, I'll show you my land—we might be able to strike a deal for your music fair."

Max got in the car with us and Morris told him we'd seen the field off Hurd Road and would like to start there. As we drove, Max pointed out some of the land he owned. My heart was beating so fast I hoped no one could hear it. We arrived back at the field and I told Ticia and Mel to wait in the car and keep Morris occupied while Max and I took a walk into what had become *home* in my mind.

"Max, can we talk about this field?" I asked. "This is the perfect place for us. It's the right size and shape and has great sight lines and great vibes." Something about the way Max carried himself told me to be completely candid with him: "It feels like we're meant to be here." I wanted to seal the deal right there in the field. We walked over the rise above the bowl.

"How much land would you say you'd need?" he asked.

"Well, in addition to this field and whatever you have surrounding it, we need another six hundred acres, including land for camping and parking," I told him.

"I still have a crop of alfalfa growing here and crops in several other fields as well," Max said. "How soon do you think you'd need them?"

"Would *now* be too soon?" I asked, with a smile.

Max laughed and pulled a pencil from the protector in his shirt pocket. He wet the tip of the pencil with his tongue and started to scribble numbers on a pad. A sharp guy, he figured how much he was going to lose on his crop and how much it would cost him to reseed the field. When he came up with a number for the bowl, it seemed a fair price and I said yes immediately. We agreed that he would calculate the other fields in much the same manner, taking into consideration whether or not he could harvest crops before we needed to prepare the ground. It was going to be a hefty sum, but I knew that this land was our Woodstock—and Max was our savior. As we shook hands, I realized for the first time that he had only three fingers on his right hand. But his grip was like iron. I was thinking, He's cleared this land himself.

Without Max Yasgur, there would have been no Woodstock. He was known in Sullivan County as a strong-willed man of his word. He had grown up on a farm with a boardinghouse where summer guests stayed. His father died when he was a teenager, so he became the head of the household. He'd studied real estate law at my alma mater, NYU, but his dream was to expand his family's property and create Yasgur's Dairy, the biggest milk producer in Sullivan County. He continued to buy up farms and land, building his dairy herd, until he reached his goal. He developed delivery routes and built a massive refrigeration complex and a pasteurization plant. All that hard work took its toll, though, and by the time we met him, Max had already suffered several heart attacks. An oxygen tank was kept handy for his use at all times, and he had an oxygen tent in his bedroom.

I called John and Joel to tell them the news: We were back in business—we had the perfect spot for the festival. John was guardedly optimistic on the phone but immediately agreed to come upstate the next day to work out the final arrangements with Max. I hoped he and Joel would recognize this for the miracle it was when they saw the land for themselves. I then called Artie and Joyce Mitchell and told them to let everyone know we had a home. I phoned Stan and told him to gather every set of plans we had and get back to Bethel ASAP. Mel returned to Wallkill to organize the move so the trucks could begin hauling everything on Monday.

The next day John and I met with Max, his son, Sam, who was a lawyer, and their banker. We had agreed on a $50,000 fee, plus another $75,000 to be held in escrow to cover any damages that might occur, and John had brought cashier's checks in that amount. After negotiating the other terms of the lease, including what we could and could not do to the land, we signed the papers at 10 P.M. that night.

MIRIAM YASGUR: It takes Michael about fifteen or twenty minutes to charm you, and having spoken with him for a while, he really put us at ease. He explained the way it was going to be, and he made it sound like everything was going to be so simple and not anything that big. He has a way of ingratiating himself—I think he's a born con man. Even though you know you're being had, you can't help but like him. John came across as a very straight person—and probably one of the most honorable young men I ever met.

JOHN ROBERTS: After the deal was closed, we were driving toward New York, and Michael Lang, as usual, had the final word. "You know," he said, "when we start working on that pasture up there, there'll be so much going on, we'll lose track of the provisions of the contract that we've violated. Of course," he added after a considerable pause, "Max'll probably lose track too."

JOEL ROSENMAN: Max wanted to make sure he got that fifty thousand before some other dairy farmer did. Having said that, I'll say this about Max, he never asked us for another dime after we paid him.

By Friday, July 17, it started hitting the papers that we were moving to White Lake. At first Max was a bit coy about it, telling the press that he was still deciding whether or not to rent us the land, but I knew Max's handshake was his bond. He was a man of integrity and an idealist. I don't believe the money alone was what motivated him. Max was willing to rent to us to give us a fair chance to accomplish our dream—much as he had done with the dairy. We showed him all our maps and detailed designs for Wallkill, and he was impressed by our diligence—this wasn't something just thrown together. He wanted to be paid for his land, but in return we also got his loyalty.

We still had to meet with the White Lake officials and get any necessary permits. After what we'd just been through, we were nervous about that. Max promised to help us as much as he could, and we had a preliminary meeting with Bethel town supervisor Daniel Amatucci over the weekend. He didn't think there would be a problem but set up a special meeting for us with the town board for Monday, July 21. We were moving as fast as we could.

As Wallkill officials were preparing a cease-and-desist order to be served on Woodstock Ventures to kick us off the Mills site, we were already out of there. Talk about closing the barn door after the horse has gone! We'd started by emptying the barn of everything and moving the furniture, files, and supplies to White Lake. I made a deal with Elliot to rent his entire motel through the festival and into September, in the process pulling the El Monaco out of foreclosure. The motel also became a ticket outlet. We set up offices in three shabby rooms, and moved ourselves and some of the staff and crew into the rest. We also established festival headquarters in the old New York Telephone Building in neighboring Kauneonga Lake. Near Max's property, Penny found a shuttered hotel called the Diamond Horseshoe that could house 150 or so workers. It needed some renovation to be habitable, but the owners rented it for a song. Chris Langhart and his team started making enough repairs so that it had running water and electricity—but not much else.

By Monday, we were already contacting the electric company, the phone company, and other suppliers to bring power and communications to the property. Jim Mitchell ordered some trailers to use for production offices on-site near the spot where the stage was to be built. At the Mills site, we'd planned to truck in water, but Max's fields were conveniently located adjacent to a small, crystal-clear lake named Fillipini's Pond.

On July 19, the *Kingston Freeman* reported:

> Woodstock Ventures have contacted two sources in Sullivan County about the prospect of holding the exposition in the area. The *Freeman* contacted Max Yasgur, owner of a 2,000 acre farm in the Town of Bethel, who

confirmed . . . the possible use of his property as the site for the exposition. Yasgur stated that he had not yet decided whether to make his property available but added that he expects to speak with representatives of the exposition tonight.

The mystery surrounding the homeless happening was further heightened today when a Town of Bethel resident stated that he will hold a press conference Monday to reveal information about a "White Lake Music Festival"—Elliot Tiber refused to confirm rumors that the Aquarian Exposition and the White Lake Music Festival were one and the same.

While I owed Elliot a lot for making the call that had brought us here, the last thing we needed now was a loose cannon. I canceled the press conference and told him if he opened his mouth again before checking with me, we would be gone from his motel in a heartbeat. I did not want anyone to jump the gun by announcing anything before getting through the session with the town board.

Another problem came to us compliments of our real estate agent, Morris Abraham. He told me that we had to come up with ten thousand dollars for some unnamed officials if we wanted to be sure any approvals or permits necessary would be granted. We had planned to give him a finder's fee for connecting us to Max, but this reeked of extortion. I felt that if we paid them off, it would taint the entire effort and somehow come back and whack us in the head. Karma works in every direction. Stan and I talked it over and we decided to let Max know what was happening. On the way over to Max's, we agreed that instead of paying off Morris and his partner on the board, it would be wise to donate the money to the local hospital fund as a sign of our good intentions.

When I told Max about the payoff demand, he blew his top. "No way are you to pay a bribe to Morris Abraham! I'll find out who's at the bottom of this and make sure there are no obstacles to your music fair—and if there are, I'll make public this bribery attempt!" Max had become our staunchest ally. He liked our idea of donating the money to the hospital too, and we promised to follow through. John agreed and the donation was made to Bethel Medical Center.

On Sunday, July 20, we took a break from our preparations for the town hall meeting to watch the lunar landing and see Neil Armstrong walk on the moon. The irony! America was putting a man on the moon, and we were just trying to land on *earth*.

Monday night, Don Ganoung, Mel, Stan, and I arrived to meet with town supervisor Dan Amatucci, the Bethel Town Board, and the Bethel Zoning Board. The room was tiny, and we all sat together around a table. Bethel residents showed up, but there was just enough space for a few to stand. Some peered through an open window.

Mel presented a hastily drawn plot plan for Max's land, which was filed with the zoning board. We identified the plot of land where we wished to hold the festival: three miles west of White Lake in a block bordered by Route 17B, Perry Road, Hurd Road, and West Shore Road.

We had hired a Sullivan County lawyer, Richard Gross, who told the board members that he had been advised by the Bethel town attorney Frederick Schadt that there were no zoning issues: Max's land was zoned commercial and agricultural. We promised to submit building plans as soon as possible for the board's approval.

Max spoke eloquently on our behalf, urging the boards to approve the festival: "All they are asking is fair play. Once we have formed a barrier against those who want to grow their hair long, we can just as well form a similar barrier against those who wear long coats or go to a different church."

"I would not stand in the way of anything if it is legal," Amatucci announced after our presentations. "We will welcome anyone to the town if they abide by the law, mind their p's and q's, and live within the law. If they do this, there will be no problem."

After three hours of discussion, we waited outside the town hall as votes were cast. While our fate was being sealed in that room, I sat alone on the building's steps, reflecting on what had to be some sort of cosmic intervention that—just hours after being expelled from Wallkill—had led us to a man like Max Yasgur and this perfect place. Coincidence or luck just did not explain it. It was karmic. We were meant to be here. As I looked up at the American flag waving from the portico over my head, I knew we would get the approvals we needed.

Both boards unanimously decided in our favor. Just after the meeting, Don Ganoung told the press: "They gave us the green light— the festival will be held as planned! We are all very excited. We have leaped the biggest hurdle anyone can imagine."

At the board meeting, we had emphasized our desire for local business involvement in the festival. Members of White Lake's small business community welcomed us with open arms. Garage owner Ken Van Loan, head of the Bethel Businessmen's Association, told the press: "This is the greatest thing that's ever happened to Sullivan County. It's a shot in the arm to the town economy. The festival will boost money spent in Bethel for lodging, food, and auto maintenance." He later estimated that we'd spent $200,000 in Bethel within the first ten days of our residency.

There were only 2,366 residents living in Bethel. That part of

Sullivan County had fallen on hard times since its heyday as a resort area in the 1940s and '50s. Families had moved on to more exotic locales for their summer holidays. Tourism and agriculture remained the main sources of income for the area. There were still a few large hotels near Liberty that catered to well-heeled Jewish vacationers from New York City—like the Neville, Grossinger's, and the Concord—but the countryside was mainly dotted with run-down bungalow colonies and failing motels. Nearby Monticello had a racetrack—but it was not what you'd call a flourishing attraction. It seemed that Bethel needed us as much as we needed them.

Not everyone was happy about our arrival. On Sunday night a crudely lettered sign made from a large piece of plywood had been placed just down the road from the entrance to Max's property: STOP MAX'S HIPPY MUSIC FESTIVAL—NO 150,000 HIPPIES HERE! BUY NO MILK. Not a good omen for us. But when Max saw the warning, it only strengthened his resolve to help make our festival a reality. That was a measure of who he was.

All the local papers carried stories about our rise from the ashes. "Comparing our reception here to that of the Town of Wallkill," Rona was quoted as saying, "we are overwhelmed! We have been getting fantastic cooperation from county, town, and village officials." Paul Marshall told *Newsday* that the cost of moving the festival would be about $100,000.

Another paper reported that we had sold seventy thousand tickets. When these numbers came out, Dan Amatucci started fielding phone calls from worried locals, about twenty the first day. "It will be worse than the grasshoppers in the grain fields," one resident told the *Times Herald-Record*. So far, though, no threat of legal action.

Max continued to speak out on our behalf: "They're pretty good kids, and I welcome them," he told the Hackensack *Record Call*. "I'm from a different generation, and we did other things . . . Just because a boy wears long hair doesn't mean he's going to break the law. I don't buy that nonsense. This is going to be something different, but I don't have any fears at all."

To assuage other residents' fears, I released a statement: "There may have been a misconception as to the total number of persons attending the festival. The 150,000 figure reported will be the *total* attendance over three days, with possibly 50,000 at any one time." This was disingenuous but necessary in those early days of Bethel.

"If residents of the immediate area are concerned over the protection of their properties," Wes assured uneasy neighbors, "we will place a security detail at their homes twenty-four hours a day." We also let it be known that helicopters would be used for traffic control, as well as to transport anyone who needed to go to the hospital. Ambulances, doctors, and nurses would be on the grounds at all times.

We knew we had to move into overdrive to get the site built—not only to be ready in time for the concert, but also to proceed so far along that nothing and no one could stop us. It was like a raid—get in, get up, and get it on before anyone had a chance to prevent it.

JOHN ROBERTS: Once Max entered the picture, it kind of freed up a generosity impulse on our part, and so we just started spending. Things were going past too quickly to think in terms of profit and loss. I swear, I *never* thought of profit and loss. I just thought of getting it on—and I've determined in retrospect why I was so careless in my thinking about it at that point. It was because I had contemplated the abyss of a total wipeout a week earlier! The three quarters of a million dollars we had spent as of July 1 was gone, plus we'd have to end up refunding about $600,000 worth of tickets, so compared to a $1,300,000 bath, everything else seemed like an enormous windfall. We were [no longer] making the calculation as to what the income was going to be. Otherwise there would be no festival, and you could hope whatever the ancillary rights were, whatever number of tickets you would sell would pay you back. Every week we were collecting tens of thousands of dollars for tickets, so we always had enough to cover ourselves, up until the last week when we moved to White Lake—and then we had quite an enormous number of expenses and no income. Some of the expenses were not anticipated. The original budget was out the window.

Everything began at once on-site. We had twenty-eight days to build what would normally take three months. On Monday and Tuesday, July 21–22, trucks started arriving with the building materials, and we completed the site layout. We convinced the utility company to run power lines from eight miles away. The local phone company rep resisted our request for numerous phone lines for the production trailers, backstage area, and security office, not to mention the hundred pay phones we wanted for the concession area. Finally, Chris Langhart called a phone company executive he knew in Ohio, who flew in to advise us. As our consultant, he managed to pressure the local phone company to get this impossible job done in the time we had left, and they brought in eight crews to do it. The phone lines eventually cost us about $20,000 to install—but New York Bell really made its money on thousands of collect calls placed by people on the pay phones during the festival.

Everybody was moving as if possessed. Our first priority was putting in roads and installing the plumbing systems. Max didn't want any underground pipes, which complicated everything, but Chris Langhart figured out a way to do it. It was like laying out and installing an infrastructure for a city. It was a massive thing to build in a month. We also got permission from Max to drill several wells to add to the water supply.

MEL LAWRENCE: We got this water-witch guy who was an albino with a divining rod, and this guy hit on everything. I think we hit water five out of eight tries.

Wes started working out the new parking arrangements. We realized we'd have to rent more land around the area for parking lots—we hoped to use the system we'd devised for Wallkill to bus people to the site. Eventually, we'd spend another $25,000 on land rentals.

A hiring office at the El Monaco was set up, just some tables in the area in front of the office. It seemed like everyone within a hundred-mile radius who was under thirty and could handle a hammer showed up to apply for work. We hired about seventy carpenters and laborers to build the seventy-by-eighty-foot stage, the lighting and sound towers, the artists' pavilion, and fifty or so concession structures. Within a day or two, we had over two hundred workers preparing the land and campgrounds, including the first group of Hog Farmers, who'd arrived in the Road Hog. As the weeks went by, these numbers would increase to over a thousand.

Chip Monck and Steve Cohen arrived with their blueprints and designs. Steve appointed his assistant Jay Drevers, a twenty-one-year-old carpenter from the Fillmore, as foreman in charge of constructing the stage. Mel got all those telephone poles rerouted to White Lake. We signed a contract with a garbage-disposal firm, which would use compactors to deal with the garbage before hauling it away, and we arranged with Portosan to provide and service the portable toilets.

From the first days, foul weather plagued our progress on the Bethel site. Rain complicated getting the fields cut and cleared, and slowed down the construction of the roads. Some patches had to be laid down three or four times, as the roadway would just sink into the mud after a particularly hard downpour. Members of the work crews slogged through mud and high grass, wet to the knees.

"The kids don't mind this," Rona told one newspaper. "This is part of their thing, the same as the guys who go hunting or fishing in the rain."

MEL LAWRENCE: We were really together as a team. There were guys cutting down trees so that we could build the food stands, guys building the stage, guys building the pathways through the woods. Everybody was pulling together. I tried to tell them that it was karma that was going to carry us through this. If we treated this land, which was so beautiful, with respect—by not driving our trucks across where the people were going to be but rather using the roadways—that karma would come back to us. Everybody bought into that. And it was raining like crazy all the time. Everybody was getting B-12 shots once a week at the local clinic. That was great!

I'd wake up in the morning and there'd be 150 impossible things to accomplish that day. I'd knock them off one by one, then wake up the next morning and start all over again. I stayed in the moment, so the pressure would never get to me. I loved the challenge and the ballet of all those moving parts. Over time, it did get to almost everybody else. When someone on staff would wander off into the woods, mumbling, "I'm done, I can't take this anymore. Everything is on me and we're never going to make it!" I would bring them back: "I know it's hard and the pressure is on, but it's not just on you. It's on all of us. Believe me, together we'll get this done."

Everybody knew what we were up against. The telephone-company men worked around the clock for us; the power company did the same. Everybody really pitched in, in a great way. It was infectious. Given the time we had, this was an undertaking of heroic proportions, and just about everyone rose to the occasion.

JOEL ROSENMAN: Michael got good people. He wasn't sure, I think, who he needed, and so he got maybe twice as many people as he needed, and we paid maybe a lot more than we had to pay. But I think it's to his credit that he put together a group of people who overkilled greatly what was necessary to do the project.

From the New York office, we started notifying managers and agents about the change in location and added a contract rider to that effect. Most were cool with it, though Creedence Clearwater Revival sent word through their management that they "didn't want to play in a cow pasture!" Fortunately, they changed their mind. The Jeff Beck Group did cancel—not due to our venue change, but because they had broken up when their lead singer Rod Stewart decided to join the Faces.

We added a few more blues-rock acts—Texan Johnny Winter, an amazing slide guitarist; the Keef Hartley Band from England (Hartley was a drummer who'd played with John Mayall); and another British group, Ten Years After, featuring Alvin Lee, the fastest guitarist around. I also booked Mountain, a new power trio formed by the great producer Felix Pappalardi, who'd worked with Cream, the Youngbloods, and others. Pappalardi played bass and Leslie West was the frontman, with a huge voice and a blazing guitar style. These were all bands who'd been inspired by the original bluesmen like Robert Johnson and Muddy Waters.

At Steve Paul's Scene, I'd discovered a kind of throwback fifties group called Sha Na Na. They were a bunch of Columbia University students who played rock and roll classics and dressed like it was the fifties. Their name was inspired by a lyric in the old doo-wop hit "Get a Job." They wore their hair slicked back in DAs and did dance routines. I thought they would be a fun addition, acknowledging our rock and roll roots while giving the audience a chance to lighten up. I went backstage to see them after their set and offered them the date. By this time, everyone knew about Woodstock, and they were stunned to be invited.

I signed Sly and the Family Stone through Hector Morales. I loved their sound—rhythm and blues and soul that rocked—and Sly's lyrics ran deep. He'd been one of the first acts we booked, but I dropped him because he was getting a reputation for canceling shows. Hector assured me that Sly had been making his summer dates and that Woodstock was important to him, so I rebooked them and hoped for the best. We thought we had the Moody Blues lined up too, but the band's manager wrote that "an album being made . . . in London is not turning out very well" and that the group had to cancel their trip to the States to finish it.

While everything was blowing up in Wallkill, I'd received a letter from Apple Corps Ltd. Though John Lennon still couldn't get into the country, they offered me a couple of their new artists: James Taylor and Billy Preston. Apple also wanted to send over an experimental film for us to project and a silver plastic installation to stand in for the Plastic Ono Band. Because of the scramble for a new site, the letter languished in the site office and did not get my attention until it was too late. They all would have been great additions to the weekend—even the conceptual substitute for the Plastic Ono Band.

Rumors were rampant about Woodstock—before the Wallkill debacle, various papers reported that Lennon and possibly Dylan would be there—but now we needed to get the word out that the concert was still on. Wartoke made phone calls and sent out a flurry of press releases to hundreds of newspapers about the change in location.

JANE FRIEDMAN: At that point, we were constantly being asked by everybody what was happening with Woodstock. We didn't want

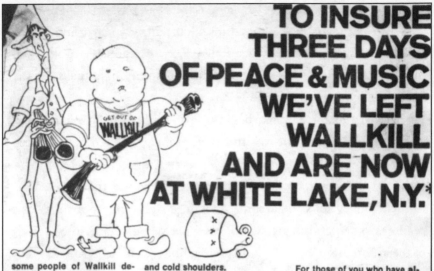

TO INSURE THREE DAYS OF PEACE & MUSIC WE'VE LEFT WALLKILL AND ARE NOW AT WHITE LAKE, N.Y.*

some people of Wallkill decided to try to run us out of town before we even got there.

They were afraid.

Of what, we don't know.

We're not even sure that they know.

But anyway, to avoid a hassle, we moved our festival site to White Lake, Town of Bethel (Sullivan County), N. Y. We could have stayed, but we decided we'd rather switch now, and fight Wallkill later.

After all, the whole idea of the festival is to bring you three days of peace and music.

Not three days of dirty looks and cold shoulders.

Just one more word about those *concerned* citizens of Wallkill

Our lawyers have been instructed to start damage proceedings immediately.

Now to something a bit more pleasant.

Our New Site.

It's twice the size of our original site. (Who knows, maybe the people of Wallkill did us a favor?) That means twice as many trees. And twice as much grass. And twice as many acres of land to roam around on.

For those of you who have already purchased tickets, don't worry. Your tickets, even though printed Wallkill, will of course be accepted at our new festival site at White Lake in the Town of Bethel.

We'd also like at this time to thank the people of Bethel for receiving the news of our arrival so enthusiastically.

See you at White Lake, for the first aquarian exposition, Aug. 15, 16, and 17.

Woodstock Music & Art Fair

White Lake, Town of Bethel (Sullivan County), N. Y.

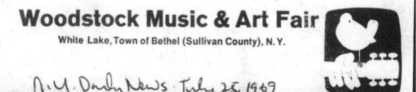

N.Y. Daily News. July 25, 1969

it to die, so we kept the information flowing every day. When it became controversial, we tried to engage people into taking a side. It was a brilliant campaign.

Because it made national news, losing Wallkill was probably the biggest publicity boost we could have gotten. To make the most of it, we decided to create an ad to place in the *New York Times,* the *Daily News,* and other papers explaining what had happened and giving information about our new location. We commissioned Arnold Skolnick to draw a caricature of two hillbillies holding shotguns, standing next to a jug of moonshine.

The ad ran for a week, beginning July 25. Now it seems a bit heavy-handed, though it was funny. It probably helped to sell thousands more tickets.

A few days later, on July 28, a benefit was held at the Village Gate to raise money for scholarship funds to enable "ghetto artists" (the predecessors to graffiti artists) to exhibit at Woodstock. This was part of the art program we had planned, reaching out to artists of all types to have their work shown and sold at the festival. Performers at the benefit included Marian McPartland, Les McCann, and Roberta Flack. John Morris had also come up with the idea of bringing Native American artists from New Mexico on the Hog Farm Express plane we had chartered to transport the Hog Farm. He contacted some members of the Hopi tribe, who agreed to fly out on August 7 with Hugh Romney and the others.

July 28 also marked the date of our first press conference in White Lake, as well as another meeting at the town hall with police, local officials, and state health department representatives. It had been one insanely busy week since we'd gotten our okay.

But trouble reared its head again. A group of angry residents showed up at the town hall with their own brand of Concerned Citizens Committee petition. This committee included two members of the zoning board who had voted yes the week before. Now, banding with some of Max's neighbors and a few other residents, they were citing Woodstock as "a public nuisance, a health menace, and conducive to traffic congestion creating fire and health hazards." They planned to do what they could to stop the festival. We spent eight hours answering questions and showing our plans to local officials. Finally, they agreed with us that there was no time or reason for a town meeting regarding our festival.

Our victory celebration was short-lived, though. The next day we were twice served with papers to appear before Judge George Cobb in Catskill; actions had been brought against us by a group of four summer camps who claimed we were disrupting their business, and another injunction was filed by summer-home owners with properties next to Max's.

"The apparent bed of roses into which Woodstock Ventures' Aquarian Exposition nestled last week has turned into a briar patch," is how the *Times Herald-Record* put it. I couldn't have agreed more.

eight BETHEL

_____

"What would you do if a kid with long hair handed you a joint?"

"I'd arrest him!"

"Sorry, we can't use you."

In a room above Ratner's, next door to the Fillmore East, I'm watching the screening process for our Peace Service Corps. Wes; Lee; Joe Fink, chief of the ninth precinct in the East Village; and John Fabbri, a former chief of police of South San Francisco, are interviewing hundreds of New York City cops. About five hundred have made the first cut—and we're making sure they have the right attitude to work at Woodstock. I don't think I've been surrounded by so many police officers since the would-be busts in Coconut Grove. Only this time, most of the cops are on our side.

We're spending $100,000 on security, including the salaries for John Fabbri, Wes Pomeroy, Don Ganoung, and Jewell Ross, a retired captain of the Berkeley police. These are enlightened guys who don't lose their cool when dealing with large crowds of kids—like those who packed Golden Gate Park during the early be-ins. Joe Fink has been a huge help as well.

Wes hired Jewell Ross to write a procedural manual, and he came up with the Peace Service Corps. Wes also got permission from New York City police commissioner Howard Leary to put notices in all the precincts, advertising for police to come and work for us.

All the candidates had to fill out a questionnaire, and those whose answers showed they thought along the lines of what we wanted were called into this screening process.

Wes addresses the assembled: "We want you to work a rock festival upstate, where thousands of kids will be relaxed and easygoing and dressed in lots of different ways. You have to be comfortable with that. No weapons of any kind will be allowed—no guns or nightsticks. Your role is going to be to help people—it's what you do most of the time, anyway, as a police officer. And if the kids need to know how to get help, you help them. We don't expect there to be any violence, but there might be people who become ill or disoriented, and we want you to take care of them like a cop would on the streets of New York. It's really a piece of cake to go up there and not have to worry about enforcing the law, okay? Just be nice—and we'll pay you fifty dollars a day for being nice."

A few cops get up and leave. But finally around 350 think this is a great way to earn some extra money and spend a day in the country. Lee takes down their sizes for their "uniforms," which will be bell-bottom jeans and a red T-shirt with PEACE *on the front and our dove and guitar logo on the back, a windbreaker, and a pith helmet.*

I hired a company called Intermedia Systems, headed by Gerd Stern, to help Wes and Don Ganoung design parking and do camping logistics. I'd first met Gerd in 1966, when he supplied some of the black-light posters, fractals, and other items that I bought to stock the shop in Florida. Based in Boston, his company had expanded, and he and his staff were also producing all the signage we'd need. We figured on about two thousand signs to be placed throughout the festival site to guide people to various areas and provide information. Intermedia had hired Alton Kelley, the Family Dog poster artist from San Francisco, to supervise the design and production of the signs at the site. He set up a little silkscreen printing shop and was soon creating signs like: PLEASE LET MAX'S COWS MOO IN PEACE and GROOVY WAY. Intermedia's coordinators helped us figure out how much space we'd need for camping, determined by the number of tickets sales—and our land needs kept growing.

We signed a contract with an aviation company to supply helicopters and pilots to be on call through the festival weekend. We rented more land behind the stage from Max's neighbor to construct a heliport, which Chris Langhart designed. Miles of Christmas lights supplied lighting there and in the camping areas.

Our increased attendance projections had greatly impacted the number of food concessions we needed. After the Wallkill debacle, Nathan's had dropped out, and Peter Goodrich's candidate of last resort was a makeshift company called Food for Love.

Peter had met Charles Baxter, Jeffrey Joerger, and Lee Howard in the Village; unfortunately, they didn't have much experience in the food business: Joerger sold antiques, Howard ran a rehearsal studio, and Baxter organized the three of them into the catering outfit for Woodstock. Their attorney helped them set up a lopsided deal with us. They'd order enough food for 150,000 to 200,000 people, but we had to front them the $75,000 to cover the cost of food, supplies, and wages. They would reimburse Woodstock Ventures with their concession income, then we'd split profits fifty-fifty. None of us liked this arrangement, but we were pretty much stuck.

JOHN ROBERTS: Only one of them had some kind of food-catering experience. Peter Goodrich basically said, "They're the only game in town. They've already made inquiries about hot-dog buns and Coca-Colas and equipping themselves. I don't think anyone else can come in here in two weeks and do it. They can do the job—it's no food or them."

Booking the catering for the performers proved an easier task. One morning, from out of the blue, a limo arrived at El Monaco and Barry Imhoff stepped out. A big guy, about five ten and three hundred pounds, Barry had catered events for Bill Graham. He'd driven up from New York to show me his wares. At this time of day, there were maybe a hundred kids milling around the parking lot, looking for work or just hanging out. It was a very funky scene. Barry was clutching a suitcase and said, "Guess what I've brought you? Come on out to the car!"

People gathered around the limo, and Barry propped the case on the hood, opened it, and showed me the first portable telephone I'd ever seen. "If anyone on the planet needs this right now, it's *you*!" he said. It was almost like science fiction.

I realized Barry was warming me up for the *real* reason for his visit—catering. I was already uncomfortable with the whole limousine thing—very uncounterculture-like—when he popped the trunk and, as if uncorking a genie from a bottle, lifted a huge silver tureen cover to reveal a monstrous bloody roast steaming on a silver platter. The kids crowded around as Barry sliced off huge chunks of beef and handed them out to the throng, soliciting their endorsements. That telephone would definitely come in handy—but, in the end, Barry's brisket lost out to omelets from David Potbelly (Levine), known for his restaurant across from the Fillmore. Though Barry didn't get to cater the artists' pavilion, Bill Graham would ask him to stock his trailer at Woodstock with a fridge full of steaks.

On August 7, eighty-five members of the Hog Farm, including seven babies, plus fifteen Hopi artists flew from Albuquerque on American

Airlines flight number 281 into JFK airport. Wartoke turned their arrival via our chartered jet into a major photo op. Reporters packed the place—and Hugh Romney proved to be a spokesman with star quality.

HUGH ROMNEY: We had no concept of the magnitude of things until we got to the airport and there was just all this world press—a wall of it. They're asking me if we're doing security and I thought, "Oh my god—we're the cops! I can't believe it!" And off the top of my head, I said, "Well, do you feel secure?" And he said, "Well, *sure*." And I said, "Well, it's working, then!" Another guy asked, "What are you going to use for crowd control?" And I said, "Cream pies and seltzer bottles!" I noticed they were all writing it down. God knows what else was discussed.

The whole idea of the Hog Farm handling security came about through an innocent remark Mel had made to the press a week before. We had never asked them to do this and it was just as much a surprise to Hugh Romney when asked by the journalist. We always thought that they'd help get things together in the camping area as keepers of the peace—but that the off-duty cops would handle security. Nonetheless, a couple of photos of the Hog Farm's arrival ran in the *New York Post* with the caption: "They will act as an auxiliary security force, assisting 346 vacationing New York City cops being paid $50 a day plus room and board to keep order at the festival, expected to attract 100,000 persons a night." That caption would soon come back to haunt us.

John Morris, always stylish, booked limos to transport the Hopis up to Bethel, and we chartered a Trailways bus for the Hog Farm. In Bethel, the dozen earlier arrivals who'd driven out from New Mexico had already set up tents, tepees, lean-tos, and psychedelic buses in the camping area. They'd been joined by twenty or so Merry Pranksters, including Ken Babbs, who'd driven Furthur, their legendary bus, from Oregon. We'd paid their travel expenses after a fee was negotiated with Ken Kesey (who at the last minute decided not to come). Members of the Ohayo Mountain Commune in Woodstock and people from other groups showed up as well. It quickly turned into a huge scene, and they'd hang out around a kitchen they set up in a wooden geodesic dome. They would all gather in the morning for yoga before breakfast, then Stan would divide them up into different crews, according to what their abilities were—from digging fire pits, to clearing trails through the woods, to stacking wood, to building the free stage. The only problem we had was when pest-control people showed up to spray DDT to get rid of all the mosquitoes. The Hog Farm was hip to the ill effects of pesticides long before the general public knew anything about it. They threatened to leave over that, and we stopped the spraying.

One of the Pranksters, Paul Foster, devised a special Hog Farm logo—a flying pig with wings—which Alton Kelley silk-screened onto red strips of fabric. These were handed out as armbands to the communal members and their ever-growing group of volunteers. In the evening, they'd all gather around the campfire. Sometimes Wes Pomeroy and his wife and daughters would join them, and Stan spent a lot of time there.

STAN GOLDSTEIN: The Hog Farm had swelled to many hundreds of people. The word went out, and we welcomed a commune from here, a group from there who came a week or two before the event— unofficially unsolicited—to join us. The Orson Welles Theater, which was a communal theater group out of Boston, showed up in buses and brought motion-picture projectors and screens to show movies on the campgrounds. They were a very capable and well-organized group of people. We got this force of people who were *of* the festival, but not employed *by* the festival, who by this time knew what we were doing and had a pretty good idea of how dedicated we were to taking care of the people who showed up. So there was this reservoir of people to address problems and assist people. Once these groups came in and got oriented, we all ate as a group at the Hog Farm kitchen. We had meetings every day, with work assignments and discussions of how things needed to be done and what the problems were.

In an effort to prepare the grounds for novice campers, we got the Hog Farm to blaze the trail. Stan, Hugh, and Hog Farmer Tom Law, who also taught yoga, showed other early arrivals how to set up camp. Then those people would, in turn, set up camp in a different area—so when others began to arrive, there would be a campground operation already in place with community fire pits and cords of wood in each area. This unofficial organization was happening continuously all over the property. Just about anywhere folks went, they'd find someone who had an idea of how to set up camp and how to get anything they needed.

WES POMEROY: The [Hog Farm] said, "We're all equals, there is nobody in charge, and no one speaks for everybody else." Except obviously, there were some who were leaders. They always had some kind of yoga in the morning and I'd get up there and sit on the ground and I was just *there*. Somebody would blow on the conch shell and people would come wandering over, and we'd all just talk.

They were very effective and good, and I'm glad they were there. Their roles were clear, but their parameters were ambiguous, and trying to structure it any more would have been just a useless piece of work. So when I did want to talk to them, I'd just go up there and wander around—sort of hang out and shoot the shit. We got along fine, and Hugh Romney is a very good friend.

Stan was really the guy who interacted with them the closest. He knew them best, but we all got along very comfortably. We all lived together, and they knew who my daughters were, so I had no worries about my daughters—they were safer there than any other place I knew. I found out a long time ago that kids are going to do what they want to do anyway, so why make a damn fool of yourself?

HUGH ROMNEY: About a thousand people came in and were on the various crews. We were supplying people, as they rolled in, with plastic to make their little shelters with. Stan and the promoters were extraordinary to be able to look beyond the Day-Glo to see what we could actually do.

We set up a campfire, and it was so large, I said, "We need a giant marshmallow!" We drove around for twenty miles and bought all the marshmallows out of every store, and squished them together and made a giant marshmallow on a pitchfork at the campfire that night.

The humor was the bond. I put together a bulletin board, and one of my fortes is that I'm very quick with a staple gun and paper, and we cut a hole in the side of the bulletin board so you could stick your head through it and make 4- and 5-D announcements. One day, as I stuck my head through to make an announcement, there was Max Yasgur and his whole family. The grass-roots human revelation that came to Max Yasgur from that really opened him up. It was a real "just folks" kind of a vibe that he locked into.

The Hog Farm set a tone that was passed from person to person, like a joint, welcoming everyone. Soon we were all welcoming each other. Hog Farmer Lisa Law (who was then married to Tom Law) took charge of stocking the free kitchens they would organize to feed people who were without means or supplies. She and Peter Whiterabbit traveled to the city to buy supplies: something like 160,000 paper plates, 1,500 pounds of bulgur wheat, 1,500 pounds of rolled oats, 225 pounds of currants, and lots of nuts and dried fruit. We gave her $3,000 to cover the first batch of supplies, which also included knives and stainless-steel cooking pots, since she was opposed to using aluminum. She ran out of money and went to the Village office, and Joyce gave her another $3,000 to finish the shopping.

LISA LAW: They just handed it to me. There wasn't any problem at all. I used the money frugally. My job was to make it as easy as possible for the people in the kitchen so they could produce the biggest amount of food. And Yasgur kept us supplied with yogurt, milk, and eggs. We'd get these flats of eggs every day. We were purchasing them from him, but it was right there from his dairy farm, so it was really nice. Right away the campers were arriving, so we were cooking continuously and trying to get our act together for what we were going to do.

I still hoped to add a few more surprises to the show, particularly some artists living in Woodstock. Paul Butterfield agreed to perform with his Blues Band on Sunday night. Fred Neil had moved up from Coconut Grove. His song "Everybody's Talkin'" was the theme song for *Midnight Cowboy* (and would soon become a huge hit for Nilsson). This made him even more reclusive than he already was, but he said he'd play Friday night. We added him to the press release listing the lineup. Then, a couple of days before the show, he called and said he wasn't going to make it.

Bob Dacy—whom I'd known in the Grove and now ran Woodstock's Sled Hill Café—arranged a meeting for me with Bob Dylan at his home. Dylan's songs were important in my life, as they were in the lives of countless others. I just thought I'd tell him that we'd all love to see him there, unannounced, of course. His wife, Sara, made lunch and we all talked about what I had planned. I explained the reasons why I hadn't made an offer to have him officially on the show. I knew he was uncomfortable with the mantle of "prophet" that he'd been tagged with by the press. He'd rarely played in public since 1966. Bob was the most important artist of our generation, and because of my respect for his artistry, I underestimated the side of him that is about business. Maybe if I'd offered his booking agent a large enough fee, he'd have played—like he would at the Isle of Wight festival not long after Woodstock. In any case, during the two hours we hung out, he was cordial and said that maybe he'd stop by.

Later that week, Al Aronowitz wrote in the *New York Post*:

> The day before, it had rained so hard the mud was deep enough to give you a good headstart to China . . . The owners of the Woodstock Music and Art Fair were busy acting like people who had half a million dollars to spend. Meanwhile an hour and a half away, where Woodstock really is, Bob Dylan was coping with rumors that he was going to make a surprise appearance at the festival. "I may if I feel like it," he said. "I've been invited, so I know it'll be okay to show up . . . My opinion of that festival is not any different from anyone else's. I think everyone is probably going to have a good time, but I wouldn't blame them if they didn't."

A few days after the festival, I was crossing Tinker Street in Woodstock and happened upon Bob, riding in an open Jeep with Bernard Paturel from Café Espresso. As they drove by, I waved and gave a sort of "sorry you didn't make it" shrug. With a grin, Bob tipped his hat and nodded back with what I took as a "me too." (Twenty-five years later, Bob would finally take the Woodstock stage.)

As at Miami Pop, I planned to film and record the festival, only this time Artie and I had a bigger vision for the film. We had been trying to sell the movie rights, but so far, no luck. D. A. Pennebaker had filmed the Monterey Pop Festival, but the movie had been a flop, so studios saw concert pictures as loss leaders. Early on, Artie and I had talked about the importance of capturing the building and preparation of the site. I had become friendly with Alan Douglas, whose multimedia company was active in music, film, and photography. He agreed to help fund some of the early filming and offered to raise the money to make the picture. In addition to documenting the setup, we discussed sending film crews to California, Texas, and Ohio to travel to New York with groups of people, documenting their experiences en route to the festival and beyond. Unfortunately, with the move to White Lake, time just got away from us and we couldn't pull off the far-flung filming.

ALAN DOUGLAS: I kept pushing him—"Michael, we've got to get started"—so it was about two weeks before the festival was to begin and there was no film deal yet. Although we were basically a recording company, we were making books and films and other things and there were what we called "underground filmmakers" around my office and I had a film-editing suite downstairs. So I said, "We'd better send some guys up there and start shooting," because at that point, they were building the stages and they were preparing the fields, and I thought that if, in fact, they were going to do a film, that would be an important part of it all. I had two hippie filmmakers from London working with me, Malcolm Hart and Michael Margetts, and a well-known New York filmmaker,

Marty Topp, so we equipped everybody. I gave them the film and rented cameras and sent them up to Woodstock a couple of weeks before, and the first two weeks of preparation that you see in the film was shot by our people.

Michael and Malcolm were juiced and jumped in with both feet. They rented a car from Avis, removed the top of the trunk, and Michael would shoot from there while Malcolm drove. It seemed as if they were always shooting, day and night. They even got a shot of Wes Pomeroy's daughter Ginny riding horseback with a Hog Farmer.

When Joel arrived in Bethel the week of the festival, he was a bit nonplussed and unsure where to put his energy. We were still dealing with permit issues, and the box-office operations needed attention. I was hoping he would focus on those areas, but Joel seemed more interested in trying to figure out what I was doing. He was particularly upset by the film crew Alan Douglas had sent. It seems he saw this as self-aggrandizement on my part, and he repeatedly denigrated the wisdom of spending any time or resources on making a movie. Joel, of course, would later become the beneficiary of our efforts, when the film became Woodstock Ventures' greatest asset.

I really liked the documentary work of the Maysles brothers— David and Al—and we met several times with them and their producer Porter Bibb. David and Al checked out the site and seemed interested in making the film independently but were having trouble finding the financing. They recommended Wadleigh-Maurice Productions to shoot the performances. About my age, Michael Wadleigh was a Columbia University medical school dropout who'd become a filmmaker. He had won an award for his documentary *No Vietnamese Ever Called Me Nigger*. Producer Bob Maurice was a tenacious guy determined to make the film. With a handheld camera, Wadleigh had recently filmed some exciting live-music performances of Aretha Franklin and James Brown, and was eager to do more. Wadleigh-Maurice Productions had been working with an experimental new split-screen editing machine that could result in three different images onscreen at once. They thought it was the way to go to capture the excitement of a live performance. Their associate producer Dale Bell began gathering 16mm film stock and putting together a team with enough cameras to shoot three days and nights of performances.

DALE BELL: The Saturday before the festival began, our little group of six people in a couple of cars went to White Lake and met Michael Lang for the first time. If I had any wisdom at all, it was to say, "Let's shoot it, let's hold on to the negative, and let's wait for people to come to us, because once we have possession of the negative and we have recorded it, we are in control." That was part of the philosophy that Bob and Michael and I were developing. So we went up there and left a camera and sound and a producer behind. It was like, "You're the placeholders and you just shoot whatever walks and talks."

I wanted to hire someone to photograph the event, and Chip recommended Henry Diltz. Based in L.A., Henry had just shot the cover of the debut album by Crosby, Stills and Nash. Before becoming a rock photographer, he'd been in a folk group in Hawaii. It turned out that he had known Mel there, and he fit in with everybody right away.

HENRY DILTZ: I enjoyed going down every day to where they were building the stage. It was like a huge battleship—it looked over this green field and the blue sky and it was really like an ocean. These hippie girls who ran the kitchen would bring lunch out to the site where guys were all building this thing. Michael Lang had some kind of an old motorcycle that he'd come riding on through the alfalfa fields with his leather vest on and his curly hair. He looked sort of like a cherub. Chip and Michael and Mel were like brigadier generals. People were issuing orders and getting stuff done and things were carried out in a very crisp and efficient—but very friendly—way.

PENNY STALLINGS: Michael was inventing it as he went along. He was so intuitive about the way he operated that it all worked. You had all of these guys almost afraid of Michael—which was really fun for those of us working for them. To see them sort of befuddled, not knowing how to deal with him. That was quite fun to observe. Michael was the quiet, mysterious presence deferred to by the guys who were older and who were the "real deal" in terms of having some experience doing concerts and promotion and working at the Fillmore. Many of us younger staffers saw Woodstock as a very political event—we were going to show the world who we were, how big we were. But Mel and John and Chip didn't necessarily look at it that way. They were just working, not smoking pot, not amused by the whole hippie ethos, didn't live with us, didn't hang out with us—they weren't buying into it. Michael, their boss, did.

You had the dreamers who would come in—like Tom Edmunston—who would say, "We're going to have a giant scented sphere and everyone will touch it." And what that would be and how you would build that, no one knew. Michael liked those ideas—he wanted those ideas, wanted that input. On the other hand, how would you really do it? Well, you wouldn't. The artists who came up from Florida—Ron Liis and Bill Ward and Buster Simpson—they actually did do art installations. They did some really wonderful and zany art there, but there were many other extremes, too, that just sort of evaporated along the way.

BILL WARD: Ron's a born leader—he's six four and looked like a hippie. He had a big beard and wore a vest with bells on it. He was a good artist, and had a good eye for things and took over the crew, and they built everything. Eventually, Mel got me to try to talk to Ron, who was driving him crazy. Ron would just do things his own way, whatever was expedient. Apparently at one time—I wasn't there when this happened—he purloined the stage crew's forklift and a fistfight ensued. Ron was inclined to just take whatever he wanted.

We had a great crew: Buster Simpson was a friend of Ron's from the Middle West, and he came out. Buster is now a very successful sculptor in Seattle. Buster really had his head on straight, and another on the crew, Herb Summers, is a very talented artist, a good thinker, and easy to get along with—and they all pitched in. Buster and his girlfriend did those outdoor conceptual sculptures. They made an open tepee and suspended a large rock in the middle by ropes, and they built a vertical structure with baby chicks in it.

PENNY STALLINGS: At one point, Buster wanted to get a little girl in a polka-dot pinafore just to skip through the festival. That was the kind of thing they were doing—just wonderful.

Throughout the lush green bowl that opened out to the stage, the crews dug holes and placed poles with beautiful appliquéd banners Mel had commissioned from a guy in the Bronx. Five feet long with peace symbols and other designs, the banners quickly vanished once the audience arrived.

We realized we needed a footbridge between the artists' pavilion and the stage, so Chris designed one. That was the thing about Chris; if I could imagine it, he could build it. This one rose about twenty feet above the road and provided an awesome view as you walked across it.

Chris calculated how much weight it needed to support by quizzing John Morris about Jimi Hendrix's weight and the weight of the typical groupie and multiplying that by ten or twelve. Some of the artists from Miami painted gorgeous murals to decorate the sides of the bridge.

In those last few weeks before the festival, we were also scrambling to get our medical operation set up. Early on, we'd been seeking advice from the Medical Committee for Human Rights in New York, and Don Ganoung and Wes had been in discussions with doctors in the Wallkill area, but we had to start over in Sullivan County. Bill Ward recommended Bill Abruzzi, a doctor in nearby Wappingers Falls, whom he had met volunteering during the civil rights march from Montgomery to Selma in 1965. Completely sympathetic to our cause, he signed on and began designing a medical plan. Based on our audience estimates at the time, he recruited six doctors, thirty-six nurses, and eighteen medical assistants (for whom we covered malpractice insurance) at a cost of close to $16,000. (Eventually numerous volunteers would pitch in, totaling some twenty-five doctors and two hundred nurses.) The three local hospitals were put on alert. Don Ganoung also hired a local ham-radio group to help us with on-site communications. He notified the local employment office to solicit workers for the duration of the festival weekend: We needed seventy parking lot attendants, three hundred workers for the food concessions, and two hundred people to pick up garbage around the site each day. Mel located a company with a huge trash compactor—one of the first of its kind—to have on-site to help with cleanup.

The more money we spent, the better we were treated by the community. We were buying materials locally and hiring residents, and as that happened, it changed some of the negative attitudes in town and began to endear us to them. More and more White Lake residents got into the Woodstock spirit. They became supporters because they liked what we were doing, and they saw everybody working hard. During those last two weeks before the festival, it seemed as if thousands of people offered to help in every way.

JOHN ROBERTS: We didn't want to repeat a lot of the same mistakes that we'd made at Wallkill. So we paid a lot of attention to the politics—who we had to know, what we had to do, who we had to convince, who we had to stay clear of; there was a lot of work done in those areas. PR became extremely important.

Don Ganoung and Rona continued to take the lead in our public relations, but were occasionally joined by Elliot Tiber. Elliot insisted on putting the Earthlight Theatre troupe at our disposal and offered the El Monaco as the site for a free preview of festival theater for the White Lake residents. Talk about a disaster. Before a crowd of old-timers, farmers, and families, the actors stripped off all their clothes as they performed a scene from *Oh! Calcutta*. The townsfolk went running.

Somehow a rumor got started that Peter and I planned to have a big shipment of pot at the festival, supposedly sent up from Miami. The story went that the Monday before the festival the boat carrying our supply was stopped by the Coast Guard just off the Keys. All untrue.

The countdown began on Monday, August 11, as thousands of people began to filter in. We'd announced that the campgrounds would open on Wednesday, but that did not seem to deter those who wanted in early. We were on a twenty-four-hour clock trying to finish the stage, the towers, the concessions, the roads, the parking lots, the plumbing, the drinking stations, the medical facilities, and the kitchens, and take care of the hundreds of other details still to be completed. People were arguing over manpower and equipment. There just wasn't enough to go around.

The fence around the perimeter was only partially up, and I didn't see any sign of ticket booths. I assumed that Joel and Keith O'Connor, who handled the box-office operation from the Woodstock Ventures office, were overseeing their delivery and placement, but somehow the ticket booths never appeared. I later learned that local garage owner Ken Van Loan had attempted to tow two dozen or so to the site at the last minute but got stuck in traffic with the very first haul and had to turn back.

We'd been so busy getting ready we'd nearly forgotten about our recent legal troubles. Paul Marshall had assured us that the attempts to stop the festival by the summer camps and home owners wouldn't amount to anything. We wouldn't know for sure until mere days before opening day—when they met before the judge on Tuesday, August 12. Paul, Don Ganoung, and Wes arrived that day in Catskill at 10 A.M. to meet with the state supreme court justice, and it turned out that Paul, as a kid, had gone to one of the camps filing the complaint. He chatted up the camp owner, "Uncle Davy," before the proceedings—which helped, I think.

During the court session, Paul noted that we'd spent $1,400,000 and were committed to another $300,000 by the time the festival was over; by then, we'd sold 124,000 advance tickets. Finally, after a long day of Wes, Don Ganoung, and Paul Marshall making assurances that we had the means to protect the petitioners' properties, they all agreed to drop their complaints.

Our final legal hurdle was over. In just three days' time, the Aquarian Exposition would open on schedule.

nine AUGUST 13–14, 1969

"Our concession stands aren't ready! A hundred thousand dollars' worth of food is going to rot, thanks to you! Who needs this? We're splitting from here unless we renegotiate our deal!"

"You asshole! You were supposed to have your shit together, and you're just using this as an excuse to sweeten your deal!" With that, Peter Goodrich slams his fist into Jeffrey Joerger's face.

I didn't see that coming.

As Jeff goes down, he yells, "You motherfucker! You hit me!" He goes for a knife he has stashed. Lenny Kaufman, whom I've hired as special security, catches this, and when our eyes meet, I nod and he moves toward Joerger to restrain him.

"I'm getting my gun!" Jeffrey shouts as he backs into his trailer and slams and locks the door.

It's Thursday morning—the day before the festival—and people are pouring in. We've lost count since yesterday, but we've probably got sixty thousand people already nestled in the bowl and camped in the woods. The guys from Food for Love showed up Tuesday night and have been pissed off ever since because their booths are only halfway built—our crews keep shifting back and forth between the priority projects yet to be completed before opening day. The stage is still not finished. The incessant rain has resulted in a mud pit around its perimeter, which delayed the installation of the concrete footing until just a few days ago. The same abysmal weather conditions have also slowed progress on the concessions for crafts and food. Even the roads we'd built keep turning into swamps.

"Look, Jeffrey, let's work this out!" John Roberts yells into the slammed door of the trailer. "We'll have a meeting tonight and resolve this situation." John says he wonders about Joerger's sanity, and I'm thinking, Gun?

John, Mel, Joel, and I see that we have a problem. We've got the free kitchen at the Hog Farm with plenty of granola and brown rice, but if Food for Love doesn't come through with hot dogs and hamburgers, we're going to have thousands of angry, hungry kids on our hands. We radio over to Wes and fill him in on the situation.

"Work it out with them—do whatever it takes," Wes advises. "The last thing we need are starving kids, especially since we don't have any New York City cops."

The last two days before the festival were forty-eight-hours of non-stop fires to be extinguished—*literally* and figuratively. On Wednesday, Lee got a call at the telephone building office that set the tone for what was to come.

The week before, Joe Fink had come up and surveyed the area and all seemed fine with our plan for the "vacationing" police to work in shifts over the three days. We had made arrangements to house, feed, and transport the cops from the city, with the stipulation that they would not bring weapons. But then, in the East Village, the Up Against the Wall Motherfuckers started handing out antagonizing leaflets: "Let's all go to Woodstock and greet the New York fuzz who'll be unarmed and give them a real warm welcome." On top of that, Chief Leary saw the photos of the Hog Farm's JFK arrival splashed over the papers and read that they'd be joining New York's finest on security detail. So he pulled the plug on the whole thing.

On Wednesday morning, a teletype went out to every precinct in New York City: "It has come to the attention of the Department that certain members of the force have been engaged to do various work assignments during the Woodstock Music and Art Fair . . . Permission will not be granted for extra employment where, as a condition of employment, the police officer's uniform, shield, gun or exercise of police authority is not to be used." It was understood that whoever went against orders could be fired. Joe called Lee with the bad news that the 346 cops we'd selected weren't coming. When Wes found out, he was livid.

WES POMEROY: Chief Leary shut the door on us . . . he sent out orders that no New York cop's going to work up there. It was because of the Hog Farm! He said he'd just found out about it, which was bullshit—and so here we are with our whole Peace Service Corps gone to hell.

LEE MACKLER BLUMER: Wes and Joe Fink started plotting how to overcome it. We were feeling overwhelmed already from seeing the numbers of people who were on the property before there were gates and knew that security was in deep danger.

Wes felt betrayed by the brotherhood of police, and even the *New York Times* ran an editorial admonishing Leary for withdrawing the police at the last minute. Joe stayed in contact with Wes all day, promising to convince some of the men to disobey orders and surreptitiously moonlight for us. Wes reached out to local police agencies and prison officials to try to get people to fill in but was turned down by most. We had to do something—the police were part of the strategy we'd used to convince town officials to let us do the festival. In addition to wanting cops as peacekeepers, we needed them to direct traffic and deal with medical emergencies.

I didn't want to take any chances with not having any sort of professional security. There were going to be numerous cash payments, between the gates and concessions, so I called a friend, Lenny Kaufman. A former biker, bouncer, and adventurer, Lenny was always steadfast in tough situations and I trusted him completely. I had him round up six or seven men he had absolute confidence in and told him to bring them to the site that night.

Wednesday was another rainy day and it made some of the final electrical work very dicey. The trailer next to the main electrical terminal had stairs that were "hot." The electricians couldn't ground them for some reason, so every time you walked up the steps, you'd get a shock. They rushed to complete the elevator for transporting amps and equipment thirty feet up to the stage from the loading area.

Bill Hanley arrived with the special equipment he'd designed to carry the sound as far away as the outer reaches of the grounds. He'd built a custom mixing board and deluxe speakers and had taken out a $3 million insurance policy on the equipment. Cranes were used to place six speakers and horns on top of the towers, and monitors were bolted to the front of the stage. Eddie Kramer, whom I'd met with Hendrix at Miami Pop, would record the concert, along with Lee Osborne, from a sound trailer behind the stage. Ahmet Ertegun had bought the audio rights for Atlantic—Crosby, Stills and Nash's label.

In addition to the main stage, Hanley put in a smaller sound system for the free stage over by the Hog Farm. There, we'd finished a puppet theater and the playground area the day before. We'd been installing a chain-link fence around the entire site, separating the free area from the section closer to the main stage. I later found out what was happening to some of the fences from Abbie Hoffman's friend Roz Payne.

ROZ PAYNE: I got there a few days before the festival and camped with the Hog Farm. There were teams of workers putting the posts and wire fences around the property to keep people out who didn't have tickets. Every night after they would leave, Paul [Krassner], Abbie, Jean-Jacques [Lebel], and I would take down the fence. We left the posts, but took down the wire. We'd do other actions too. We found a sign that said NO TRESPASSING, and Jean-Jacques wrote over it with paint PEOPLE'S BULLETIN BOARD, and we put that up instead. We made a sign that said HO CHI MINH TRAIL for the main pathway through the woods.

All along, we put the word out to the Movement people that there would be free areas. I knew they were crafty enough to sneak people in, but I thought that between advance ticket sales and people buying tickets at the gate, we would do okay financially. With all the rain delays, I stopped caring about the fences and focused on getting the stage and sound together so the concert would start on time.

We finally realized that Steve Cohen had overdesigned the stage roof. For two weeks, the weather had prevented us from putting all the pieces of the puzzle together. The wooden trusses turned out to be way too heavy for our purposes. We never got them properly covered with canvas to make them rainproof. The roof was meant to have cross trusses where the lights would hang. But we couldn't get the cross trusses up, so Chip would eventually light the whole show with twelve Super Troupers from the towers. "We have 650,000 watts sitting under the stage rusting!" Chip would remind us.

We rented two massive cranes for a thousand dollars a day to assist in the construction of the stage and towers. The cranes became trapped next to the stage because the wooden fence encircling the stage, and other construction, prevented us from getting them out before people started arriving.

CHIP MONCK: What we needed was a real heavy-duty rigger with a full company behind him, and production direction that was exceptionally solid, and grown-up and heavy-duty contractors. But we didn't have them, and everybody said, "Don't worry, it'll happen." We didn't have a contractor. We should have done it as though we were constructing a building. There should have been a site supervisor, there should have been an ironworker, a couple of welders. The design was terrific, and it had layers and layers of canvas that were almost like fish scales. It would have been beautiful. We should have had a complete crew that was nothing but staging. We had only four guys who were doing scaffolding. It was a big mistake. You can't do things like that on a dime. We were all fairly overcome by the size of the thing.

I rented the lights from Charlie at Altman Stage Lighting in Yonkers. In the end he was really pissed off because his five hundred C-clamps—at six dollars apiece—were all locked tight with rust. So they had to be thrown away. There were three arcs, precisely 100 feet out on the left and 15 degrees right of the center line of the stage; there were another three on another tower. And then almost 15 degrees off your exact right and left were two more follow spots. So we only had the ten. That was just enough—there was no ambience, there was no background, there was nothing else. The only other scenic element really was what we call a carnival socket, which are the little lamps that usually hang in an old-time used-car lot, with the piece of cable and lots of little lightbulbs—we had little 7$\frac{1}{2}$-watt lightbulbs, one every foot, and they were on the guy wires that held the scaffolding towers in place. And that's all, so you wouldn't walk into them in the dark, but also they gave some sort of flavor.

We kept experiencing a drop in water pressure—we had fourteen miles of water pipes that began springing leaks once people arrived. Chris had brilliantly placed plastic cases with vintage army crank phones at locations along the pipeline, so that when a leak was found, a call could be made from the spot and the crew could more quickly fix the problem. We had hundreds of DANGER signs made up and placed next to the pipes to prevent people from stepping on them and causing more leaks.

It was obvious there were going to be lots more people than we'd originally told Max, so I went over to his house to talk to him about it. People were already coming by the tens of thousands. "We were thinking up to two hundred thousand people would come, but it looks like it could be more," I told him. "But we'll take care of it."

I barely got the words out before he ducked back under the oxygen tent in his bedroom. Miriam was worried about the crowds and chaos being a strain on Max—rightfully so, because it would have been a big strain on anyone. When he emerged, after his dose of oxygen, Max seemed unfazed. He knew the size of the facility we were building and that our preparations were as sound as possible. For two weeks, he'd been there constantly with us, and I guess the numbers didn't come as a complete surprise to him.

WES POMEROY: [By Wednesday], there's no more time for planning. You just deal with what you've got, that's all. A lot of people would call and say, "What are you going to do about this? We've got a lot of people out here in my field!" We negotiated with them and we'd commit ourselves to buy the crop. People were coming in there and camping all over their young alfalfa and ruining their crops, and we were in a bind. We just made sure that if the claim was correct and we were able to verify that, we'd take care of it.

It was very much like a military operation logistically. The dynamics are all the same—you do all the planning you can, and you get all your supply lines built, and you get all your supplies ordered that you need to have—food, latrines—and you get going, and if those lines break down, then you build other lines.

We had a detailed shift plan for security, covering general patrols and direction and admission to the parking lots. With the New York cops out of commission, Wes conceived a strategy with the state police that included one-way traffic and certain roads that would be open only to emergency and service vehicles. When Wes called the state troopers on Wednesday to put it into effect, the man who headed up the designated New York State Police barracks decided not to cooperate and refused to implement the traffic plan.

STAN GOLDSTEIN: Not only did we now have no more traffic plan to implement, we also did not have police to stand on the roads and direct people to the leased parking lots. When people didn't know where to park, they simply parked wherever they could, which turned the roads into what they turned into. As a little sidelight: The New York state cop in charge of that barracks who refused to cooperate with us is the fellow who subsequently was in charge of the retaking of Attica prison. He gave the order to fire and later tried to cover up the fact that he and his men killed the hostages.

When the state police tossed our plan, they set up a roadblock at the nearest exit off the thruway, where they'd stop any suspicious-looking cars and search them. Eight kids were arrested on various drug charges, some for possession of pipes. We'd arranged for lawyers to come up to offer free legal advice for these very circumstances.

Eventually, there'd be about eighty drug busts—not too bad, though, considering the numbers who came.

Short Line had added extra buses from Port Authority in New York to Bethel to meet the demand, and a few people were flying into the small Sullivan County airport, but most were traveling to the festival by car. As caravans began to stream into White Lake, the townsfolk hung out on the sidewalk, watching as if it were a circus parade.

Abbie Hoffman later told a funny story about the Short Line bus ride from New York that his wife, Anita, related.

ABBIE HOFFMAN: Anita told me about how this bus was comin' up the thruway and how it was all freaks and everyone laughin', singin', and passin' around dope, and the bus stalled in traffic and the kids saw this cat standin' in the road needin' a ride and they all started jumpin' up and down and yellin', "Pick him up! Pick him up! Pick him up!" and the bus driver began sweatin' all over and shoutin' out things about company regulations and other kinds of horseshit. A sort of instant people's militia was formed and they'd started up the aisle when all of a sudden the bus doors opened and this freak with a knapsack on his back came aboard. Everybody was jokin' and clownin' and even the bus driver felt better. He didn't accept the joint a cat tried to lay on him but he scratched the guy's shaggy head of hair and smiled.

Short Line later ran an ad quoting bus drivers about the joys of transporting kids to Woodstock. One of the drivers, Eugene Jennings, said, "We were stuck in traffic for three hours up there and the only noise I heard was jokes about the EXPRESS sign on the bus. Their fashion may be a little sloppy, but they were clean and generous. It's sort of live and let live with them."

After a couple hours of sleep Wednesday night, I woke up to the first sunny, cloudless day I could remember in over a week. This has got to be a good sign, I thought. Sure enough, some problems worked themselves out on Thursday, though others developed in their place— like the Food for Love standoff. By that afternoon, as Joe Fink had promised, police began arriving from New York, reporting for duty.

WES POMEROY: Finally on Thursday, we got word that a bunch of cops wanted to talk to us. They showed up and said, "We're here, we want to work," so I sent Don Ganoung to talk to guys like "Robin Hood" and "Errol Flynn." They were all using aliases. They wanted to be paid in cash and more money than we had promised. We felt like we were being extorted but we had no way out of it. We did hire them for twelve-hour shifts for a hundred dollars a day, which is double what we were going to pay—and we had to pay them in cash. I was very angry about the whole thing, but there was nothing I could do. There was another level of security we used, guards for houses and farms. They were special deputy sheriffs—we set up a guard service for those folks who lived there.

That evening, Wes and John Fabbri called me over to meet the 276 cops who showed up for orientation and to receive their "uniforms" and walkie-talkies. "Here's the boss," they said as my introduction. Amazingly, nobody laughed. I reminded the police that their job was to help people, not to hassle them for petty offenses. To have a good time. And not to get *too* high. That drew a laugh.

The other good news on Thursday came from Artie—he'd finally gotten us a film deal. From his years in the music business, he had two contacts at Warner Bros. who had the clout to make a deal. Before coming to Warner Bros., Freddy Weintraub ran the Bitter End in the Village and Ted Ashley owned the talent agency Ashley's Famous, which handled the Cowsills—whom Artie had managed. Ted had become president of Warner Bros. Pictures and Freddy vice president. Artie met with them on Thursday.

ARTIE KORNFELD: I said to them, "If there's a riot and everybody dies, you'll have one of the biggest-selling movies of all time. If it goes the way we hope it will go, you'll have a wonderfully beautiful movie that will make us all a lot of money." We sat there with pencil and paper and wrote out our movie deal—fifty percent split, Warner and Woodstock Ventures after negative costs, then we had to bring Wadleigh in to make a deal with him to do the direction, and that was the movie deal. It was for a hundred thousand for film footage—it was only signed by Ted Ashley and me. That's how it happened. And then I got into a limousine and went upstate, and the limousine broke down, and my wife and I wound up hitchhiking up to the festival.

JOYCE MITCHELL: I was at the meeting that Artie Kornfeld had with Freddy, and one of the questions Freddy asked me was "How many groups do we have releases from?" This was after Michael had sent me to try to get releases, and I think we had releases for maybe half a dozen acts—and none of the majors.

Michael Wadleigh signed on as director with Warner Bros. on Friday. The studio ended up giving us another $50,000 that day for extra helicopters to transport artists to the site. And when the musicians arrived, Artie would walk with them from the artists' pavilion to the stage to get their permission to be filmed. They would be paid an additional 50 percent of their performance fee for film rights. The movie would make lifelong careers for many of the acts who performed that weekend. Some artists, though, would never agree to be in the film; Neil Young (who joined Crosby, Stills and Nash right before their performance) and the Grateful Dead said no (they didn't appear in the Monterey Pop movie either). Albert Grossman refused to allow any of his artists to be in the film, though Warner Bros. eventually got Richie

Havens on board—the Band and Janis Joplin would finally appear in the director's cut twenty-five years later.

At one point, we could have owned the film outright. Before Artie signed the Warner Bros. deal, Bob Maurice contacted John Roberts, pleading with him to invest $100,000, which they really needed to pay for Kodak raw stock, cameramen flying in from the West Coast, and other expenses. In exchange, Woodstock Ventures would own all the rights. It was a gamble and John was so overwhelmed with our skyrocketing costs and underwhelmed with what he saw as potential for the film, he said no. He thought it was unlikely that a documentary film would ever make a cent.

All afternoon on Thursday, people poured into the site. The film's associate producer Dale Bell, Michael Wadleigh, and their crew arrived, including documentary cameramen David Myers and Al Wertheimer, among others, and editors/assistant directors Thelma Schoonmaker and Martin Scorsese, just out of NYU Film School. John Binder, the unit supervisor, later remembered asking Michael Margetts for the lay of the land, who told him, " 'When I see something interesting, I just press the button'—that set the tone for the whole movie. You couldn't organize Woodstock, and nobody did."

> DALE BELL: I had put together eighty people in four days to get them up there by Thursday morning, after begging, borrowing, and stealing all of the camera gear so that we would have the same interchangeable gear—lenses, magazines, cameras, motors. Thank God for Michael and Chris Langhart and Steve Cohen and Chip: I had asked for a lip on the front of that stage—plywood four-by-eights, strung at about four feet below the level of the stage so that our guys would have absolutely perfect camera angles. We

knew that everything was going to be handheld. We knew that we needed eight magazine changers and assistant camera people under the stage all the time when there was music, just changing magazines and keeping track of who shot what, and what camera roll it was.

Some of the film crew began shooting local residents and their reactions to the festival, as well as people abandoning their cars on clogged roads, which by midafternoon on Thursday were already backed up for miles. Tiny Route 17B was becoming a twenty-mile-long parking lot, and we started hearing reports that the delays on the larger Route 17 were beginning to back up into the New York State Thruway.

PARRY TEASDALE, UNDERGROUND VIDEOGRAPHER: I was twenty-one that summer and knew the area because my grandmother had a summer house nearby. I got there early in the week, set up camp, left briefly, then came back with some friends on Thursday night. I remember feeling, as we were walking along Hurd Road, that we were in a sea of humanity. Everyone was going only in one direction—*in*. And there really wasn't any room for vehicles, they couldn't make it in. It was way too crowded. All around me it was dark, and all you could hear were people walking and talking quietly. Occasionally somebody would sing, or somebody would bang on a drum, but I felt what I thought it must be like to walk on a pilgrimage in India.

ROB KENNEDY, FESTIVALGOER: I was sixteen and hitched from northern New Jersey with three of my friends. We split into groups of two and hitchhiked up Route 17, and interestingly enough both groups hit Bethel at sunset on Thursday, so we didn't have too much trouble reuniting. It was a fairly long walk in, and we stopped as we got closer to the festival grounds to set up tents and eat something. By the time we did that, my friend Mark had found the festival site and came back beaming. We were all getting off on acid pretty heavy and wandered on to the festival. We brought meager supplies that got consumed rapidly. But I don't remember being hungry much. We all had tickets that proved to be totally unnecessary. I had sent for my Friday ticket by mail and bought my Saturday and Sunday tickets last minute from another friend who didn't go. Once we were on the festival grounds, we pretty much staked out one area so we wouldn't get lost from each other. On acid, the numbers of people were overwhelming. The concept of finding your way back to a huddle of four friends when you went to piss was mind-boggling. So we pretty much hunkered down in one spot from Thursday night through Sunday morning. I don't think any of us believed there were that many hippies in the USA. We were the only freaks in our high school at that time. We knew there were some in surrounding towns, but we had no idea. That was one of the most empowering aspects of Woodstock. We realized we had the numbers.

We put out calls to all the suppliers and staff who had not shown up and urged them to get there immediately before they got stuck in traffic. Dr. Abruzzi finally arrived, and seeing how many people were already there, he arranged for more medical supplies and personnel. Urgent calls went out for additional helicopters as it became obvious we needed them not only to transport sick people but to ferry supplies.

John, who arrived Wednesday morning, and Joel, who'd been on-site since Monday, were really upset about the thousands of people already inside the bowl. All along, we'd said the camping area would be free. But now it looked like the prime spots in front of the stage had already been taken by people who arrived early—before fences, ticket takers, and booths were in place. John talked to Wes about how to handle the thousands of people already inside, and he advised him to let it go, that there was no way to clear out that many people without inciting a riot.

WES POMEROY: It was like being in combat, everything was changing. But you knew what you had, so you just changed with it. It didn't get really hectic until just about the day before. When all the people started coming at us, we saw them coming in and we started dealing with them as best you could. We knew that we would have no fence and no gate—and that was a great disappointment. But the fence was irrelevant, and there was a hole dug under the fence—and the idea was that they'd quietly let out the word that you could sneak in if you wanted to.

BILL GRAHAM: I went up the day before. I walked around constantly and it was a sight to behold. I thought at the time that it couldn't come off smoothly because it was such a huge thing and there were no blueprints. It was a first. I knew there were going to be some faults—namely traffic. Ninety thousand mice trying to get into one hole, there had to be some problems.

Thursday night, John, Joel, Peter Goodrich, and I met again with the Food for Love guys at their trailer. They wouldn't venture outside but sent their attorney to tell us they refused to operate the food concessions unless they got 100 percent of the profits, after reimbursing the $75,000 John had fronted for food. John had really counted on this income and we were all outraged at their extortionary tactics—but as Wes advised us, we agreed to their demands in hopes of fixing it afterward.

Later that night, the Diamond Horseshoe, where nearly two hundred of our staff had been staying, caught on fire and everyone had to flee—luckily no one was hurt. Probably more than half the people staying there were at the site, up all night working. The fire trucks couldn't get through the jammed roads, but those at the hotel managed to put out the fire. Apparently it was an electrical short in the basement that started it.

Journalists who were arriving in droves kept asking me if we were going to pull it off, was there going to be three days of peace and music? Was the audience going to be peaceful, or would there be violence and chaos like at the other festivals?

"If it turns bad," I told a reporter from the *Washington Post,* "they're not turning against anybody but themselves. Our festival is being done by the people who *are* the culture. If it can't be done this way, then I was wrong, wrong about *everything*!" Ticia, who was by my side, as she had been for the past few weeks, spoke up. "If it comes out the way we dreamed it," she said, "then people are going to have a different view of this culture—of *us*." Ticia couldn't have been more right.

"Take charge and keep moving"—Harry Lang's words would come back to me many times that weekend.

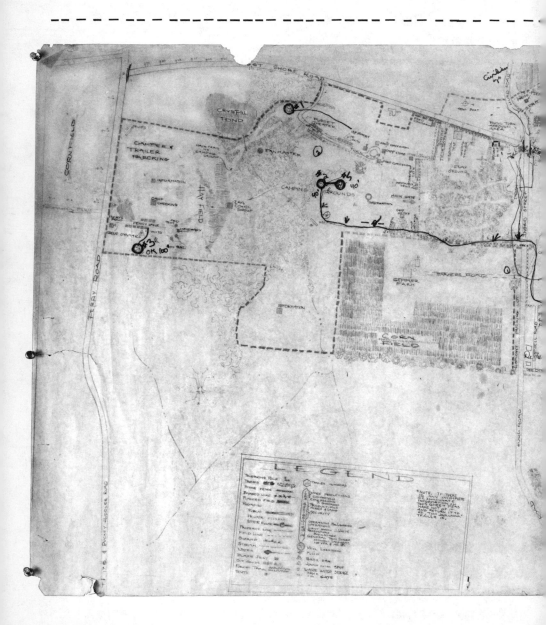

THREE DAYS OF PEACE AND MUSIC

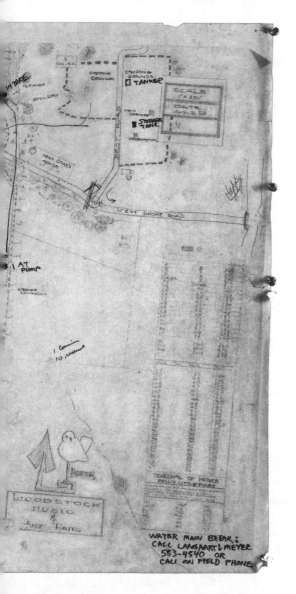

FRIDAY, AUGUST 15

Richie Havens
Sweetwater
Bert Sommer
Tim Hardin
Ravi Shankar
Melanie
Arlo Guthrie
Joan Baez

SATURDAY, AUGUST 16

Quill
Country Joe McDonald
Santana
John Sebastian
Keef Hartley Band
Incredible String Band
Canned Heat
Mountain
Grateful Dead
Creedence Clearwater Revival
Janis Joplin
Sly and the Family Stone
The Who
Jefferson Airplane

SUNDAY, AUGUST 17

Joe Cocker and the Grease Band
Country Joe and the Fish
Ten Years After
The Band
Johnny Winter
Blood, Sweat and Tears
Crosby, Stills, Nash and Young
Paul Butterfield Blues Band
Sha Na Na
Jimi Hendrix

ten AUGUST 15, 1969

"Hey, Richie, how about going on in about an hour?"

"No, man, not me! Get somebody else! I don't want to be the first act out there!"

"Come on, your band's here—you can handle this! Think about how cool it will be—to be the first artist onstage."

"No, man, my bass player's not here. And if the show's starting late, and I go out there, the crowd's gonna go crazy and toss beer cans at me!"

"Well, think about it . . ."

It's three o'clock Friday afternoon and I'm trying to convince Richie Havens to kick off the festival. We've advertised that the music starts at four—and though people don't seem restless, some have been huddled in front of the stage since Wednesday. I don't want to risk the audience waiting too long without music. I've been through that before and I don't want to repeat it.

I've been awake for nearly forty-eight hours straight, I'm on my third wind and running on fumes. We've been busy since dawn, trying to finish *a million things so we can get the music under way. This is the part I love best: seeing everything come together, the final pieces falling into place. We've been working on this thing for what feels like a lifetime—and the exhilaration of opening day, combined with the unprecedented numbers of people, is just the juice I need to keep going.*

But with the weather forecast not looking good for the weekend, there's lots of doom talk about potential disasters. Mel, Stan, John Morris, and Chip alternately accost me with problems, ranging from leaking water pipes to angry landowners complaining about trespassers to our unfinished fence (Mel recommends taking down what's left of it). John and Joel are despairing over the thousands of "freeloaders" who keep increasing by the hour. The roads continue to worsen and we're worried that crucial supplies won't make it through.

We've added to our helicopter squad to ferry in musicians staying at the Holiday Inn and Howard Johnson's in Liberty. Among the first to arrive are Richie Havens and his guitarist and percussionist. I've spotted them hanging out in the nearly finished artists' pavilion and figure I'll at least broach the idea. Richie is a pro—he started playing Village coffeehouses in the early sixties. A tall man with a powerful voice and a unique rhythmic guitar style, he's always seemed fearless. Our opening act, Sweetwater, a folk-rock band from L.A., is apparently stuck on the road driving from the motel in Liberty. Their equipment truck is in another traffic jam. I don't want to press the issue right now with Richie, but I don't let him out of my sight—knowing I may need to hit him up again in an hour or so.

RICHIE HAVENS: Me; my guitarist, Deano [Paul Williams]; and my drummer, Daniel Ben Zebulon, were squeezed into the helicopter's glass-bubble cockpit. We were sitting behind the pilot with two conga drums, two guitars squeezed between us. The glass surrounded us, top to bottom. Looking below my feet, I could see the ground clearly, as if I were sitting on air. We banked a bit to the left and the sea of trees changed into a different kind of sea, just as beautiful. My mouth dropped when I saw all those people, hundreds of thousands of them. Definitely more than the two hundred fifty thousand reported in the New York papers the following morning, a whole lot more like half a million on the first day.

It was awesome, like double Times Square on New Year's Eve in perfect daylight with no walls or buildings to hold people in place. The people filled the field and formed a human blanket across the road to the other side of the hill and into the forests all around the field, where nobody could possibly see the stage. Our helicopter landed right behind the stage. Once I got out, I looked around and saw three roads blocked by the blanket of people, especially the road on the bottom of the hill that went to the staging area.

It was quite mellow everywhere I looked. Even the people nearest the stage weren't clamoring for anything to happen. It was a summer day and they were having a good time in the country. Some were smokin' pot, dancing to portable radios, or throwing Frisbees around. Some were lying in the sun or taking naps or making out under blankets. But most of all they were meeting or hanging out with each other. No matter where they came from or how old or young they were. The vibes were good on this spot.

The last twenty-four hours had been a nonstop race against time. The crew worked through the night, trying to finish the stage and—as the sun came up—finally setting the forty-foot wooden turntable in place. If we can just keep going, I thought, I'm certain everything will be fine.

As if in answer to this thought, a beautiful woman arrived backstage with a large plastic bag of white powder. A good Samaritan had ordered a pound of cocaine to distribute to the various crews who'd been working all night and now had to get through what was sure to be a sleepless weekend. At about 8 A.M., all the crew heads gathered backstage in front of the production trailers. Just as the powder was dumped onto a card table to be divided and distributed, the clouds suddenly opened up and rain poured down like a fire hose. Before anyone could move, the sparkling granules turned into a gooey mess. People scrambled for the white paste as it ran in rivulets into the ground.

The gods had spoken again.

Last-minute decisions had to be made. I approached Chip Monck and John Morris and told them they were to handle MC duties. John had already been on the mic, testing it on Thursday when Bill Hanley and his team got the PA up and running. John has announced concerts at the Fillmore and loves the spotlight. Though Chip's never done this before, he is articulate and has an authoritative presence that will make him a good MC.

CHIP MONCK: At seven in the morning on the first day, Michael came over to me onstage while I was working and said, "Chip, since there's not much lighting to do, you have another job, master of ceremonies." All of a sudden, you can actually hear my knees knocking together! I was terrified! He was just, "Do the job and get it done." The first thing I announced was for people in the bowl to stand up and move back from the stage. Then all of the little notes started coming up about "Harold, please go to the blue tent in the back for your pills for your diabetes"—of course, that meant somebody was going to make a dope deal.

By Friday morning, at least two hundred thousand people were packed into Max's fields. With the fences down, we all knew it was impossible to collect or sell tickets—even though people were looking for places to buy them—but we kept batting around ideas on what to do. I could not locate Keith O'Connor or Joel, so I called Mel to find out what had happened to our ticket operation. He said he was out of the loop. Apparently, the portable booths to be staffed with ticket sellers had never arrived.

The original plan was that the gates to the main field would open at 1 P.M.—but, of course, there were no gates. Artie thought we could get women "dressed in diaphanous gowns" to pass the hat—and he hadn't even been dosed yet. When I saw the cameras filming our rather tense discussions, I ushered everyone away from the lens. Though I wanted Woodstock to be documented, there are limits.

Later that afternoon, after talking to John and Wes, we came to terms with what a couple hundred thousand people already knew. John was devastated. I had John Morris make an announcement from the stage, stating the obvious: "The concert is free from now on." Following the applause, he went on: "The people putting this on are gonna take a bath—a big bath . . ." Our hope was that this message would inspire people to pitch in and help their neighbors; we were all in this together no matter what.

JOYCE MITCHELL: We were pretty sure it was going to be a free festival long before it was announced. It was a combination of all the various underground groups who came to Michael, plus the fact that we knew we could never get that damn fence built in time. There was an awful lot we knew that we didn't share with other people. It wasn't conspiratorial—it just *was*. It was really clear from Michael's point of view that what was important was getting the festival on.

WES POMEROY: I felt like I was letting them down, like somehow I had failed, but I had to be honest: I told John, "There's not anything we can do about it—I can't protect your money," and I suggested that if they wanted to, they could set up a couple of places where they encouraged people to donate. I thought that would be pretty effective, because people were feeling grateful. Some people were asking, "Where do we give our money?" But for some reason, that wasn't carried forward.

Chip and John kept reassuring people from the stage that the concert would begin soon. We started playing the new Led Zeppelin and Crosby, Stills and Nash albums over the PA and the vibe seemed good. At one point Stephen Stills called John Morris in the production office. David Geffen or someone had told him about the crowds and he and the band were getting nervous about the gig. "Listen to this—we're playing the record and people love it!" John reassured him, holding the receiver out so Stills could hear "Suite: Judy Blue Eyes" followed by applause. "Okay, we'll be there!" Stephen said. "We're coming in by helicopter Sunday."

At one point, Bill Graham turned up backstage. John Morris tried to engage him and commiserate about the traffic difficulties and crowds of people. Bill was at a loss; no one had ever had to deal with the things we were facing. "It's time to stop being a promoter—and be a producer!" he told me. "You've got all these people here! What are you going to do with them?" "We're going to take care of them, Bill," I said, as I climbed the stairs to the stage.

Around 4 P.M., I was at a sort of command post Chip had set up off to the side of stage right. That's where I would spend much of the weekend. I heard the roar of motorcycles and saw a group of about twenty bikes coming up West Shore Road, right behind the stage. Concern swept over me for a moment when I realized it was a gang of bikers from the city. When they passed by, I noticed how polite they were being to the people moving aside so they could get through. As they moved on, they were swallowed up by the crowd.

ROB KENNEDY, FESTIVALGOER: The audience was one living, breathing organism. There were no boundaries. There were naked people, high people, straight people, and every kind of people in between. It was a very cool crowd. A funny story: One of my friends brought a *very* large Sherlock Holmes–type pipe. The stem was at least ten inches long and it had a huge bowl that *always* induced cough attacks. After a particularly bad fit of hacking, another of our friends got furious and heaved the thing as far as he could behind us into the crowd. The pipe owner got really upset and started yelling, "Throw it back. Throw it back!" Suddenly it reappeared—still burning—right upside the head of the guy who threw it away. Instant karma!

In the woods near the concessions area, a casbah of drugs and paraphernalia sprang up. Wares included an assortment of acid, THC, mescaline, peyote, mushrooms, several varieties of grass and hash. Booths sold rolling papers, pipes, roach clips, cigarettes.

People kept pouring into the site all day. It took eight or more hours to drive the one hundred miles from New York. Traffic came to a standstill on the thruway miles before hitting exit 16, which led to a very clogged Route 17. Eventually, the state police would no longer allow cars to exit there. The twelve-mile-long Route 17B had stopped moving since Thursday night. By Friday afternoon, traffic was tied up within a twenty-mile radius of the site.

GREIL MARCUS, MUSIC JOURNALIST: The intrepid *Rolling Stone* crew thought it would be bright to beat the traffic, so we left the city early in the morning and headed up . . . We got to Monticello, a little town eight miles from the festival . . . Eight miles of two-lane road jammed with thousands of cars that barely moved. Engines boiling over, people collapsed on the side of the road, everyone smiling in a common bewilderment. Automotive casualties looked like the skeletons of horses that died on the Oregon Trail. People began to improvise, drive on soft shoulders until they hit the few thousand who'd thought of the same thing, then stopping again. Finally the

two lanes were transformed into four and still nothing moved . . .
A lot of kids were pulling over and starting to walk through the
fields. Beat-out kids heading back told us nothing moved up ahead
and that we had six miles to go. It was a cosmic traffic jam, where
all the cars fall into place like pieces in a jigsaw puzzle and stay
there forever . . . It was an amazing sight, the highway to White
Lake: It looked, as someone said, like Napoleon's army retreating
from Moscow.

JONATHAN GOULD, FESTIVALGOER: We cut from the herd of cars mired on
Route 17B and struck off on our own. After a couple of miles of
dusty gravel road, we came upon Sullivan County's tiny airport,
which turned out to be more of a strip than a port, surrounded
by a collection of shabby hangars and utility buildings. I have no
memory of any of us articulating the next step in our plan. For my
part, I was wearing what any seventeen-year-old self-respecting
crypto-hippie/wannabe rock musician who had just returned
from London would wear for a three-day outing in the boondocks
of upstate New York: a closely tailored suede sport jacket, a blousy
yellow shirt with balloon sleeves, and a pair of crushed velvet bell-
bottom trousers. My hair came down to my shoulders; aviator sun-
glasses completed the effect. My friends Tom and Chris were more
modestly dressed—in my recollection, they wore denim from
head to toe. Our costumes implied a narrative: I was a rock musician, these were my roadies. Imbued with this fantasy, we walked
across the parking lot and joined a line of about twenty-five col-
orfully dressed people on the edge of a weedy patch of tarmac
where the helicopters were landing and taking off. The only thing
I remember was the feeling of waiting for someone in a position of
authority to say to us, "What the hell do you think you're doing?"
The helicopters kept landing and taking off, each one carrying
two passengers seated beside the pilot. Eventually it was our turn.

Chris and I crouched low and ran across the tarmac (we'd seen this on TV), climbed into the bubble-shaped glass cabin, clicked our safety belts, and away we went.

I'd never been in a helicopter before, much less seated in the open doorway of a low-flying helicopter as it hurtled across the hilly farmland of upstate New York. It was a blessedly short trip. We came up over a rise and there, arrayed in a great bowl below us, was the largest assemblage of people I had ever seen. We circled once over this multitude and descended toward an open patch of ground that was just to the left of the stage. Throughout the flight, Chris and I had avoided eye contact as we channeled all of our attention into trying to look like the sort of people who flew in helicopters all the time. Now we braced ourselves for the moment of truth when we would touch down and our role as brazen imposters would be exposed. Sure enough, as soon as we landed, a pair of fierce-looking hippie-roadie types came running toward the helicopter. (I remember thinking, At least they aren't cops.) One of them leaned into the doorway and shouted over the engine roar: "Do you need anything?" Did we *need* anything? Well, no, not just now, thank you. We unbuckled our seat belts, climbed out of the glass bubble, assumed our now-expert helicopter crouch, and ran across the field, escorted by the two hippie-roadies, who were giving us a quick orientation course. ("The backstage area is over here. The food tables are over there.") Tom's helicopter landed a few moments later, and he too emerged unchallenged. We were at Woodstock, our feet on the ground, our heads in the clouds.

By the end of the day, Wes had made an announcement for local radio stations, asking people not to attempt to travel to Woodstock, that we were at capacity. An estimated one million people tried to get there on Friday and had to turn back.

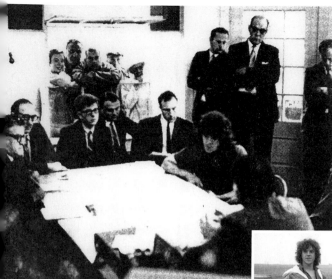

Above
Bethel residents peer through the window while we meet with town officials to make sure we can have the festival in White Lake

Below
Me, Chris Langhart, and Ticia

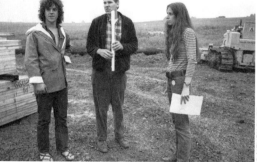

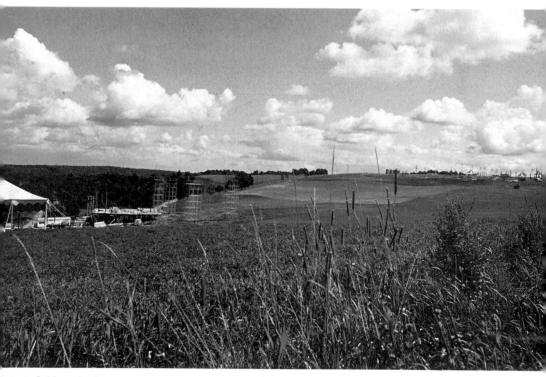

Max's field, eight days to go

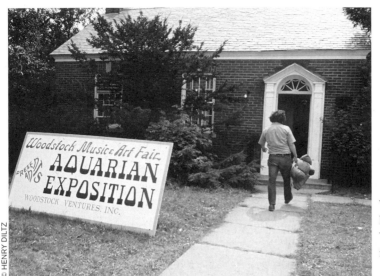

Woodstock Ventures headquarters at the New York Telephone Building in Kauneonga Lake

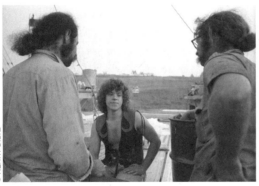

Stage designer Steve Cohen, me, and stage construction foreman Jay Drevers

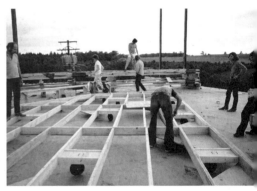

Building the turntable for the stage, August 11

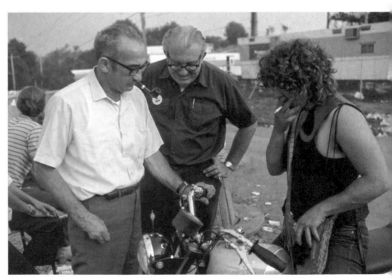

Max Yasgur (left, with pipe) and me

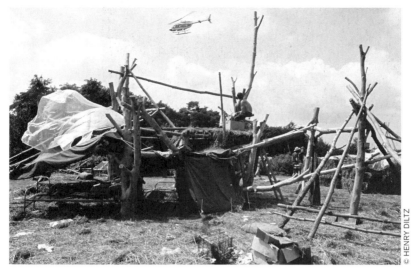

Our jungle gym in the kids' park

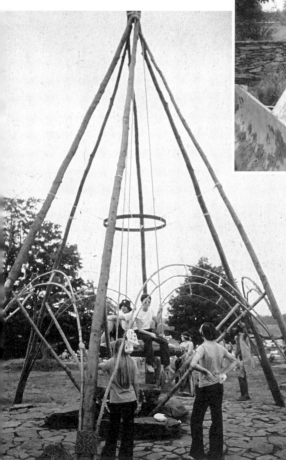

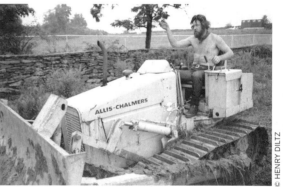

Above
Artist Ron Liis

Left
A wooden sculpture created by
Buster Simpson

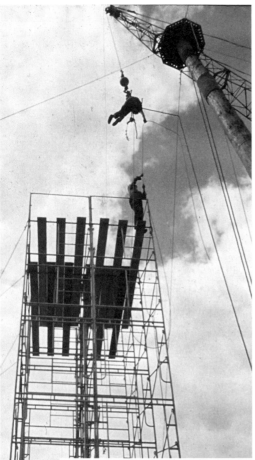

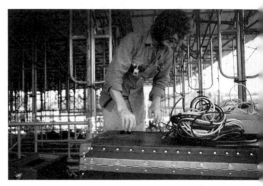

Above
Chip sorting through a maze of wiring under the stage

Left
A rigger in midflight

Below
Filmmakers Malcolm Hart (center) and Michael Margetts (right) at the local garage

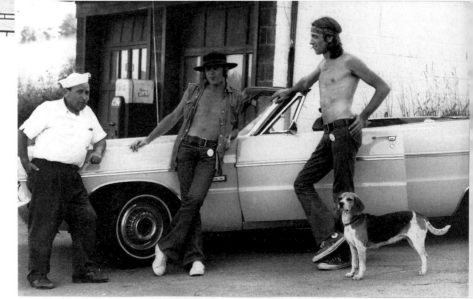

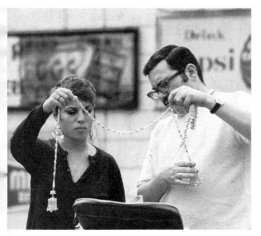

Rona Elliot takes a break to buy jewelry

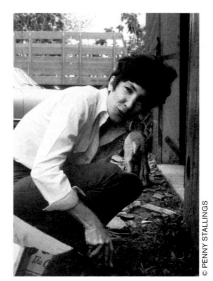

Jean Ward preparing the ground

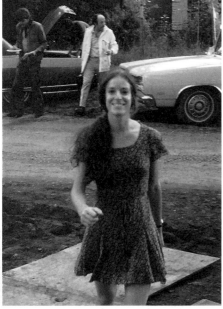

Ticia in White Lake; Peter Goodrich is in the back to the right

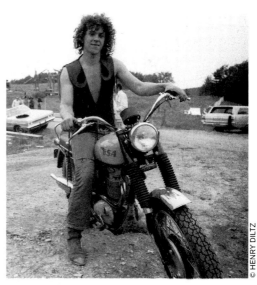

Checking on the campgrounds

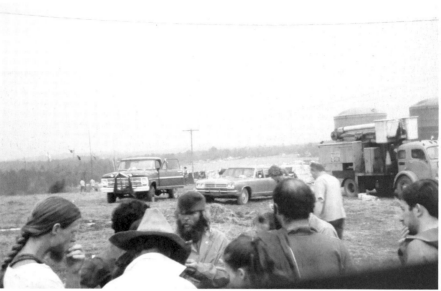

Setting up camp with the Hog Farm (*from left*): Tom Law, Hugh Romney, unnamed Hog Farmer, Stan Goldstein, unknown

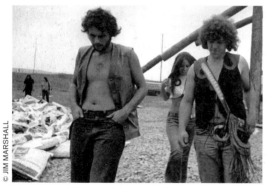

Artie and Linda Kornfeld and me

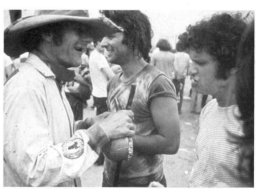

Hugh Romney, Abbie Hoffman, and Paul Krassner (*from left*)

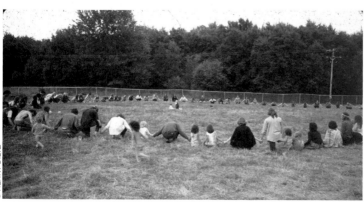

Hog Farmers make a circle to show the helicopters where to land

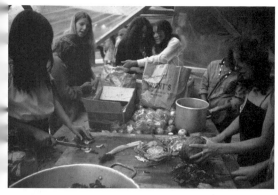

The Hog Farm free kitchen

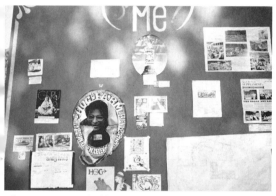

The Hog Farm's bulletin board, with Mel peering out

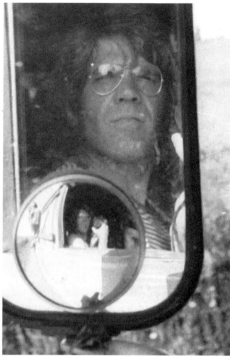

Henry Diltz's self-portrait using a Hog Farm bus mirror

© HENRY DILTZ

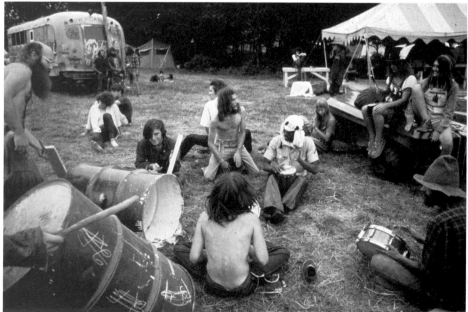

© HENRY DILTZ

The Hog Farm camp

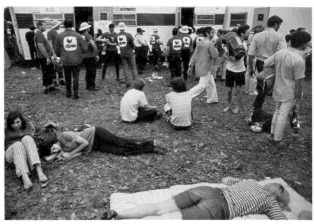

Top
Peace patrol meeting

Middle
Merry Prankster Ken Babbs and
artist/photographer Ira Cohen

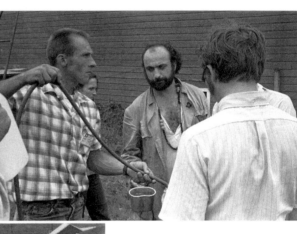

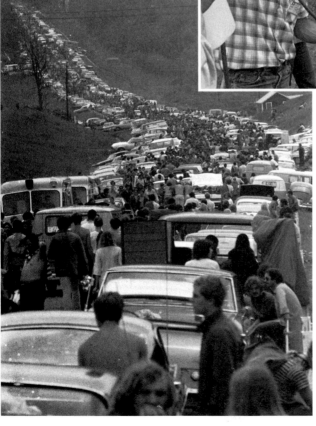

Traffic jam, August 15, 1969

PENNY STALLINGS: It was like the earth tilted as the entire baby boomer demographic tried to get there.

JOYCE MITCHELL: My office was a trailer and it was there that the *New York Times* reporter called the paper and said we were a disaster site. I wanted to choke him, but you know, "freedom of the press." I was just on the other side of the footbridge, and I was running communications—messages to the stage. I was fighting with Jimi Hendrix's agent to try to get him to come.

I had originally wanted Jimi to play an unannounced acoustic set on Friday to kick things off, but he hadn't turned up yet. By four thirty, I knew we had to get someone ready to go onstage. The only other possibility besides Richie was Tim Hardin. When I approached him, he was strumming his guitar and singing to himself in the artists' pavilion. "Hey, Tim, you want to open this thing up?"

"No way, man! I can't go on now—not me, not first! I can't deal with that!" He looked at me in desperation. "I'm waiting on my band."

I knew he was fragile—he'd only recently kicked a heroin habit by getting on methadone and I didn't want to push him. Tim was a friend, and I was a big fan of his music and was hoping he'd be at his best onstage. This could be a big break for him.

It had to be Richie—I knew he could handle it, and his powerful but calm demeanor was just what we needed to set the tone for liftoff. Regardless of what he said, he was ready and needed the least preparation and gear. When he saw me coming, Richie looked scared, and tried to walk away.

RICHIE HAVENS: Here was Michael walking slowly toward me and I knew exactly what he was going to say. I could see his smile getting larger and larger as he came closer. Then he cocked his head to one side and said, "Richie, please help us out. Oh, man, you've *gotta* help us out."

When I realized he was serious this time, I could feel my heart start to freak out. And I was pleading with Michael. I said, "Michael, I'm supposed to be number five, not one."

"Please, Richie, man, please!" I was finally convinced.

At 5:07 P.M., dressed in an orange dashiki and white pants, Richie Havens walked out onto that huge stage with his big Guild acoustic and propped himself on a tall wooden stool. Flanked by his percussionist and guitarist, he started talking to the crowd like he was at the Café Wha? "You know, we've finally made it! We did it this time. They'll never be able to hide us again!"

"Get Together," "I'm a Stranger Here," "High Flying Bird," "I Can't Make It Anymore," "Handsome Johnny." After about forty minutes of playing an energized set of folk tunes, Richie stood up from the stool to end his performance. We still weren't ready with another act, so I gave him a nod to keep going. Like the trouper he was, he just kept going and going. He'd get up to leave the stage and we'd send him back. He didn't have a set list to draw from—but returned with song after song, and his band followed along. Finally, drenched with sweat, he gave us the look that this—his sixth or seventh encore—was it.

RICHIE HAVENS: I'm back out there one more time, when finally I've completely run out of songs and know I've got to get off, no matter what the situation is. So I started tuning and retuning, hoping to remember a song I've missed, when I hear that word in my head again, that word I kept hearing while I looked over the crowd in my first moments onstage. The word was: *freedom*.

And I say to the crowd: "Freedom is *what we're all talking about getting. It's what we've been looking for . . . I think* this *is it*."

I start strumming my guitar and the word *freedom* comes out of my mouth as "FREE-dom, FREE-dom" with a rhythm of its own. My foot takes over and drives my guitar into a faster, more powerful rhythm. I don't know where this is going, but it feels right and somehow I find myself blending it into an old song—"Sometimes I Feel Like a Motherless Child"—a great spiritual my grandmother used to sing to me as a hymn when I was growing up in Brooklyn. It's a beautiful song, a song I hadn't played in six or seven years. The rhythm is strong and my foot is driving me.

Deano and Daniel are following along, getting into it, chanting phrases back at me. But "FREE-dom" is always there, like an unspoken bass line or a distant refrain. This was the same feeling I'd been experiencing all along. The feeling that Bethel was such a special place, a moment when we all felt we were at the exact center of true freedom. I'm singing it, "FREE-dom, FREE-dom," picking up the rhythm another beat, and the pulse of it is carrying me and connecting the whole Woodstock Festival for me in my very last moments onstage. I felt like I could feel the people I couldn't even see on the other side of the hill . . . "Clap your *hands! Clap your hands!*" And they all did!

As I watched Richie walk offstage after his incredible set, I spotted my father, a big smile on his face, sitting on the downstage scaffolding. The best seat in the house.

How to follow Richie? Artie and John Morris supplied the answer in the form of Swami Satchidananda, an Indian spiritual leader who wished to say a few words to the crowd. My old friend Peter Max, who'd been studying meditation and yoga, had brought the swami and a group of his followers to Woodstock.

ARTIE KORNFELD: There was no discussion about it, because as soon as it came up, Michael thought it was cool. I was looking at it as "what a great vibe to put out." He put a wave of peace out there.

JOHN MORRIS: There's this teeny-tiny little man in a robe . . . I brought him up onstage and he sat there and in his squeaky voice talked to the people . . . It was part of the calming influence. It was like an invocation.

Though not booked to perform, John Sebastian was a familiar face hanging out backstage. After his band the Lovin' Spoonful had broken up the previous year, he'd been spending time in California, living in a commune with the Firesign Theatre and writing songs for his first solo album. He'd just happened to run into the Incredible String Band at the Albany airport Friday morning and they invited him to join them in the helicopter we'd sent to pick them up.

JOHN SEBASTIAN: I ended up backstage mainly because I knew everybody; these were all people I had played with, hung out with, sat around tables smoking dope with. This was absolute community. I felt very much at one with the whole group. I was quickly given all the passes I would ever need, and started wandering around backstage. Everyone was coping simultaneously with the fact that it had become a free festival. The mechanics about getting people on and off the stage had been thought about, but it was a monumental task. So all those who weren't onstage found themselves helping with food or helping with lodging, helping any way they could.

I wandered around and found an eight-by-eight Volkswagen bus tent that had become a dressing room. I felt like I was right at home. I swept out the tent and began to batten it down a little bit. It had been put up very fast and people obviously had bounced around inside of it and shaken its moorings. So I started to fasten it down and Chip Monck came along at one point, and says, "Geez, you know about this." And I said, "Well, I have been living in a tent just like this for the last couple of months." He said, "Terrific, you're in charge of this tent." I said okay. The entire Incredible String Band put all their instruments inside. They had an oud and a twelve-string, and a sitar, and mandolins, and banjos. We're hiding this stuff in the extremities of the tent so none of the moisture would get in.

It was still early, so I decided, I'll make a circle around that crowd—just to see what's going on. It was a long walk, took three hours. I wandered up into the wooded area where there was a jungle gym, various craftspeople had set up their little worlds. Incredibly magical to wander through this area and see the various factions of this community of souls who had come together. I was not recognized at all.

We had saved an area backstage for friends and family. My mother and father were amazed by what they saw. They wanted to stay for the whole thing but had left their dog in their car and had to leave to check on her. Soon they would call to say that because of traffic, they were unable to reach their car. I sent a helicopter to pick them up, then their dog Jody, and take them to Monticello. It was like my life flashing before my eyes: I'd invited Ric O'Barry from Miami, who'd also tried to get Fred Neil to come. Peter Max was there, and lots of friends from Woodstock, the Grove, and Brooklyn. I'd barely been home in weeks and my relationship with Sonya had pretty much come to an end—but she was there, along with other friends from the Grove. I'd invited Train but they were in the studio, finally recording their first album for Vanguard, the same label as Joan Baez and Country Joe and the Fish.

CHRISTINE OLIVEIRA, FESTIVALGOER: I was friends with Michael and Sonya in Coconut Grove and moved to Woodstock not long after they did. After watching Michael run in and out of town, planning the festival for months, we had to go, and he gave us tickets. We were camping near the Hog Farm off to the side, and we were, I guess, sort of the elite, but I didn't know that. Our area had its own little amphitheater, so the people who performed would come over and play where you could hang out and nobody would see you. The Hog Farm was really together in terms of getting food organized for people and staying on top of sanitation. I hate crowds, so I mostly stayed in this part because you could hear everything anyway. I thought, "This is a once-in-a-millennium thing." A lot of it I attribute to Michael's energy drawing it there.

The first day I sat in that audience in front of the main stage for four hours, and finally I thought, "I can't sit here anymore." It was not a bad crowd, but I had to get up. Most people were so stoned. They were fifteen, sixteen, seventeen years old, and had never been away from home. I was already twenty-six. From the stage, they'd call, "So and so, come and get your diabetes medicine," and that was a shock to me because I had never heard of so many people being diabetic.

I got up and walked around. There were pipes lying across the ground, and the water system broke down, and the roads weren't really in properly to get the cars in and out. They were building the stage right up to the last minute. They were even working on stuff while the first acts went on.

They had this little village and woods, with concessions and beautiful stuff—leatherwork and tie-dye, but it was the whole culture. It was gorgeously set up, with a big jungle gym and a playground. It was this magic utopian village.

ABBIE HOFFMAN: It got to be a really beautiful scene with people looking out for each other. I got Bobby Neuwirth, Rick Danko, John Sebastian, and others to come down and do a little concert at the free stage. It was quite special. Joan Baez waited for an hour in the rain to go on, without telling anybody who she was.

JOHN SEBASTIAN: Rick Danko and I went over to the large tent where the Hog Farm was cooling out acid casualties. The people were lying on canvas cots, and [Hugh Romney] was walking around in a white outfit. Every kid who came in would come up to him and say, "Hey, man, take these and don't let me ever see them again." Rick and I tried to think of all the songs we could play for the mentally disoriented. It was hard-core easy-listening music.

Little impromptu jams were going on backstage too. At one point, Jerry Garcia and Mimi Fariña were singing and playing together. On the main stage, the Friday programming was easing in. We'd located Sweetwater, and they finally arrived, after we picked them up in a helicopter. But they suffered through some sound problems due to all their instrumentation, including flute, cello, keyboards, conga, drums, bass, and two lead vocalists, Nancy Nevins and Albert Moore.

ALEX DEL ZOPPO OF SWEETWATER: We had a fairly eclectic band. We had a mixed racial, mixed gender band—Italians, Jews, Mexicans, Irish. We'd take anyone! Seven people and very strange instrumentation—no guitar. We were unfortunately a complicated act to stage. We were used to going on without a sound check, but we weren't used to *being* the sound check! And from what we know, Albert ran into someone he knew and dropped a little of that brown acid, which was not a good idea.

FRED HERRERA OF SWEETWATER: We were the first electric group onstage, with mics for the amps and drums. So we were essentially the sound crew's sound check. They were adjusting levels all the way through our set, so everything was intermittent. I could sort of hear from the main speakers what was going out to the audience. But I could not hear what was going on on the other side of the stage, and they could not hear us. We were trying to listen to our amplifiers, but we were so spread out that even the bass I played, which was cranked up quite a bit, would just get lost. It would just get sucked up outside in the air there.

With a haunting tenor voice, singer-songwriter Bert Sommer performed "Jennifer," "She's Gone," Simon and Garfunkel's "America" and other ballads, while sitting cross-legged onstage, backed by electric guitars. Artie would produce his next two albums.

More of the musicians had been showing up at the Holiday Inn in Liberty, and we sent Joyce over in a helicopter to make sure everything was okay there.

JOYCE MITCHELL: Everyone was at the motel, and they were fighting over rooms—there weren't enough rooms. Janis was there. I tried to cool her off in the lobby because she was very drunk and very demanding. The Grateful Dead were sweethearts. They said they would share rooms. The Who were there and it was difficult to get Keith Moon settled down. The son of a bitch tried to rape me! I had to really push him to get out of his room. He was grabbing me.

ELLEN SANDER, MUSIC JOURNALIST: Several miles away, the culmination of pop history was unfolding, but a couple of hundred of its superstars and their touring staff were stranded at the Holiday Inn. The Airplane and the Who had just played Tanglewood a few days before, so they were already there. Somebody had changed a $5 bill at the bar and put all the quarters into the jukebox, playing "Hey Jude" sixty times end to end. The whole bar sang along with the chorus, linking arms, swaying from side to side and laughing, among them Jack Casady, Marty Balin [both of Jefferson Airplane], Janis Joplin, and Jerry Garcia. A high-stakes poker game was going on at the corner of the bar. Later [folk singer] Rosalie Sorrells and Jerry Garcia sat on the floor with guitars and sang folk songs together. Judy Collins headed a long luncheon table in the dining room with [record executives] Clive Davis and Jac Holzman in company.

After darkness fell, Tim Hardin finally said he was ready to go on. His band had arrived, but he stepped onstage alone with his guitar, playing some of those gorgeous songs he'd written, like "If I Were a Carpenter" and "Reason to Believe." His set started out strong.

GILLES MALKINE, GUITARIST FOR TIM HARDIN: I was twenty and playing rhythm guitar with Tim. He did the first half of the set solo. But then, halfway through, he brought out the band. You could not see the end of the crowd. It was like all of humanity looking at you. And most everybody in the band was okay with that, I think, but I was pretty frazzled. I was at the end of my tether. He suddenly threw a title of a song at us that had not yet been written. His wife, Susan, had written a poem called "Snow White Lady" about heroin, so he said, " 'Snow White Lady' in F," and he put this crumpled piece of paper on the keyboard and started playing, and so we just went along with him, but it was a disaster. He was kind of chanting— it was a single chord and he was looking for the tune in there. Okay, you might do that in a café somewhere, but Jesus Christ, the whole world was looking at us! From that first tune, we started to get a little better, but any other crowd would have walked out on us, we were that bad. It was so disastrous that afterward I quit the music business for many years.

I was disappointed when things fell apart onstage for Tim. But once it was over, he was relieved and happy.

About ten thirty, we were getting Ravi Shankar ready to go on when it started thundering. He was telling Al Aronowitz, "I am frightened in case something goes wrong with so many people," but once he got out there, his playing transcended the problems of the weather. The vibe was intense. When those spiritual moments would happen, you could really feel them. You could feel everybody coming together.

GILLES MALKINE: One act that was miles above everybody else was Ravi Shankar. There was no speaking, it was all pure music. What he did with that crowd was amazing, just with music. And at certain points in the performance, people would stand up and yell because of where he took them. They say it takes several lifetimes to make a sitar player. I believe it, because talk about leaving your mind behind! And just going with the music and with the flow and with a couple of others you've played with all your life, like Ustad Alla Rakha, who was the tabla player. He woke up that audience and took them along with him on this soaring musical journey. Nobody else could touch that.

AL ARONOWITZ, REPORTER FOR THE *New York Post*: Shankar was in the midst of his performance when the rain began falling, accompanied by a few lightning bolts, and the water was frightening. The rain began collecting in the canopy atop the stage and threatened to collapse it. At another point, festival guards expressed the fear that the stage, built on scaffolding, was beginning to slide in the mud. The harder the rain fell, however, the more determined the crowd seemed to stay. Huddled around bonfires, most of the audience waited an hour while the music was interrupted because the water threatened to short the electrical equipment. But even in the rain, the crowd gave standing ovations.

The darkness and the heavy rains caused some false alarms and fears about the stage's sturdiness. Because it was built on the rise of a hill, we were concerned that it was going to move. It may have a bit, but there were poles set in concrete, and if it moved at all, it could have been only a few inches. The tarp hanging over the stage filled with water, so Saturday we used the crane to push the tarp up to empty it. Otherwise a ton of water could have come down on someone's head.

After Ravi Shankar's set, the folksinger Melanie wandered up backstage with Artie Ripp. A friend of Artie Kornfeld's from the record business, he was working with Melanie and had suggested that she play a few songs with her acoustic guitar. She was fairly unknown then, but from the first verse of "Beautiful People," she really connected with that unique, quavering voice of hers. All alone up there in the dark, she managed to totally tap into thousands of people huddled together before her. Inspired by what happened, she would go home and write "Lay Down (Candles in the Rain)," which became her first big hit in 1970.

> MELANIE: It was magical. I had my first out-of-body experience. I started walking across the bridge to the stage, and I just left my body, going to a higher view. I watched myself walk onto the stage, sit down, and sing a couple of lines. It started to rain right before I went on. Ravi Shankar had just finished up his performance, and [Chip Monck] said that if you lit candles, it would help to keep the rain away. By the time I finished my set, the whole hillside was a mass of little flickering lights. It was an amazing experience to be there, to be in that time and live through that group of people who were acknowledging each other, as if we were all in one family. Woodstock was an affirmation that we were part of each other.

The lighting of candles would set a precedent that carries on to this day. The candles became lighters, which have since become cell phones.

The rain threatened Arlo Guthrie and his band's performance, but we decided to go for it. By then Arlo, thinking he was off the hook, had dropped some acid. He wasn't up for going on, but we talked him into it. He did a great set, opening with "Coming Into Los Angeles." He carried on a kind of one-sided conversation with the audience, stopping in the middle of Dylan's "Walking Down the Line" to follow a loose thought. Everyone loved it.

Joan Baez, who was pregnant, did not seem at all put out by the delays. She brought a cup of hot tea to Melanie, who'd been coughing. At one point, Artie and I were standing together and he was saying, "How am I ever going back to Fifty-sixth Street after this—it's changed my life," trying to explain to me what he was going through, when Joan walked up and said to him, "I think he knows." She had a good sense of humor, taking it all in stride even when Abbie Hoffman handed the renowned pacifist a switchblade as a gift.

Finally, just after midnight, Joan went onstage. She started her set with the uplifting gospel song "Oh Happy Day." She looked out into the crowd and told them about her husband David Harris, who'd just been imprisoned for draft resistance, then sang his favorite old union ballad, "Joe Hill." Her next song was inspired by her sister Mimi, "Sweet Sir Galahad," and Joan joked that it was the only song she'd written that she would sing in public. After the folk songs, she moved into some country-rock numbers cowritten by Gram Parsons, "Hickory Wind" and "Drug Store Truck Drivin' Man." Then Joan's moving, unaccompanied "Swing Low, Sweet Chariot," followed by "We Shall Overcome" ended the first day of music around 2 A.M.

JOHN MORRIS: At the end of Friday night, we still had so many things to do that were stacked up. It was more like it was the first round, and "What can we do here? What can we shore up? Where are we? What's happening? What are we lacking? What are we doing?" We worked all that night. They were out there and we had to take care of them somehow. We had to make it work.

Friday felt like an eternity, but an eternity in heaven. Against all odds and despite the infrastructure being stretched almost to the breaking point, we were living—at least for the moment—in the kind of world we had envisioned.

There had been a million moving, spinning parts, all coming together, and I was in my element. After about a two-hour nap late Friday night in one of the trailers, I was ready to start doing it all over again.

eleven AUGUST 16, 1969

"If we don't get the cash, we're not going on!"

It's late Saturday afternoon and the Grateful Dead's road manager, Jon McIntire, and the Who's John Wolff have cornered me by my production trailer. Emotions are heating up. It's the road manager's job to get paid before the band hits the stage.

"Look, we'll give you a check," I tell them. "The check will be good after the weekend. Everybody's in the same boat—there is no cash on the site. The gates are down, it's a free concert, you know what we're up against—"

"That's not good enough—it's got to be cash or else no music," Wolff repeats. We owe them the second half of their fees: the Dead $3,375 and the Who $6,250. I don't know how we could get the money in time for them to go on.

"We're in a real bind for cash," I repeat, "but I will give you a check now and you can go to the bank Monday morning and cash it, and I promise it will be good."

"Only if it's a certified check," they insist.

It dawns on me how to get these guys to let their acts play. Deep down, I know the Dead won't pose a problem; their friends are here, they'll play no matter what. Jerry Garcia has already been jamming at the free stage. The Who, on the other hand, might be looking for an excuse not to perform. They still seem pissed off that they agreed to play what will turn out to be the most important show of their career. Since Pete Townshend arrived, he's been scowling at everyone and keeping to himself. This peace-and-love thing isn't for him.

I look straight at Wolff. "If that's your decision, I'll go out and make the announcement that the Who won't be performing because we have no cash."

The Who are important musically and are one of the best live acts around, so this is a bit of a gamble. I know I'd never make that announcement. But, with all the changes in lineups and the unscheduled acts, the audience probably won't even notice if they don't play.

Wolff and McIntire exchange glances. "Forget it!" Wolff says before they stomp off. That's the last I'll hear from them until Monday, I think.

M el Lawrence was the first of our staff up on Saturday morning. At dawn, he walked around the site to make sure everyone had made it through the rainy night okay. Mel was into preemptive action and wanted to take care of business early.

MEL LAWRENCE: After this incredible Friday night, people just slept in the bowl—right in the spot where they were. All these people were asleep and it was quiet, and I made my way down to the stage and the production offices, where everybody's asleep too. It was maybe six or something, and I knew we had to clean up the place, so my crew and I got garbage bags and we put them all along one side of the bowl in a line.

When the crowd began to wake up, Mel went up onstage and made a little speech about "why don't we just clean up our areas? We're going to pass along garbage bags for you to put your trash in, and then we'll pick them up." That worked. We put on some music, and we were off to Saturday.

ABBIE HOFFMAN: The morning after the rains came . . . a cat came out of his tent and made a fist at the sky: *"Fuck off rain, we're staying here forever!"* It was then that the battle began for me. It was then that I felt at peace. It was about 5 A.M. and I had a hunk of brown canvas over me with a hole cut out for the head. I reminded myself of General George Patton inspecting the troops of Normandy as I walked around assessing the damage. The main performance area had turned into a huge slide of mud, people, collapsed tents, overturned motorcycles, cans, bottles, and garbage galore—man, there was more fuckin' garbage unloaded in Woodstock Nation that night than in the Lower East Side during the entire garbage strike.

Our plans for garbage removal were extensive. They were based on calculations made by Peter, Stan, and Mel. We had estimated the number of cups, plates, cans, bottles, and food wrappers we'd use in a day. We weighed what we thought would be the average size, multiplied it by four days, and then multiplied that number by two hundred thousand. With that information, we contracted for the largest trash compactors available and placed them strategically around the site. We would collect the garbage, take it to the compactors, then load it into trucks to haul to a local dump. A pretty good plan, and it worked beautifully the first day—until we got to the "haul it away" part—traffic was just too heavy to make it through.

With radio reports about traffic jams and a lack of supplies coming in, rumors about food and water shortages, chaos and misery were rampant in the ill-informed media. To the press, it was a disaster area. I knew things were not that bad. I made my way around the site to see for myself. Going through the crowds, I ran into Mel, who was working on a fix for one of the lines of overflowing Portosans. The honeywagons had been able to service them on Friday, but by Saturday they were getting stuck trying to get off the site. Mel resorted to a variation of one of our earlier sanitation plans: dig deep trenches and backfill them with earth after each dump. We got a backhoe in to dig a trench a hundred feet long, wide and deep, and that's where the waste would go.

MEL LAWRENCE: The trench was on top of a hill. That's where they dumped the waste. And the next year, I heard they had a great corn crop there!

MIRIAM YASGUR: Kids were running motorcycles through our fields planted with corn right across from our office plant. They were breaking cornstalks, and Max promptly called Michael and said, "Do you know they're destroying this field, which is not part of the land that I rented to you at all?" It didn't take very long until a whole group of young kids came out and put signs all around the field: DON'T RIDE THROUGH THIS FIELD . . . THESE ARE MAX'S CROPS. Nobody ever rode through the field again. They kept going around it. People were camping along the sides of the road, and they started coming up my driveway and I went out and I said to the young people, "Look, we cannot have people camping along the driveway. Our men are working, they have to get in and out." They moved. Nobody camped on my driveway. Nobody camped near the dairy.

The board of health had sent a guy to the site on Friday morning to inspect everything. According to Mel, he could have had us shut down. But he brought his daughter with him and she disappeared as soon as they arrived. He spent the entire weekend looking for her—and never got around to filing his report. I'm sure his daughter was having the time of her life.

In the early morning, I headed over to the Hog Farm and Movement City. Unbelievably, en route, I ran into my old friend Ellen Lemisch. She hopped on the back of my bike, and we talked as I took her on my rounds. At one point, she said, "Do you realize what you've done, Lang?" That shook me, as I suddenly did realize that this was now something we had *done*—no longer something we were trying to do. All our spirits had set sail days ago and Woodstock was now moving under its own steam.

Throughout the day, between sets and whenever I thought things were under control, I'd take a few minutes to get on my bike and check out our not-so-little city—the hospital tents, the heliport, the free stage, the various campgrounds, Movement City, the free kitchens. Communications between the different areas on-site were limited, so that was the only way to get a real-time take on the situation. Everybody seemed to be holding it together. I said a quick hello to Paul Krassner, who was hanging out at the Yippie booth.

PAUL KRASSNER, YIPPIE COFOUNDER AND PUBLISHER OF *THE REALIST*: Woodstock fit our original vision of what the protest at the Chicago Democratic Convention should have been the year before: an alternative event with music, a special community with people who shared the same value system where you couldn't separate the idealism from the irreverence.

STAN GOLDSTEIN: The crowd began to be its own self-policing, self-regulating, self-controlling entity.

There were makeshift lean-tos, tepees, pup tents, shelters made out of bales of hay. Just as we'd hoped, sprinkled around the perimeter were little encampments of people sharing everything. I noticed fewer and fewer people manning the Movement City booths set up by various political organizations. The entire gathering had become Movement City.

TOM SMUCKER, ACTIVIST AND WRITER: We got up there with our MDS literature. And we set up our booth with the others. And behind it was this printing press that was going to run off a newspaper each day . . . Abbie Hoffman was there, SDS, Motherfuckers, Peaceniks, swamis, Meher Babaites, the Hot Chow Mein truck guys, we were all there, trying to pick up on it . . . But the booths were never used. The scene [at the festival] was so far-out that people started leaving [our area] right away. Literature got rained on or was never distributed . . . You took the massive energy, the freedom . . . all the good music, and general friendliness, and dug *that* . . . In the rain and mud, water shortages, heat and cold, the Hog Farm served the *people*, whatever their ideology.

More important than politics was *community*. All these different people coming together and getting along, sharing. The Hog Farm kept several food lines going, and though crowds were queued up at the Portosans and phone banks, no one seemed to mind. People were calling their friends and telling them how great things were. Word started to get out that the picture was quite different from what was being painted by the media.

The only complaints I heard were from people buying tickets to exchange for burgers and Cokes at the Food for Love concession stands. The lines were long and then they had to wait a second time for the food. Jeffrey and company had mismanaged their supplies, and they were already running low. So they started overcharging for cold hot dogs ($1 each, when the going price was a quarter), which people had to stand in line hours to get. This really pissed off the Motherfuckers and some of the other Movement City people, not to mention the hungry kids.

Because of reports of shortages, local groups in Sullivan County banded together and gathered thousands of food donations to be airlifted to the site. People who showed up after walking for miles told stories of townspeople offering them food and drink along the way. Stories hit the press of price gouging, but I think most of the residents of White Lake were giving what they could.

BILL WARD: We'd left the site Friday night to try to make it to the Diamond Horseshoe, got stuck in the jam, and abandoned the car, walking five miles to the motel. Saturday morning I got up early and went back to the car. There were cars everywhere, abandoned all along the road. There was garbage and people everywhere. A nice little old couple along the street had all these hippies camped out in their yard, and they were bringing them food and water, and people were sharing Cokes and stuff. All these groups of people who appeared to be so different were all standing around chatting and sharing things.

TOM SMUCKER: The few inconveniences gave everyone something to do and developed a reason for cooperation, which made you feel good.

GILLES MALKINE: Everybody rallied to help each other, to be like family, to play in the mud, to share, to help. A lot of the townspeople felt it too. People said over and over, "The kids are wonderful. We helped them. We ran out of food too." It was a wonderful thing and brought out the best in everybody. The rain was almost like, "Okay, it's time to wash now, it's time to clean up, and let's not forget where we are." It wasn't threatening, and it didn't dampen the spirit at all. It was like, "Oh, now we've got to put up with this—well, we will." And it was funny and made the mud fun.

CHRISTINE OLIVEIRA: After it rained, it was awful. It was mud city! I didn't get that wet because I stayed under the tent, but the mud factor was just unbelievable. We couldn't get to the concession stands because of the mud slide. It became a joke. We brought a lot of food, and you could always get something. We were right by the Hog Farm. They had macrobiotic food, very healthy vegetables, rice—it was tasty.

ABBIE HOFFMAN: There were banks of pay phones, and we had one pay phone where our organizers would be the only ones in line. After some hours on Saturday, the festival owners gave us walkie-talkies, gave us access to a helicopter. It was kind of interesting, because the people flying the helicopters were, of course, National Guard. And they were ready to go to Vietnam—they were military types, and here we were, the antithesis. But when it came to things like saving lives and getting out good information about not drinking certain water, all of a sudden the casual sex and the nudity and the drug smoking, and the fact that we were against the war, didn't matter. So in a sense, we were all Americans. And I can't remember a single moment of friction.

PARRY TEASDALE: A friend of mine was wandering around the site and told me on Saturday there was a guy doing video over in Movement City, and I said, "Somebody else doing video—how can that possibly be?" It was so new, I thought I was the only one around who had it. There was David Cort, and he had some portable video equipment, so I said, "Why don't I get some of my equipment to your site?" I took it over to Movement City—my monitor, my camera, my recorder—and we set my system up at this kind of lean-to booth, so people could come by and see themselves and talk. At this time, seeing themselves on a video screen was a novelty. David and I also went around together and shot sequences of people who were working in the medical tent and people bringing in water—interviewing people and recording what was going on around Movement City.

HUGH ROMNEY: There was an amazing energy, and once you surrendered to it, you could just keep going. That energy just took over. It was a sensational feeling to be used by the energy. What ran Woodstock was the spirit of volunteerism, that instant life-support system.

More and more people, some who'd been traveling since Friday, continued to arrive. As the crowds mounted, the number of people who needed medical attention increased. Most of the cases were people who'd cut their feet on broken bottles. Helicopters transported serious cases to Sullivan County hospitals. By Saturday, there would be some twenty doctors and fifty nurses on-site—and more due in. Horribly, we found out early Saturday morning that a seventeen-year-old, Raymond Mizsak, from Trenton, New Jersey, was killed after being run over by a tractor while he slept in his bedroll next to the road. It was devastating news. There would be two more deaths on Sunday, one from a heroin overdose, the other from a burst appendix. Over the course of the weekend, two babies were born—one in a car stuck in traffic on the road and the other in a local hospital after the mother was airlifted out in a helicopter.

The community reached out to help: when the local facilities were overwhelmed, a high school in Monticello was transformed into a hospital ward. A regional airlines, now defunct, Mohawk, volunteered the use of a forty-seat plane to fly in Don Goldmacher and June Finer from New York City's Medical Committee for Human Rights, along with other medical personnel and supplies. We expanded our medical operations by turning the staff "canteen"—a huge pink-and-white-striped tent—into another field hospital.

PENNY STALLINGS: Peter Goodrich was in charge of what was supposed to be the workers' break tent. By Saturday afternoon it was clear that none of us were going to get any sleep, let alone stroll over to the canteen for a meal. So I proposed to Peter that we convert the tent into a medical clinic. People were getting cuts and sprains from walking barefoot in the mud. And there were enough bad trips to fill a mini psycho ward.

There was fire in Peter's eyes as he informed me that he had no intention of relinquishing his tent. Peter had decked the last person he had had a disagreement with—so it took all my courage to tell him that I would take the responsibility for making the change. In other words, this was going to happen—and I would fight for it if I had to. Seething with rage, he turned and sloshed through the mud, ranting all the way. To my relief, Chris Langhart had no problem with taking an order from me. Along with two of his guys, he ran water and electricity lines into the tent with dazzling speed. Other crew guys laid plywood down on the wet ground and brought in the cots, blankets, and medical supplies that had been delivered to us by the National Guard.

Abbie Hoffman, whose father had been a medical-supply distributor, jumped in and became a huge help, lending his activist ingenuity to tense situations. He worked with the doctors in the medical tents and assisted the Hog Farm. Originally bad trips and broken bones were being treated in the same facility and that was not working out. A separate trips tent was created and operated by the Hog Farm, which solved the problem. The Hog Farm's method to deal with a bad trip was to gently talk the person down, offering love and comfort until the worst was over. Then they'd ask the person to stay on and help the next one who came in freaking out.

ROZ PAYNE: I was helping Abbie in the hospital tent with Don Goldmacher and June Finer. June was a fabulous doctor who worked in clinics, and Don worked in a methadone clinic in the South Bronx, and they were always at all the demonstrations.

ABBIE HOFFMAN: Signs went up fast: CUTS, WAITING ROOM, ADMISSION, VOLUNTEERS, REST, EMERGENCY, HEAT TABLETS. Old friends began coming over. Abe Peck, ex-editor of the *Chicago Seed* and one of the best cats alive, ran the volunteer operation. Roz Payne from Newsreel took over information control and kept the visitors out of the area.

A local politician requested that the National Guard, which was bivouacked nearby, supply helicopters. The guard agreed, and their helicopters transported donated food—in all, something like ten thousand sandwiches, water, fruit, and canned goods were donated by people all over Sullivan County. The first National Guard chopper couldn't find a place to land near the free kitchens, so it left until someone reached Stan. He rounded up a massive group of people in a field near the kitchens, got them to hold hands and form a giant circle, then sit down. They placed a marker in the middle to indicate the landing spot. Once they landed, everyone in the circle became porters, unloading the helicopter and transporting the food to the free kitchens.

At some point during the afternoon, a *New York Times* reporter grabbed me for an interview. I quickly told him, "It's about the best behaved five hundred thousand people in one place on a rainy, muddy weekend that can be imagined. There have been no fights or incidents of violence of any kind." A state police official told the same reporter he was "dumbfounded by the size of the crowd. I can hardly believe that there haven't been even small incidents of misbehavior by the young people."

HENRY DILTZ: Behind the stage there was a lake and everyone would go nude swimming. They were really like gypsies. They all took off their clothes and went swimming in the pond. Then I got out and went up to the wharf and started taking photos and nobody cared. I took this beautiful photo of one girl kind of bobbing around in the water with lily pads. Looked like a Pre-Raphaelite painting.

JANE FRIEDMAN: We walked around and we weren't on acid or any drug, but it was like being on a drug, just feeling the total relaxation of this entire huge group of people. Everybody was relaxed. There wasn't any tension, there wasn't any stress, there wasn't any anger, there weren't petty squabbles. Probably it was all the drugs, but at the same time, it was this big mass of wonderful serenity. And the artists were really cool. Everybody was very proud to be there.

Quill, the band from Boston that had performed the public-service concerts for us in Wallkill, opened the show on Saturday a little after noon. After a rainy morning, it had turned hot and humid. Quill had all kinds of percussion instruments they threw out to the audience to get people to play along. They were an upbeat young band in the unenviable position of getting things going while the sound was being adjusted. So they played free-form jams and psychedelia-tinged songs like "They Live the Life" and "That's How I Eat."

By then, John had corralled Joe McDonald into playing to keep the crowd happy while we set up for Santana. He was due to go on with his band the Fish on Sunday, but when John spotted him hanging out, he grabbed him. There'd been talk that Joe might go solo anyway, so basically John convinced him somehow that there was no time like the present to give it a try.

COUNTRY JOE McDONALD: I said I didn't have a guitar. I didn't even have a guitar pick, just a matchbook cover. They gave me a rope for a strap.

I just sang a mixed-bag folk set. Not too many people were paying attention to me. I was watching them and they were talking. They knew Country Joe and the Fish, so I wasn't really surprised. I was just Muzak or something. I knew my job was just to go up and kill time. But after about an hour, I got more confident, I figured I had nothing more to lose. Boredom brings on confidence. I stopped playing for a minute and went over and asked [my manager] if I should try out the cheer. I came back out.

And I said, "Give me an F." And everybody turned and looked at me, and said, "F."

Then I said, "Give me a U." And they yelled back, "U!" And it went on like that. And I went on singing the song and they all kept staring at me. My adrenaline got really pumping.

Though the crowd might not have connected with Joe's acoustic "Ring of Fire" or "Tennessee Stud," they totally got the "Fish Cheer" and his wry antiwar song, "I Feel Like I'm Fixin' to Die Rag," which became a Woodstock anthem and a highlight of the movie. Hundreds of thousands of people singing along to "So it's one, two, three, what are we fighting for? Don't ask me, I don't give a damn. Next stop is Vietnam" made quite a statement against the war.

Between sets, Hugh Romney ended up onstage making announcements, becoming an audience favorite in the process.

HUGH ROMNEY: I was working pretty much full-time with the drug talkdown situation, busy moving from one situation to the next. How

I ended up getting onstage was that I had some announcements to give Chip to make, and I was also on his case because he'd made this announcement about avoiding the "blue acid." Chip said, "Come on up and do it yourself." He had no problem letting me talk on the microphone, and the only times I ever went up there were when I had something to say toward the collective consciousness. Later, when the rains came and they were announcing it was a disaster area, I said, *"There's a little bit of heaven in every disaster area!"*

Hugh calmed people's fears about the "bad acid." "It's not *poison*," he said from the stage, "it's just poorly manufactured."

Santana was up next, and I was really looking forward to their performance. I hoped they would boost the energy level of the day. Hardly anyone had seen them on the East Coast, though they'd been playing around the Bay Area for a couple of years.

CARLOS SANTANA: We got to Woodstock at eleven in the morning. We'd heard it was a disaster area. They flew us in on a helicopter. We hung around with Jerry Garcia and we found out that we didn't have to go on until eight at night. They told us just to cool out and take it easy.

One thing led to another. I wanted to take some mescaline. Just at the point that I was peaking, this guy came over and said, "Look, if you don't go on *right now,* you guys are not going to play." I went out there and I saw this ocean as far as I could see. An ocean of flesh and hair and teeth and hands. I just played. I prayed that the Lord would keep me in tune and in time. I had played loaded before, but not to that big of a crowd. Because it was like plugging into a whole bunch of hearts—and all those people at the same time. But we managed. It was incredible. I'll never forget the way the music sounded, bouncing up against a field of bodies. For the band as a whole, it was great.

GREGG ROLIE, SANTANA VOCALIST/KEYBOARDIST: We played to each other. Carlos's back was usually to the audience because we played like jazz players. And 500,000 people happened to be there. You can see the first ten or twenty thousand; after that, it's all just hair and teeth. So there was nothing to be afraid of. If I had known what it was all about and what Woodstock ended up meaning, I probably would have been frightened to death.

With its monster rhythm section, Santana was the first group that really got everyone up and dancing. I flashed on my parents' nightclub where people did the mambo on Saturday nights. Carlos Santana had merged that Latin sound with rock and roll and it was phenomenal. On "Soul Sacrifice," Michael Shrieve played one of most amazing drum solos I have ever heard, with the percussionists joining in and Carlos's soaring guitar building everything to a crescendo. The audience went nuts—it was obvious another star was being born.

MICHAEL SHRIEVE, SANTANA DRUMMER: The size of the crowd was so big, it was like standing on the beach and looking at the ocean, and you see the water and the horizon and sky. It was a sea of people as far as you could see. We were like a little street gang there making music together and hoping that it went over. But when I look at the drum solo I took, it drives me crazy because of some choices that I made, in terms of stopping the groove and going really soft. But for the audience it worked. It was very tribal.

People continued to pack the bowl, while more and more artists and friends filtered in backstage. While we cleared the stage of Santana's equipment, Chip Monck spotted John Sebastian and grabbed him to play a few songs onstage. He had dropped some acid but went on anyway, talking to the audience like they were old friends.

"This is a mindfuck," he told them and started a kind of acid rap before doing "Rainbows All Over Your Blues," "Darlin' Be Home Soon," "Younger Generation." By the time he finished, the sun had come out. John has since said it was his worst performance ever, but I thought it was wonderful how he embraced that huge audience as family, reinforcing the idea of our gathering as a new community.

HENRY DILTZ, PHOTOGRAPHER: I got behind John Sebastian onstage and took a shot of this lone figure in this colorful jacket with this sea of humanity in front. John and his tie-dyed clothes, standing there and giving the peace sign. All little bumps of heads off into infinity. All the way over to your left, and all to your right. And the hillside totally covered with camps and tents.

JOHN SEBASTIAN: I've spent years living down the outfit I was wearing— it was tie-dyed Levi's jeans and jacket. My Woodstock "suit of lights," as someone called it.

ALAN DOUGLAS, PRODUCER AND MUSIC EXECUTIVE: My guys ran out of film on Thursday, so we loaded the car on Friday to supply them with more film and cameras. There were six of us with cameras and film in everybody's lap, and by the time we got there it was late. We finally got to a place where the cars were all parked on both sides of the road as far as you could see. The police stopped us and said, "I'm sorry, this is as far as you can go," and we explained that we had what the camera people needed, and they said, "Sorry, you have to stay here, you cannot go any farther than this," and made us park the car. I said, "Where is the site?" and they said, "It's just a couple of miles," and they pointed to a forest and a path.

We all got out carrying stuff, and we walked for eight hours to get there. We were imbibing refreshments the whole way. We missed Friday night completely and got there Saturday morning. Everybody was so wasted we just fell down when we got there.

Michael had made arrangements behind the stage for his friends and family, and everybody pitched tents. We were deeply involved in a Lenny Bruce project at that time, so a young lady named Doris Dynamite fixed our tent up and had a Lenny Bruce flag flying in front of it. I was lying in the tent most of the day, and finally in the afternoon I walked to the stage, and the crowd was amazing. Michael always says, "The crowd was the star." He was right. They were just so inspiring. I never heard the musicians play the way they did, and of course, all you could see was the whites of their eyes. The whole place was hallucinating, so it was always a little bit unreal.

ELLEN SANDER: By Saturday afternoon, there was a break in the weather. The Airplane were due to play late at night, to close the show, but they wanted to see the festival, as did all the performers at the Holiday Inn. Stories of the size of the crowd and amazing mess came in hourly. Finally, a caravan of at least a dozen cars assembled. Among those gathered was Bear—Augustus Stanley Owsley III, previously known as the acid king of San Francisco, a renowned soundman and keeper of the stash that could levitate the entire festival. And escorting the Airplane, their old ladies, and this mammoth stash were four state troopers who headed the caravan and brought up the rear, escorting a good dozen cars right into the festival area.

The stars and their guests unloaded and walked to a pavilion where fruit, wine, sandwiches, and punch were plentiful and flowing. Somebody immediately began putting acid into a huge vat of punch. A few moments later they were caught in the act and ten gallons of punch was poured out on the ground, but not before some of it had gone into the bloodstreams of people unsuspectingly drinking what had been poured into paper cups. Al Aronowitz, alerted as to the contents of his glass as he was drinking, spat and sprayed a mouthful out, cursing angrily.

We walked a monkey bridge from the performers' area to the stage, a suspended path of slats that went twenty feet up from the ground, over the wall separating the stars from the main mulch and affording them a star's-eye view of those *hundreds of thousands of people,* meadows full of them, stretched out over a field about a half mile away. And all of them were on their feet, dancing to Santana's Latin-based rock; they were like a great writhing mass of T-shirts and bottles of pop and smiles, with clouds and clouds of sweet pungent smoke rising from within their midst.

One thing I was careful about all weekend: to never drink from a cup or open bottle handed to me. I didn't want to get dosed. I was just too involved in the moment and had too many balls in the air to step outside that consciousness. Before the end of the weekend, Artie and Linda had been dosed, and even Mel and Joyce, both usually pretty straight, dropped acid.

Though Garcia, Owsley, and other members of the Grateful Dead had arrived early, Bob Weir and Dead manager Rock Scully showed up on Saturday after their limo got stuck on the highway and they had to walk in.

ROCK SCULLY, THEN MANAGER OF THE GRATEFUL DEAD: The couple of hundred tabs of sunshine acid that I'd stashed in a silver art nouveau case were leaking out down my leg under the relentless rain. My pores were saturated with the stuff. My mouth was smeared with this Day-Glo acid, my hand a giant raw orange claw, my pants bright saffron. There was a river of orange acid trailing behind me and strange, mutant strains of vegetation were beginning to sprout in my wake.

BOB WEIR OF THE GRATEFUL DEAD: Once I got there I camped out in a tent about a half mile from the stage. I sort of drifted around. It was muddy. There wasn't enough food or facilities. But everybody was pretty much into it, they were gonna make the most of it.

PAUL KANTNER OF JEFFERSON AIRPLANE: We always liked to go into water of untested depth, so we went to Woodstock with open minds. And it was fucked up, which was good. If it would have been completely organized, then it would have been *really* fucked up. But the sense of chaos and anarchy—two of my favorite words—prevailed and made it what it was. No fences, no security, none of that shit.

I got high on acid, walked around, hung out. People were setting up tents and campfires, cooking, swimming, and dancing. It was like a children's crusade, a great social experiment. It simply hadn't happened before. It was akin to white-water rafting in that you never know what's around the next bend and you're not even worried about it because you're too busy pushing yourself off the rocks.

After John Sebastian, we kept things moving, and readied the stage for the Keef Hartley Band. The group played a mix of jazz, blues, and rock. Drummer Keef Hartley had been a member of John Mayall's Bluesbreakers for several years, and his new band had expanded the blues sound to include horns. They covered an old Sleepy John Estes song, "Leaving Trunk," in an extended jam that segued into originals like "Sinnin' for You" and "Just to Cry."

Up next was the Incredible String Band, whose folk-psychedelic improvisations featured banjo, oud, mandolin, and keyboards. Lead singer Robin Williamson started the set by reciting a lengthy poem. From Scotland, the band was inspired by old English folk music and Indian ragas, like Ravi Shankar's modal music. You could hear this

MICHAEL LANG

blend in songs like "When You Find Out Who You Are." They were the forerunners of today's freak-folk movement.

Canned Heat kept the crowd pumped up, playing "Going Up the Country" and some boogie blues, including one they improvised on the spot and later called "Woodstock Boogie." I didn't get to see much of their set because of my confrontation with Wolff and McIntire over the money issues for the Who and the Dead.

I later found out that after they left my trailer, they cornered John Morris with the same threat. As John was the one who'd pushed the Who to agree to Woodstock, he felt obligated to get them paid. He knew that he had absolutely no shot with me, so—going off the reservation once again—he called over to Joel at the telephone building. He convinced him that the Who and the Dead wouldn't play without cash, spicing the demand with the image of a rioting mob enraged by the no-show.

Joel set out to solve what he didn't realize was a trumped-up dilemma. He called Charlie Prince, manager of the White Lake bank where we'd opened an account, and told him the situation. Shuttled by helicopter, Charlie let himself into the bank, locked up on a Saturday night, searched for some blank cashier's checks, and filled them out for us. That's how much some of the townspeople believed in us.

Mountain was on by the time I got back to the stage. They played a harder blues than Canned Heat, with Leslie West's growling vocals and blistering guitar. They were another new face and the crowd loved them, especially on standards like "Stormy Monday" and a Jack Bruce epic, "Theme from an Imaginary Western." Not to be outdone by Canned Heat, they came up with their own song at the festival, which they called "For Yasgur's Farm."

LESLIE WEST: I think I had the most amplifiers of anybody there. It was paralyzing because that stage, that setting, was some kind of natural amphitheater. The sound was so loud and shocking that I got scared. But once I started playing, I just kept going because I was afraid to stop.

More and more artists had appeared in the pavilion area. Mountain had brought a bunch of roast chickens with them, which they were sharing with Janis Joplin and her band. Janis was pouring champagne for everyone. John Sebastian was running in and out when not tending to the "dressing room"—the VW camper he'd been overseeing.

JOHN SEBASTIAN: At this point I was mainly engaged in keeping the tent dry. Because of the rains, Sly Stone was having trouble staying clean. He had much more spectacular stage gear than other folks. I was trying to loosen him up at one point and I walked over and his sister was grumping about something. I said, "Gee, is there anything I can do? Use the tent or something?" And Sly said, "Oh, she just needs a little red meat, and she'll be fine."

I wonder if Sister Rose ever found her way over to Bill Graham's trailer and all those steaks.

Next up: the Grateful Dead. By then, a combination of the weather and hallucinogenics proved their undoing. As they were loading their heavy equipment onto the forty-foot turntable onstage, the platform's wheels collapsed. This caused a delay, which was lengthened when the Dead insisted that their soundman Owsley Stanley rewire the stage for their set. Tinkering with the sound system and their hook-ups resulted in constant shocks from the guitars.

ROCK SCULLY: We're getting ready to put our equipment onstage. It's all on risers, but our gear is so heavy it breaks the wheels of the risers and we have to move everything in by hand, which takes forever. In the meantime, incessant nightmare announcements are coming over the PA. *"Please everyone, get off the tower, someone just fell!" "Don't take the brown acid, there's bad acid out there!"* They don't say what the thousands who have *already* taken it should do . . .

I make the mistake of thinking, What more can happen? And then suddenly, as if someone pulled a cord—darkness falls. The wind picks up and the stage starts vibrating, physically quaking. Our beautiful giant light-show screen has turned into a sail and is moving the stage through the sea of mud like the good ship *Marie Celeste*. It is starting to slide, it is, uh-oh, tipping over, and Dicken, my brother, has to climb up the mizzenmast and slash the screen with a bowie knife. Not a good omen, Captain . . .

In the middle of their very first number, "St. Stephen," this crazy guy we know runs out into the middle of the stage and starts flinging LSD off the stage. After all those announcements! Okay, his acid is purple, but it *looks* brown. Oh no, it's the brown acid—the acid you're . . . *not supposed to take.* When Garcia sees this mad, crazy guy throwing what looks like brown acid off the stage, something he might under normal circumstances have thought droll and antic now looks ominous. He is asking himself the question men zonked out of their minds on psychotropic substances should never ask themselves: *"Why me?"*

To make matters worse, the Dead are playing horribly. They just cannot get started, can't get it right. Not one song. And the sound is awful, and it is windy and blustery and cold. Finally the Dead set finishes up with "Lovelight," but even Pigpen's surefire rabble-rouser can't quite pull it off. *Thank God that's over!*

JERRY GARCIA: Jeez, we were awful! We were just plumb *atrocious*! I was high and I saw blue balls of electricity bouncing across the stage and leaping onto my guitar when I touched the strings. People behind the amplifiers kept yelling, "*The stage is collapsing! The stage is collapsing!*" As a human being, I had a wonderful time hanging out with friends and sharing great little jams. But our performance onstage was musically a total disaster that is best left forgotten.

BOB WEIR: It was raining toads when we played. The rain was part of our nightmare. The other part was our soundman, who decided that the ground situation on the stage was all wrong. It took him about two hours to change it, which held up the show. He finally got it set the way he wanted it, but every time I touched my instrument I got a shock. The stage was wet and the electricity was coming through me. I was *conducting*! Touching my guitar and the microphone was nearly fatal. There was a great big blue spark about the size of a baseball, and I got lifted off my feet and sent back eight or ten feet to my amplifier. Some people made their careers at Woodstock, but we spent about twenty years making up for it. It was probably the worst set we've ever performed.

TOM CONSTANTEN, GRATEFUL DEAD KEYBOARDIST: The audience was nice and vinegary by the time we got on. They looked like one of those Hieronymus Bosch paintings, with ten thousand grotesque bodies. The electricity during the performance didn't bother me, but because everyone else was so frazzled it made the tempo hard. It was not an especially long performance. I think we played for forty-five minutes. Everyone was glad to get off, we felt like an android jukebox.

With the Dead scrambling offstage around 10 P.M., we tried to quickly get ready for Creedence Clearwater Revival. I think the Dead's experience made Creedence nervous too, but they didn't show it. They were practically a hit machine by then, and they played with conviction and intensity: "Born on the Bayou," "Green River," "Bad Moon Rising," "Proud Mary," "I Put a Spell on You." On and on, with John Fogerty's bluesy voice, guitar leads, and masterful harmonica playing, and a great finale of "Suzie Q."

STU COOK, CREEDENCE CLEARWATER REVIVAL BASSIST: You couldn't see anything. We had some technical problems. After the first song, we weren't sure there was anybody there. It was quiet. But some guy, way the hell out there, yelled, "We're with you!" Okay, I guess that's who the concert's for. And on and on we played, and we had no idea what we were involved in. Later, it started to dawn on us just what had happened, and we thought we'd never ever see anything like that again.

JOCKO MARCELLINO, SHA NA NA DRUMMER: I had taken some mind-altering stuff and it wasn't FDA-approved, I'll tell ya. I thought, "I've got to be alone," and there were 500,000 people! So I wandered up to the top of the hill to try to get it together. Creedence was rockin' "Born on the Bayou." And hearing that put me back in the groove.

JOHN SEBASTIAN: Creedence Clearwater delivered a set that was every bit as important and delicious as any other performer at Woodstock. I think they may not have had any other serious competition besides Sly Stone and Jimi Hendrix. It was so tight and so wonderfully strong, particularly in my psychedelicized state. But Fogerty came off that stage and said, "*Well, you guys really screwed that one up.*"

Janis Joplin and her new band, a kind of Stax/Volt Revue with horns, were next. I was a little disappointed in their performance. Of course Janis's voice was as amazing as ever, but she kept turning around to give direction to the musicians, who'd played with her only a couple of times. At one point, she let Snooky Flowers, a funky R & B vocalist, take the lead on Otis Redding's "I Can't Turn You Loose"—and kicking off her shoes, she seemed happy dancing and strutting around barefoot. Her devastating testifying on "Try (Just a Little Bit Harder)" and "Work Me Lord" crushed the audience, and they begged her not to stop. At the end of her long set, after a gut-wrenching "Piece of My Heart" and "Ball and Chain," I almost expected everyone to just collapse in a heap.

ELLEN SANDER: Janis Joplin danced with them as if they were one, they shouted back at her, they wouldn't let her off until they'd drained off every drop of her energy.

Everyone was primed for Sly and the Family Stone—who were ready to put on a SHOW. They were decked out in fantastic outfits—Sly in white fringe, Sister Rose in her platinum wig and fringed go-go dress, and bassist Larry Graham in a feathered hat with matching suit. Their performance was beyond phenomenal—"M'Lady," "Sing a Simple Song," "You Can Make It If You Try," "Everyday People." During the spectacular finale, "Dance to the Music"/"Music Lover"/"I Want to Take You Higher," Sly took us all to a psychedelic church as he and five hundred thousand people did a feverish call-and-response like a preacher and his congregation in a revival down South.

CARLOS SANTANA: I got to witness the peak of the festival, which was Sly Stone. I don't think he ever played that good again—steam was literally coming out of his Afro.

ELLEN SANDER: Grace Slick and Janis Joplin were dancing together, their eyes tight shut and their fists clenched and their bodies whipping around. *"Higher!"* Sly shouted into the crowd. *"Higher!"* they boomed back with the force of half a million voices at their loudest. He threw up his arms in a peace sign, a billow of fringe unfurled around them, and the audience responded, shouting "Higher" in unison and raising their arms and fingers into the air, joyously, desperately, arms and hands and fingers raised in peace signs, heads and voices crying out into the night, crying the anguished plea of the sixties, *"Higher, higher!"*

It took a while to come down after Sly's performance, but leave it to Abbie Hoffman to turn the mood around. He grabbed me backstage, saying in a panicked voice, "I just saw someone running around with a gun, you've got to help me find him!"

I didn't realize it at the time, but Abbie, after a twenty-four-hour shift in the medical tents, had decided to take the edge off. He'd popped a hit, or two or three, of acid. Not seeing anyone from security around, he and I went to find the gunman.

"I think he went under the stage!" Abbie said with total conviction, so we started looking everywhere under the massive structure where assistants were changing film magazines. After a few minutes of futile searching, Abbie stopped. He turned to me with this perplexed look and said, "You really aren't afraid to die, are you?"

I wasn't sure what to make of this, but I started to question the wisdom of this quest. When the "nut with a gun" turned into the "nut with a knife," I realized the only *nut* I was likely to run into down there was Abbie.

It was three thirty in the morning and the Who were about to go on, so I said, "Look, Abbie, whoever you saw is gone, so let's just go watch some music and chill out for a few minutes."

He agreed and we headed back up to the stage to sit with musicians from various groups who'd gathered to watch. Abbie kept fidgeting next to me. He couldn't stop talking. "I've really gotta say something about John Sinclair! He's rotting in prison for smoking a joint!" Sinclair, the manager of the radical Detroit rock band the MC5 and the founder of the White Panther Party, was set up by the cops and sentenced to ten years in prison for the possession of two joints.

"Okay, Abbie," I tried to reason with him, "there will be a chance later on, between sets or something."

But he persisted. "No, I really gotta say something! *Now!*"

"Abbie, the Who is on," I reminded him—they were about halfway through performing *Tommy* in its entirety, so I don't know how he failed to notice. "You can't make a speech in the middle of their set— let them finish! *Chill out!*"

Just after "Pinball Wizard," Abbie leaped up before I could grab him and rushed to Townshend's mic, while Pete had his back turned and was adjusting his amp. Abbie started earnestly beseeching the audience to think about John Sinclair, who needed our help. He was in his element, berating everyone for having a good time. *"Hey, all you people out there having fun while John Sinclair is being held a political prisoner . . ."* WHAM! Townshend, turning back to the audience and seeing Abbie at his mic, whacked him in the head with his guitar.

Abbie stumbled, then jumped to the photographer's pit, dashed over the fence, and vanished into the crowd below. A pretty dramatic exit. That was the last I saw of him that weekend.

HENRY DILTZ: I was right in front of the Who, on the lip of the stage. There was Roger Daltrey, with his fringes flying. Abbie Hoffman ran onto the stage and Pete Townshend took his guitar and held it straight out, perfectly, with the neck toward the guy, just like a bayonet, and went *klunk*. I thought he killed him.

Early in the set, Townshend had already kicked Michael Wadleigh in the chest while the director crouched in front of him with his camera.

Now Townshend was over the top with fury. *"The next fucking person who walks across this stage is going to get fucking killed!"* he yelled as he retuned his Gibson SG. The audience at first thought he was joking and started laughing and clapping. "You can laugh," he said coldly, *"but I mean it!"*

PETE TOWNSHEND: My response was reflexive rather than considered. What Abbie was saying was politically correct in many ways. The people at Woodstock really were a bunch of hypocrites claiming a cosmic revolution simply because they took over a field, broke down some fences, imbibed bad acid, and then tried to run out without paying the bands. All while John Sinclair rotted in jail after a trumped-up drug bust.

The Who continued with their exhilarating performance of *Tommy,* and just as the sun rose, they played raucous rock and roll classics from their days as mods: "Summertime Blues," "Shakin' All Over," and "My Generation." They were astonishing. Later, I couldn't believe the band thought they were subpar and that the audience didn't get into *Tommy.*

PETE TOWNSHEND: *Tommy* wasn't getting to anyone. By [the end of the set], I was about awake, we were just listening to the music when all of a sudden, *bang!* The fucking sun comes up! It was just incredible. I really felt we didn't deserve it, in a way. We put out such bad vibes—and as we finished it was daytime. We walked off, got in the car, and went back to the hotel. It was fucking fantastic.

BILL GRAHAM: The Who were brilliant. Townshend is like a locomotive when he gets going. He's like a naked black stallion. When he starts, look out.

ROGER DALTREY: We did a two-and-a-half-hour set . . . It made our career. We were a huge cult band, but Woodstock cemented us to the historical map of rock and roll.

The Jefferson Airplane did their best to follow the Who, but anything after that would have been anticlimactic. The sun was shining, though, and the Airplane, who'd been partying for twenty-four hours, made the most of it. Joining them on keyboards was Nicky Hopkins, who'd played with the Stones and had been slated to play Woodstock with the Jeff Beck Group. "You've heard the heavy groups," Grace Slick said from the stage, "now welcome to Morning Maniac Music." Grace's beauty took my breath away. She, Marty Balin, Jorma Kaukonen, and Paul Kantner alternated lead vocals. "Somebody to Love," "Volunteers," "White Rabbit"—they did their big hits and also longer, psychedelic jams.

GRACE SLICK: We'd been up all night and I sang the goddamned songs with my eyes closed, sort of half asleep and half singing. We probably could have played better if we'd been more awake, but part of the charm of rock and roll is that sometimes you're ragged.

They were exhausted, as were we all. Our newly created city was cast off into some crazy dreams by their trippy morning lullaby.

The perfect way to begin to day three.

twelve **AUGUST 17, 1969**

It's four thirty on Sunday, and the first act of the day—Joe Cocker and the Grease Band—have just finished their set. There's a storm coming and it's going to be a lollapalooza. I haven't seen the wind kick up like this since a tropical storm blew through Coconut Grove in 1966. The stage crew is racing around to cover all the equipment with the last of the plastic and tarps before the rains come. After three days of this, we've run through miles of plastic sheeting. Booming thunder and jagged streaks of lightning seem to be Nature's way of saying it can produce fireworks far beyond the sonics blasting from our stage.

Some of the stagehands point to previously buried cables, becoming noticeably more visible as the earth has turned to mud over the past day. These cables carry electrical wire from under the stage to the towers. One of the stage electricians is convinced the cables' outer shell is wearing away, exposing hot wire. Chip says he'll check them out but that these "horse dong" cables are impenetrable, that stomping feet can't break through the shell. They are mining cables and have a solid copper casing under the outer rubber. But while we are powwowing, someone panics and calls over to the telephone building and gets Wes's security ally John Fabbri all freaked out. He says we should shut down, and he and Joel argue over which would be worse: a violent riot or mass electrocution. I ask someone to call back and tell them we'll make sure neither happens. The cables are safe, but the stage power can't be used during the thunderstorm—we'll have to shut down for a while anyway.

I'm used to the rain. More troubling are the sixty-foot towers. On top of those towers are the massive Super Trouper lights weighing hundreds of pounds apiece. If one shakes loose, it could be disastrous. The forty-mile-an-hour winds are making the towers sway, which is a frightening sight, especially since kids are perched on the scaffolding—thousands more packed around the towers' bases. Chip sends some of the riggers to the top of the towers to lay the lights on their sides and tie them down. The towers are engineered to withstand high winds, but this storm is pushing their limits, especially with the kids' added weight. We've got to get people off them and away without causing panic. The wind is fierce—gusts are blowing rain like wet bullets, drenching everything.

John Morris reacts quickly: He grabs the mic to let the audience know what we're going to do and what they should do. "Please, get down from those towers! Move back away from the towers! Clear away before someone gets hurt! Keep your eyes on those towers." He stands alone onstage as the crew, musicians, and bystanders seek cover. Though the mic is hot, he has to get the message out before power is cut.

After two days of onstage announcing and not much sleep, John's voice is shot. I watch him give his all to help keep people safe. He's holding what could be a lightning rod in his hand, but he doesn't flinch. "Wrap yourself up, gang—looks like we've got to ride this out!" John tells the crowd we have to shut down until the storm passes, but we are here with them and *they are with each other and together we will get through this. It is a heroic moment for John.*

The morning had started under sunny skies. People woke to the sound of Hugh Romney's hoarse voice: *"What we have in mind is breakfast in bed for four hundred thousand! Now it's gonna be good food and we're going to get it to you. We're all feedin' each other."*

Stan and Hugh had worked out a plan to distribute thousands of cups of granola to the stage area. Some people who didn't want to lose their spots had not been eating.

STAN GOLDSTEIN: There were people sitting right in front of the stage dead center who wouldn't give up their piece of ground to get a sandwich, to have a vegetable, to go to the toilet. They were there and they weren't moving. Now, if a reporter walked up to them and said, "How are you doing?" "Oh, man, I'm doing all right." "How long have you been here?" "Oh, I've been here for two days, I guess." "Have you gone off and gotten some food?" "Oh no, man, I'm really, really hungry." "You haven't eaten anything in two days?" "No, man, I haven't eaten anything, I'm really hungry." And then the reporter goes away and reports that these kids are starving in front of the stage. The fact is, you couldn't have moved that kid ten feet to get some food.

The Hog Farmers loaded an open-bed truck with garbage cans lined with plastic and filled with granola. Once ready, they guided the truck through the crowd. *"Excuse me, please, truck coming through— please, would you move to the side of the road, we're bringing a truck through with food?"*

STAN GOLDSTEIN: I talked to the concessionaires who were out of food and got them to help us load all their unused paper goods to take to the free kitchen. I got another 150,000 or so potential servings' worth of paper goods as a donation from the concessionaires.

There were two fewer Food for Love stands on Sunday than there had been the day before. Angry kids and members of the Motherfuckers, fed up by the prices and the wait, burned them down Saturday night. The Hog Farmers tried to defuse the situation and at least controlled the blaze to just the two. Hugh even enlisted help from the kids when he spoke Sunday morning: "There's a guy up there—some hamburger guy—that had his stand burned down last night. But he's still got a little stuff left, and for you people that still believe capitalism isn't that weird, you might help him out and buy a couple hamburgers."

By Sunday, Woodstock now seemed like a way of life. I was almost used to it—expecting to see the things I was seeing; even the faces in the crowd became familiar. Kind of like seeing people in the neighborhood where you grew up. I guess your mind adapts to anything after a while.

Everybody had settled in, and we'd figured out how to cope with the most pressing problems, and crises like food shortages and sanitation were nearly in hand. We'd gotten into a routine of sending people out to fix the pipes to keep the water flowing—and figured out how to get trucks in and out when necessary.

To start the day's activities, someone onstage played an out-of-tune "Reveille" on the bugle. The highlight of the morning was the appearance of Max Yasgur. I'd been over to his house a few times through the weekend and Max was having a tough time, enduring several angina attacks. When Mel and I saw him approaching us backstage, we thought, "Uh-oh, problem." But as soon as we saw the broad smile flash across his gaunt face, we knew all was well.

MIRIAM YASGUR: He went over to see what was happening. He wanted to express his thanks and let them know he appreciated the way they were acting. Max came back and said, "You really can't believe what it looks like from up there!"

I asked Max to come onstage and say a few words to the audience, that they'd love to meet the man who gave them and us his land for this wonderful weekend. He seemed a bit shy about it at first, but it didn't take long to talk him into it. Chip escorted him up to the microphone and Max began: "I'm a farmer . . . ," and the people cheered. "I don't know how to speak to twenty people at one time, let alone a crowd like this." Max went on clearly and slowly, peering through his glasses at the multitudes stretching as far as the eye could see. "This is the largest group of people ever assembled in one place, but I think you people have proven something to the world: that a half a million kids can get together and have three days of fun and music—and have nothing *but* fun and music! And I God bless you for it!"

It was incredibly moving to see Max up there, overcome with emotion. Watching him address this historic gathering, I was again humbled by the miraculous course of events that had brought us to this moment.

Max was with us all the way. When he found out that a few people were selling tap water to festivalgoers, he hung a huge sign on his barn that said FREE WATER. He gave away water, milk, cheese, and butter—and asked a relative to donate bread to go with it. His daughter, a nurse, volunteered in the medical tent, and his son, Sam, helped direct traffic. "If the generation gap is to be closed," he told a reporter, "the older people have to do more than we've done."

It was time to start the music, and around 2 P.M., Joe Cocker went on. Another unknown was about to become a star. Backed by the Grease Band, he stunned the audience with his soulful vocals—and his unique stage moves. I guess you could say Joe kind of invented air guitar that day—or at least popularized it. The Grease Band had a loose approach and opened their set with a blues jam without Joe before launching into their repertoire when Cocker hit the stage. Joe took all kinds of covers and made them his own: "Dear Landlord," "Feelin' Alright," "Just Like a Woman," "I Don't Need No Doctor," "I Shall Be Released." He turned Ashford and Simpson's "Let's Go Get Stoned" into an anthem, ad-libbing a bit about his stay in New York. For the finale, he did what became his signature, "With a Little Help from My Friends." That song perfectly described the weekend and everybody knew it. His howling, expressive take transformed the Beatles hit into a Joe Cocker song. Just as they were finishing, the sky darkened. Then all hell began to break loose.

JOE COCKER: I was the only guy in the band that didn't drop acid that day and I regretted [it] to some degree . . . I didn't feel that for this mass of people I was getting through until we did "Let's Go Get Stoned," which got all of them up because most of them *were*. When we got into "With a Little Help from My Friends," I felt as we got toward the end of that tune that we'd caught the massive consciousness. I suddenly felt I'd got them to accept what we were doing. It was a powerful feeling for me. And then it was shattered when somebody yelled to me, "Joe, look over your shoulder!" I looked and saw massive clouds coming in. I just thought, Oh dear, had we done this?

Twenty minutes after we cut power, the worst of the storm passed. But rain continued to fall and we had to keep the concert shut down. I'd planned a surprise for the audience, and as Artie and I stood onstage watching a plane fly overhead, thousands of flowers cascaded from the sky.

BILL WARD: It was still cloudy and dark but it had stopped raining, and a little airplane flew over and flowers came floating down. Thousands of people stood there and looked up at the sky. They were just standing there with their mouths open. They were all wet, the place was full of mud, and they were entertaining themselves by sliding in the mud. There was a hilly pasture there, and some people had clothes on and some didn't, and they'd get a running start and flop down on their butts and slide along in the mud.

GREIL MARCUS: The kids yelled, "Fuck the rain, fuck the rain," but it was really just another chance for a new kind of fun. Odd gifts of the elements, our own latter-day saints appeared out of nowhere. In front of the bandstand a black boy and a white boy took off their clothes and danced in the mud and the rain, round and round, in a circle that grew larger as more joined them.

Moonfire, a kindly warlock, preached to a small crowd that gathered under the stage for shelter. A tall man with red-brown hair and shining eyes, barefoot and naked under his robes, he had traveled to the festival with his lover, a sheep . . . Off in the corner was his staff, topped by a human skull, the pole bearing his message: DON'T EAT ANIMALS/LOVE THEM . . . Albert Grossman, his pigtail soaking wet, was standing nearby and Moonfire ambled over to lay on his blessing. Grossman dug it. Rain simply meant it was a good time to meet new people.

Ten Years After had arrived in the wee hours that morning and were due to go on after Joe Cocker, who they knew from back home in England. The stage was still wet and I was prepared to put the show on hold until it was safe to repower. But Country Joe and the Fish insisted they could play without electricity. The storm had really put us behind schedule, and there was so much water onstage that we needed more time to clear it. The stagehands tried to discourage the band, saying it was still too dangerous to turn on the power and set up the microphones and amps. But Joe McDonald and Barry Melton wouldn't take no for an answer. They didn't need power, they said, they'd play acoustically, with no mics, no amps, no electricity. They had a ukulele, percussion instruments, and some drums.

JOYCE MITCHELL: Country Joe came in, and he said, "I've had enough of this. Those kids are out in the rain, they're out in the mud. We're playing music for them." And that's what they did. To me, he was a big hero. I can't tell you how impressed I was with the way he did that.

COUNTRY JOE McDONALD: When the electricity went out, the kids were bored. Having played a lot of demonstrations, we knew that people would respond to some kind of nonamplified noisemaking. We wound up banging pots and pans and did a little agitprop drumming. We chanted "No rain" and played cowbells, and the audience picked it up. Then we got the idea to pass out drinks to the audience. And everything was going really well until Barry Melton, who was the lead guitar player of the Fish, brought two cases of beer in aluminum cans and started throwing them into the audience and hitting people in the head. Then they started throwing things back at us.

GREIL MARCUS: The Fish kept on playing and Joe kept on smiling. They reminded me of the brave rodeo clowns that run into the pit when a rider's hurt and the bull's ready to trample him.

COUNTRY JOE McDONALD: I felt completely at home, it was really an amazing free space. In 1969 the counterculture was not a secure place to be. A lot of people didn't like you and would just come up and hit you or arrest you for being a rocker or a hippie. So it was very refreshing to be in a totally free environment where you weren't going to be trashed for being part of the counterculture. And it became very obvious to me from the word go that this was our turf.

Along with cans of beer, Barry and the band tossed out oranges and bottles of champagne. Finally, at six thirty, the sun actually came back out and we restored power. Some people had left, but those who stayed seemed almost reinvigorated by the storm. Plugged in, the Fish launched into their regular set, reprising their upbeat "Rock and Soul Music." By the time they finished, it was dusk. Ten Years After was already onstage, waiting for its equipment to be set up. Their guitarist and singer Alvin Lee was revved up and ready to go.

LEO LYONS OF TEN YEARS AFTER: We had come from a gig in St. Louis, Missouri, at 6 A.M. I'd had nothing to eat. I went down to the gig and Pete Townshend came over and said, "Don't eat or drink anything that's not in a sealed can because everything is spiked. I ended up on a trip last night, and it's really, really dodgy stuff."

We were supposed to go on just after the rain stopped and then Country Joe and the Fish rushed past us and jumped onstage before us. Because we waited so long, we wanted to get on, play, and get the hell out of there. We had tuning problems—we had to stop after the first song and retune, but the audience was great.

Around 8 P.M., Alvin Lee opened with the bluesy "Spoonful," followed by a lengthy "Good Morning, Little Schoolgirl." The band ended their two-hour set with a long improvisation, "I'm Goin' Home," which referenced several early rock and roll songs and showcased Alvin's guitar playing. He left the stage lugging a watermelon someone had passed along to him.

Iron Butterfly was booked for Sunday afternoon, but John Morris told me that their agent had called with a last-minute demand for a helicopter to pick them up in New York City. Apparently the agent had a real attitude, and we were up to our eyeballs in problems. So I told John to tell him to forget it, we had more important things to deal with.

LEE DORMAN OF IRON BUTTERFLY: Two or three times we checked out of our hotel and went to the heliport on Thirty-third Street. But the helicopter never came. I guess it had more important things to do, like feed people. It would have been great to play "In-A-Gadda-Da-Vida" up there.

Next up was the Band. I was really looking forward to their set. I'd become friends with Rick Danko and Richard Manuel. Though Rick had been hanging out for a while, the others arrived right before the thunderstorm. They seemed a bit overwhelmed, and I think they were nervous about the sound not being perfect. They were very fastidious about their production, and this was going to be pretty loose by their standards. But the festival was down the road from their homes, so this was an easy gig for them.

ROBBIE ROBERTSON: There was an area where all kinds of people—the artists, managers, record people, whoever—were mingling. Fellini faces were whipping by—it was like a gypsy caravan, a very colorful sight.

A crowd of musicians gathered onstage and watched intently as they opened with a lively "Chest Fever." Levon, Rick, and Richard alternated lead vocals as they played tracks from their album *Music from Big Pink*: "Tears of Rage," "This Wheel's on Fire," "The Weight." Some of the songs they played wouldn't come out on vinyl for a few years. I thought they sounded fantastic, but because they were musically subtle and seemed to be playing more for themselves, they didn't connect so well with the kids in the bowl.

ROBBIE ROBERTSON: After three days of people being hammered by music and weather, it was hard to get a take on the mood. We played a slow, haunting set of mountain music. It seemed kind of appropriate from our point of view. We were thinking, "Those poor suckers have been putting up with a lot of stuff, so maybe we should send out a little spiritual feeling to them." We did songs like "Long Black Veil" and "The Weight," and everything had a bit of reverence to it. Even the faster songs sounded almost religious. I thought, "God, I don't know if this is the right place for this." I looked out there and it seemed as if the kids were looking at us kinda funny. We were playing the same way we played in our living room. We were like orphans in the storm there.

When the Band finished, we made another complicated set change to get Johnny Winter on. At times like this, we really missed the use of the stage turntable. It was way past midnight and the weather had turned cool. For about an hour, Winter heated things up, playing spectacular slide on a mix of Texas blues, R & B, and early rock and roll, including Chuck Berry's "Johnny B. Goode" to end his set.

There was another big equipment shift to set up for the next act, Blood, Sweat and Tears, an eight-piece jazz-rock band with a horn section. Driven by drummer Bobby Colomby, they'd recently had back-to-back hits: "You've Made Me So Very Happy" and "Spinning Wheel." A highlight of their set, "And When I Die," would be their next one.

GREIL MARCUS: The scene onstage Sunday night was a curious one. The groups were hanging out there, performing, setting up, digging the other musicians; the Band; Blood, Sweat and Tears; and Paul Butterfield. Now, no doubt that in terms of prestige, the Band was king that night, to the other musicians if not to the audience. As Helm, Danko, and Robertson sat on amplifiers listening to Johnny Winter, stars of the past and present came over to say hello, to introduce themselves, to pay their artistic respects. David Clayton-Thomas, the young Canadian lead singer for Blood, Sweat and Tears, flashed a big grin and shook hands vigorously—a man on the way up, his group outselling everyone in the country, and impressing the audience far more than the Band did that night but still very much in the shadow of the men from Big Pink who play real music that comes out of real history.

Musicians, journalists, and plenty of others gathered onstage, eagerly anticipating the next group: Crosby, Stills, Nash and Young. Neil Young had just joined the band, and they'd played only one concert, the night before in Chicago. We all wanted to hear their debut album performed live.

GRAHAM NASH: When we got out of the helicopter, we were greeted by John Sebastian. We lit one up and had a party in Sebastian's tent—there was mud halfway up his legs. He told us graphic stories about the rain and mud. Backstage was totally chaotic.

We weren't afraid of the crowd—we were more concerned with our peers. I think Stephen and I were a little nervous that Hendrix, and the Band, and Blood, Sweat and Tears were there. And I think Neil was nervous about playing with us.

DAVID CROSBY: We were scared. Everyone we respected in the whole goddamn music business was standing in a circle behind us when we went on. Everybody was curious about us. We were the new kid on the block, it was our second public gig, nobody had ever seen us, everybody had heard the record, everybody wondered, "What in the hell are they about?" So when it was rumored that we were about to go on, everybody came, standing in an arc behind us. That was intimidating, to say the least. I'm looking back at Hendrix and Robbie Robertson and Levon Helm and Grace and Paul, everybody that I knew and everybody I didn't know.

I was also toasted because we had some of that pullover pot, that incredible Colombian gold that a friend of mine named Rocky had brought to the festival.

Around 3:30 A.M., Graham, Stephen, and David stepped onstage and started the set alone. Then Neil, bassist Greg Reeves, and drummer Dallas Taylor joined them. Stills and Young played a breathtaking acoustic version of "Mr. Soul" from their days with Buffalo Springfield. The crowd and everyone backstage were entranced. "Long Time Gone," another high point, would become the opening track of the film *Woodstock*.

GREIL MARCUS: Their performance was scary, brilliant proof of the magnificence of music, and I don't believe it could have happened with such power anywhere else. This was a festival that had triumphed over itself, as Crosby and his band led the way toward the end of it.

GRAHAM NASH: I thought we did a lousy set. When you consider playing acoustic guitars to four hundred thousand people and trying to reach to the back of the crowd with songs like "Guinnevere," it was absurd. But we certainly gave it our best shot. Sure, the "Suite" was a little out of tune, but so what?

DAVID CROSBY: We were good, thank God. It went down very well. The people who were my close friends—Paul Kantner and Grace

Slick, Garcia, and a lot of people—they were all thrilled. They said, "Wow! You tore it up! It worked!" They loved it, everybody loved it. How could you not love it? "Suite: Judy Blue Eyes"—what's not to like?

Another friend I'd gotten to know in Woodstock, Paul Butterfield, was on next—it must have been 6 A.M. by the time we got his large ensemble set up. Paul was a great harmonica player and vocalist from Chicago, and could vamp on blues for hours: "Born Under a Bad Sign," "Driftin' and Driftin'," "All in a Day." His hot horn section included saxophonist David Sanborn, and he had Buzzy Feiten on guitar. I recognized several of his band members from town.

By now the crews were fried. But everybody held on and kept going. Out in the bowl, people continued to drift away. That was a big relief, really, because the thought of a half million people trying to leave at once was horrifying. Instead of a finish, everybody was just letting it go. I had a feeling the festival wouldn't end so much as wind down—like a big sigh.

The band of twelve Columbia students, Sha Na Na, had anxiously been awaiting their turn since Sunday afternoon. They worried they'd never get to do the thirty-minute slot I'd given them. Around 7:30 A.M., they came out in their gold lamé suits and DA haircuts. They breezed through a number of early rock and roll standards like "Get a Job," "Teen Angel," and "Duke of Earl." Their enthusiasm and energy seemed to revive the sleep-deprived. Michael Wadleigh and his crew were preparing to film Hendrix, and quickly managed to capture "At the Hop" and a couple of other numbers.

JOCKO MARCELLINO OF SHA NA NA: In the performers' pavilion, we talked to all these people. We were the little kids. But they gave us a certain respect. We almost didn't play. We just snuck in. We were getting pissed. I love Paul Butterfield, but he went on forever. I didn't like him that day. Finally, we got to play right before Hendrix. By then it was a refugee camp, most of the people were gone. I met a guy, years later, who had been tripping the night before. Fell asleep and woke up when we were playing and had no idea what we were, thought he had gone on a terrific trip.

Jimi Hendrix had arrived Sunday around noon, and I'd met him and Michael Jeffrey backstage. I suggested that Jimi could go on at midnight because we'd been running late all weekend. But Jeffrey said no, he wanted Jimi to close, no matter what time. Jimi's new band had been together for only a short time. They'd been staying at Jimi's house in West Shokan and working up material to play at Woodstock.

We had rented a cottage near the backstage area, where I took them to pass the time. Occasionally Jimi would drop by the stage or performers' pavilion. At one point during the evening, it became clear that the show would not be over until early morning. I checked to see if Jimi would change his mind about the midnight slot. But Jeffrey was still set on closing.

Finally, at 8:30 A.M. on Monday, Hendrix and his band headed to the stage. The fact that only forty thousand people remained didn't seem to bother him. His set that morning would turn out to be the longest of his career—two hours. He started by introducing his new group: Billy Cox on bass, Juma Sultan and Gerry Velez on percussion, Larry Lee on rhythm guitar, and Mitch Mitchell on drums. "We got tired of the Experience and every once in a while we were blowing our minds too much, so we decided to change the whole thing around and call it Gypsy, Sun, and Rainbows . . . We only had about two rehearsals, so . . . nothing but primary-rhythm things, but, I mean, it's a first ray of the new rising sun, anyway, so we might as well start from the earth, which is rhythm, right?"

After tuning up his white Strat, he launched into "Message to Love," followed by "Hear My Train a Comin'." The band seemed suited for improvisation, and songs turned into long jams. Jimi had a serenity about him that morning, even on "Foxey Lady." Larry Lee took lead vocals on a couple of songs, including Curtis Mayfield's "Gypsy Woman." Both Lee and Jimi kept retuning their guitars, and at one point Jimi said, "We'll just play very quietly and out of tune."

The massive stage was sparsely populated compared to how packed it had been all weekend with musicians, crew, and friends. Jimi, a red scarf around his head and wearing a white fringed and beaded leather shirt, looked almost like a mystical holy man in meditation. His eyes closed, his head back, he'd merged with his music, his Strat—played upside down since he's a lefty—his magic wand. Though he was surrounded by his band, he projected the feeling he was all alone.

As he almost reverently started the national anthem, the bedraggled audience, worn out and muddy, moved closer together. Those of us who'd barely slept in three days were awakened, exhilarated by Jimi's song. One minute he was chording the well-worn melody, the next he was reenacting "bombs bursting in air" with feedback and distortion. It was brilliant. A message of joy and love of country, while at the same time an understanding of all the conflict and turmoil that's torn America apart.

ROZ PAYNE: I was working in the bad-trip tent when he started to play it. Everything seemed to stop. Before that, if someone would have played "The Star-Spangled Banner," we would have booed. After that, it became *our* song.

TOM LAW OF THE HOG FARM: I was standing right in front of him. Nobody was in the audience hardly. I felt like he was the defining poet of the festival with that piece of music. It was like taking you right into the heart of the beast and nailing it.

GRAHAM NASH: Hendrix was okay. I had heard him better. But "The Star-Spangled Banner" was unreal. As creative a two minutes as you can probably find in rock and roll.

MEL LAWRENCE: I woke up to Jimi Hendrix. I was in my trailer on the hill, and I looked down on this depressing scene of the quarter-filled bowl full of trash and people walking out on Jimi Hendrix. Then I heard "The Star-Spangled Banner" and it gave me chills.

Jimi segued from "The Star-Spangled Banner" into "Purple Haze." I thought about Miami in May '68 when Hendrix descended from a helicopter and played that song on the Gulfstream stage. It seemed that day had presaged this one.

On Monday morning, Jimi ended his set with an instrumental piece later named "Woodstock Improvisation," followed by the haunting "Villanova Junction," and finally, around 10:30 A.M., "Hey Joe."

It was over.

What had seemed an eternity now felt like the blink of an eye. Nothing would ever be the same again.

thirteen THE AFTERMATH

‒ ‒

Monday, August 18, 1 P.M.: I'm looking down on the grounds where I've been entrenched for the past three weeks. It's a very different view from what's been described to me by those who flew over during the height of the festival—when, for miles, all the eye could see was a blanket of people. A guy in Sweetwater said it looked like fields and fields of wildflowers. Now it's fields and fields of mud.

I have to get to the bank on Wall Street to meet Joel, John, and Artie, and one of the helicopter pilots has offered me a lift.

As we turn east, I spot something there, in the bowl near the front of the stage: an immense peace sign. It's made up of garbage—shoes, blankets, cans, bottles, papers, T-shirts, sleeping bags, and watermelon rinds. The kids who have stayed to help with the cleanup have created this symbol of what we all hope will be our legacy.

I keep this image with me as I head to Manhattan and the Bank of North America. Leaving the world of Woodstock for the world of Wall Street, I wonder what I'm literally flying into. John, Joel, Artie, and I will be together for the first time since Thursday. I know we have some un-pleasant financial business to deal with—I'm just not sure how unpleas-ant. Other than the time on Saturday when the Brink's truck driver arrived at my trailer and I sent him home empty-handed, this is the first time I've focused on finances since the festival began. Hopefully, any problems can be resolved. But I don't know how many checks John has written over the weekend or how much money has yet to be collected from advance-ticket outlets.

After Jimi Hendrix ended his two-hour set Monday morning, the festival was officially over. Because people had been gradually de-parting since Sunday, traffic moved smoothly, directed by three hun-dred state police, sheriff's deputies, and volunteer firemen. People hitching rides held signs with their destination, and Short Line buses ran nonstop from Monticello to New York City. One newspaper de-scribed some pretty outrageous departures: "Eleven young people rode fenders, bumpers, hoods, and the roof of a '57 Chevrolet that scraped the road surface at each bump. A reporter saw three youths tied to the luggage rack on the roof of a Ford station wagon bearing New Jersey license plates . . ."

Another paper reported that White Lake residents continued to assist festivalgoers, "obviously touched by the plight of the foodless, moneyless, housingless youngsters. Some opened their homes to them for the night and others gave away free food and water. Monticello Police opened up the small town park to provide a sleeping place for those waiting for Short Line buses."

PARRY TEASDALE: I knew a couple who lived nearby, whose son—a friend of mine—had been killed in Vietnam. When they heard about all these kids with nothing to eat, they said, "There are kids who are hungry, and we're going to feed them." They packed up every hot dog they could get and went to the festival and fed young people.

CHRISTINE OLIVEIRA: We got out of there Monday afternoon. We'd stop because we didn't know exactly which back roads to take home and we didn't have a map, and people would say, "Do you have enough to eat?" They'd come out with sandwiches.

I spent Monday morning wrapping up as much business as I could before leaving for the meeting at the bank. Mel and Stan were going to oversee the cleanup. We estimated it would take about $50,000 and a minimum of two weeks to restore the land for Max and the other farmers whose fields we'd rented. About eight thousand people were still camped in the surrounding areas, including the Hog Farm and other commune members. Many began helping to remove trash from the grounds. Mel started looking for volunteer assistance, to aid the cleanup crews we'd hired. He began with the Boy Scouts.

MEL LAWRENCE: The cleanup was really interesting. People as far as twenty miles away were calling and saying we needed to clean their barn—they were looking at this situation as an opportunity to get their property cleaned up. We had a front loader push everything into a big pile and load it onto a truck; there were thousands of sleeping bags and articles of clothing left behind.

PENNY STALLINGS: We had so much to do to clean up. Mel referred to the site after everyone left as looking like Andersonville, a Civil War prison camp. The ground was smoking from all the humanity that had been there.

HENRY DILTZ: What was left was muddied junk. Bags of food, clothes, all soaking wet and trampled in the mud. With all this stuff lying around just like dead bodies. You've seen those old pictures of battlefields on glass plates, of bloated horse bodies, cannonballs, dead soldiers lying in the field. That's what it looked like.

Staff members gathered at my production trailer. Until our financial situation was settled, I had to explain that we couldn't pay anyone. While this was going on, reporters were there asking questions. When a *New York Times* reporter inquired about our financial status, I told him we'd spent a lot more than we'd made: "So many came . . . and we had to take care of them. It was worth it." The writer went on to report in the *Times*: "Today a trailer serving as a business office was filled with young workers expecting to be paid. They were told to take only what they absolutely needed until the sponsors could obtain cash. In the spirit of sharing that has marked the weekend, champagne and cigarettes were proffered."

Stan stayed in Bethel for the next three weeks during the bulk of the cleanup and dismantling process. He created request forms so that neighbors could file claims for loss and damages or just to ask for trash removal.

STAN GOLDSTEIN: I stayed to calm fevered brows. There were two immediate fallouts: A group of very vocal, unhappy people in whose fields and lawns people had settled, who claimed all kinds of damage from the marauding hordes. Then there were the other people who said, "Wow, what a miraculous thing you guys have done . . . the kids were great . . . how did you manage to do it?!" Of course, most of the merchants and businesspeople in the area were very happy. They'd never done so much business in such a short length of time.

Various people began filing lawsuits, including the president of the Monticello Raceway, which had planned a race for that weekend;

eventually, about eighty lawsuits would be filed. (Most would be settled out of court or dropped.) Politicians started calling for an investigation into the festival. One, Representative Martin McKneally (R-Newburgh), flew over the site in a helicopter and issued a statement saying, "The stench that arose from the hill on Yasgur Farm will remain in the nostrils of the people of Sullivan County for years to come." He went on to compare the smell to "Egyptian filth." State Attorney General Louis J. Lefkowitz announced he had been contacted by officials from New York City to investigate the festival. Lefkowitz was concerned about ticket buyers who could not get to the festival. As tickets were not collected, it was impossible to tell who had made it to the site and who hadn't. John and Joel later settled on paying a lump sum of $25,000 to the state to cover any such claims.

While people were clearing the site, various tools and equipment just disappeared. We had told the Hog Farm they could take any equipment left over in their area and they took us up on it.

ROZ PAYNE: I stayed a few days after the festival was over—everyone's leaving, the piles of garbage are being left, and here we have sound equipment from the stage, we have a printing press, we have generators that are left behind, we have a field hospital. Most people are gone by this time. The Hog Farm is picking up bottles. I contacted people in New York to bring up the largest rental truck they could find. I also had a friend of mine drive up my little red Volkswagen. We filled up the U-Haul truck with the entire field hospital, except for a small refrigerator, which we put in the back of my VW. We put the printing press in the rental truck—whatever we saw, we took. Somebody took air conditioners from the trailers. We gave the printing press to the Black Panthers, which they printed their newspaper on. We gave the field hospital to the Black Panthers Free Clinic.

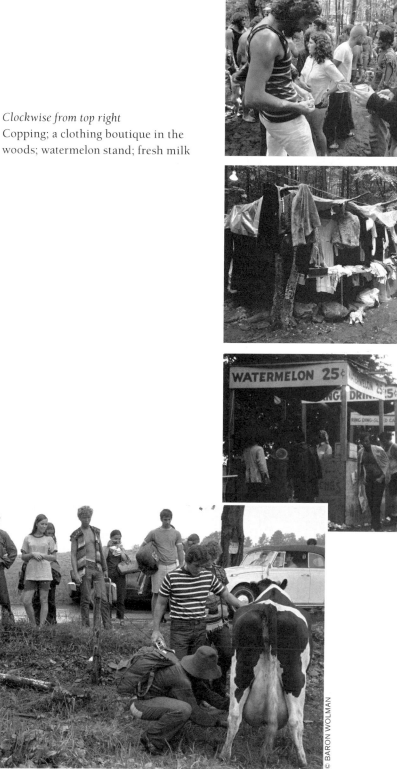

Clockwise from top right
Copping; a clothing boutique in the woods; watermelon stand; fresh milk

© BARON WOLMAN

© BARON WOLMAN

© KEN REGAN

© BARON WOLMAN

WATERMELON 25¢

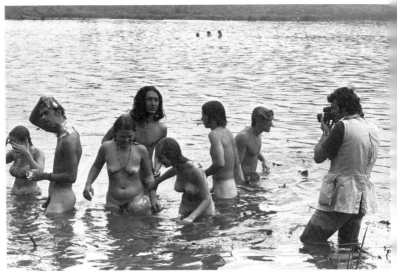

A photographer getting his feet wet

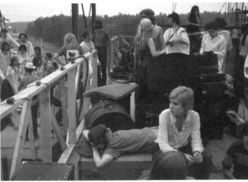

Penny taking a break at the side stage

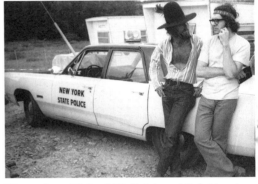

Filmmakers Michael Wadleigh and Bob Maurice

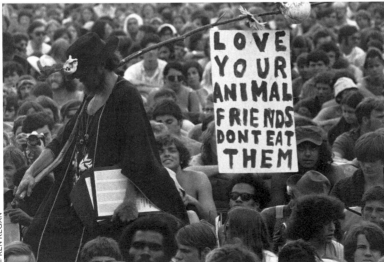

LOVE YOUR ANIMAL FRIENDS DONT EAT THEM

Animal rights at Woodstock

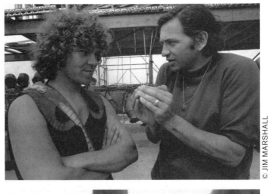

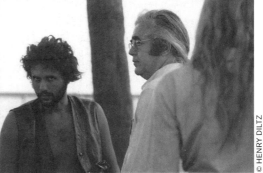

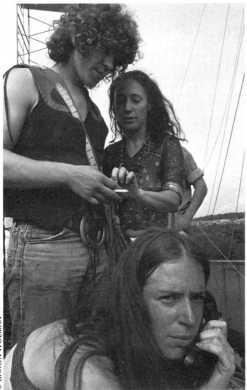

Clockwise from top left
Me with Joyce Mitchell and Ticia on the phone; me and Bill Graham; Artie with Albert Grossman; checking on Tim Hardin; Joan Baez with Joe Cocker's manager Dee Anthony and Joe's producer Denny Cordell

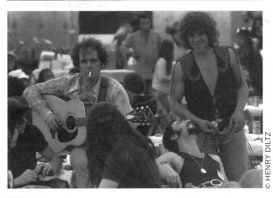

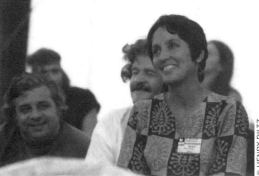

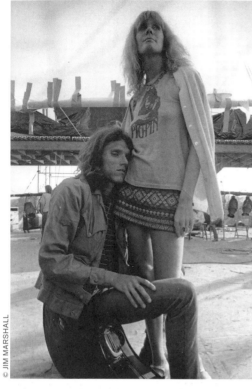

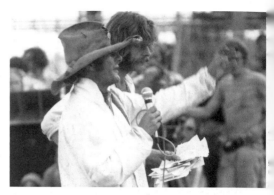

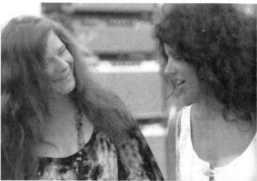

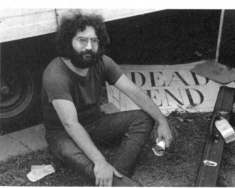

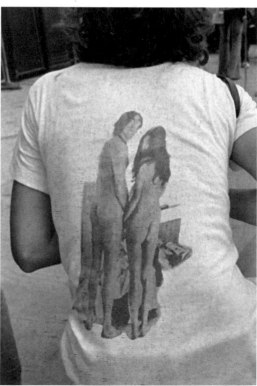

Clockwise from top left
Jorma Kaukonen and friend; Hugh Romney
and Chip Monck making announcements,
Saturday morning, August 16; Janis Joplin
and Grace Slick; John and Yoko making an
appearance; Jerry Garcia

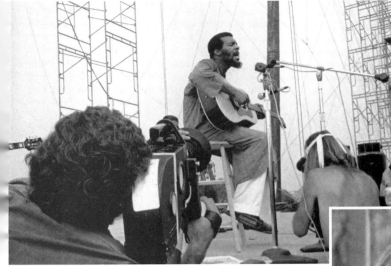

Above
Richie Havens starts the show

Right
Swami Satchidananda and his followers arrive,
August 15

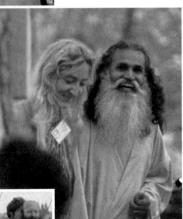

© HENRY DILTZ

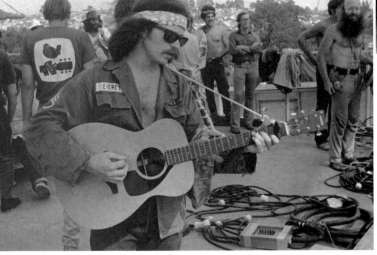

© JIM MARSHALL

Above
Country Joe McDonald getting ready to go on,
August 16

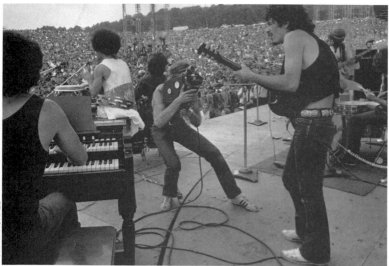

Santana

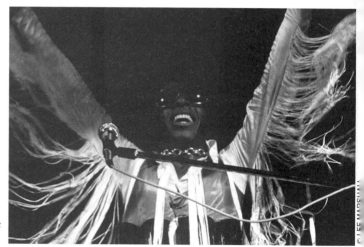

Sly Stone

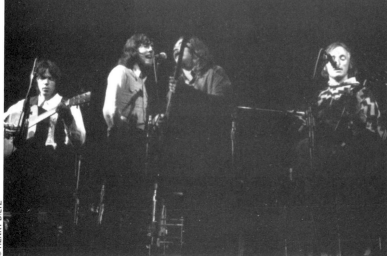

Crosby, Stills, Nash
and Young

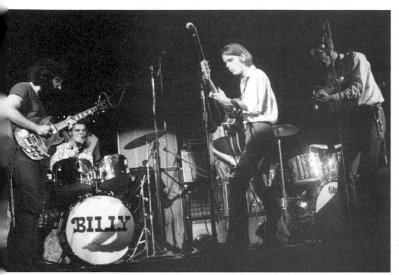

The Grateful Dead

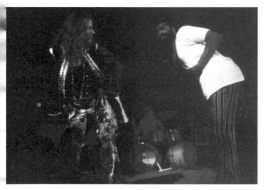

Janis Joplin and Snooky Flowers

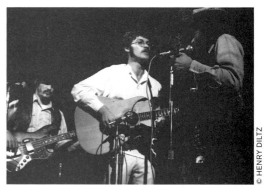

The Band

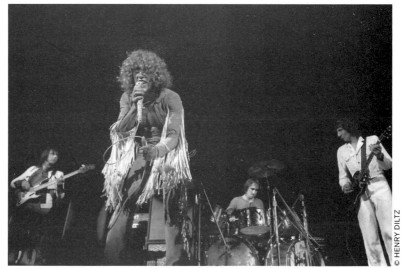

The Who

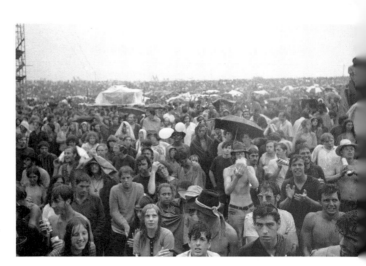

Right
August 17

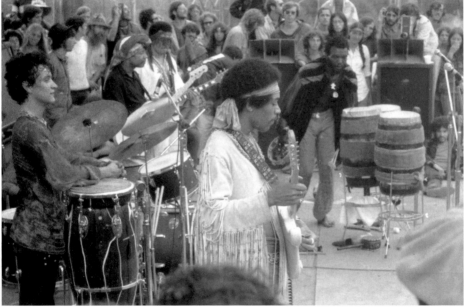

© HENRY DILTZ

Above
Geraldo Velez and Juma
Sultan on percussion,
Larry Lee on rhythm
guitar, and Billy Cox on
bass with Jimi Hendrix

Right
Max and Miriam survey
the festival site

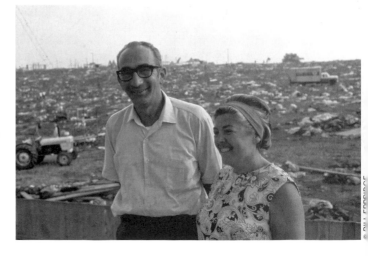

PENNY STALLINGS: The Hog Farm started loading building equipment that we had rented into their buses, and I said, "No, no, you can't do that—we need it for next year." The festival was going to happen again, I thought—from that point on, there would be a gathering of the tribes, a sea change in philosophy and political thinking in the country.

But Mel said to me about the equipment, "What do you care? Just let them take it." That was the hippie philosophy—we all share. But I knew John would be paying for it. He was a wonderful guy and I wanted him to pay for the next one the following summer.

Though some of the local officials were angry about the havoc and inconveniences, many had positive things to say. Sullivan County sheriff Louis Ratner told reporters, "I never met a nicer bunch of kids in my life," and another cop said, "When our police cars were getting stuck they even helped us get them out. I think a lot of police here are looking at their attitudes." Though there had been alarms sounded about medical emergencies, in the end, Dr. Abruzzi reported that his team had treated about five thousand people since Thursday, but almost half of the cases were cut feet. "It's about what you'd expect for a city of over three hundred thousand people," he said of the number of people they treated.

We got roundly criticized by the *New York Times,* which particularly upset John and Joel. The Monday edition ran an editorial, NIGHTMARE IN THE CATKILLS, condemning us:

> The sponsors of this event, who apparently had not the slightest concern for the turmoil it would cause, should be made to account for their mismanagement. To try to cram several hundred thousand people into a 600-acre farm with only a few hastily installed sanitary facilities shows a complete lack of responsibility.

In contrast, Max had kind words about us. Monday afternoon, he held a press conference at his farm, where he told the assembled journalists: "The kids were wonderful, honest, sincere, good kids who said, 'Here we are. This is what we are. This is the way we dress. These are our morals.' There wasn't one incident the whole time. The kids were polite, shared everything with everyone, and they forced me to open my eyes. I think America has to take notice. What happened at Bethel this past weekend was that these young people together with our local residents turned the Aquarian festival into a dramatic victory for the spirit of peace, goodwill, and human kindness."

No one was sure exactly how many people were at the festival. Aerial photographs were studied and estimates averaged around 450,000 to half a million. The White Lake historian Charlie Feldman was certain "there were 700,000 people there. The attendance estimate is based on aerial photos and there were thousands of people under trees," who couldn't be counted.

Arriving at the Wall Street heliport by midafternoon, I rushed into the executive offices of the bank. I entered a large, darkly paneled room and looked around for my partners. They were not easy to find, with all the lawyers, bankers, and bankruptcy attorneys in attendance. I finally spotted them in the president's office surrounded by John's brother Billy, an attorney; several more lawyer types; and an older gentleman who turned out to be the bank president. When I first poked my head in, I had noticed a large fish tank against the wall. I thought, Could that be piranha? It was at that moment the smell of fear and angst and anger in the room washed over me.

Unbeknownst to me, Artie had invited a couple of people along to the meeting. While still pretty stoned at Woodstock, he'd told Albert Grossman and Artie Ripp about the Monday appointment. Apparently, both were interested in forming a partnership with Artie and me. They suggested raising money to buy out Joel's and John's shares of Woodstock Ventures. They believed the Woodstock film was going to be huge and there was great value in the corporate name.

ARTIE RIPP: I was like a closet rabbi and thinking how do we make this thing work—how do you realize other opportunities after this? The undertaking itself had been like the Normandy invasion. I was friends with Albert Grossman, who was clearly a power player because of the acts he controlled and his influence in the business in general. We went on the helicopter from Woodstock with Artie. We fly to Wall Street and we go to the banker's office—and here's a guy who's got both a picture of Chairman Mao on the wall and a piranha in a fish tank in his office. Already I know this guy is off the fuckin' cliff someplace. He wants to make it clear that he's an out-of-the-box thinker and left of right and right of left and not anyplace near center.

ARTIE KORNFELD: I walked into the meeting with Artie Ripp, and the banker was throwing meat in his piranha tank. After coming from this beautiful experience, I was seeing everything that I hated about the world of capitalism.

The meeting had been going on since nine that morning. John had been writing checks all weekend to pay a long stream of people who managed to get to the telephone building. Now he and his family were going to have to guarantee over a million dollars to the bank to make good on those checks. The other option was for Woodstock Ventures to declare bankruptcy. The bank officials said they would hold all checks until Thursday, by which time an accounting of whatever incoming funds there were could be completed.

Regardless, there was no clear financial picture to be had at the meeting, or at least no one was interested in giving one to me. At a minimum, I was expecting the four of us to sit down and assess our situation and explore possible solutions. We were not without assets. We had created a huge amount of goodwill; we had the film and recordings of what had become an event of historic proportions. But it became clear that John's brother Billy was representing the Roberts family, who for all practical purposes had taken over control of Woodstock Ventures. The Roberts clan was taking an admirable position in backing John, taking us all out of the bankruptcy fire, but I sensed they had no interest in seeing our partnership continue. The die had been cast before I even touched down at the heliport.

Still, I could not help thinking about what John must be going through. It tore at me that he and Joel had not had the same amazing experience with Woodstock that Artie and I had. For whatever reason, they'd spent a miserable three days stuck in the telephone building in White Lake and now John was having to pledge his trust to pay our bills. I certainly did not have the money to pay my share, and neither did Artie or Joel. I also knew that as bad as John felt, Joel's position—he was John's partner but the Roberts family considered him an outsider—was somehow worse.

Joel and John were devastated and turned their anger and resentment toward Artie and me. John's family was similarly disposed toward us, and even Joel appeared to have become somewhat persona non grata in their eyes. It quickly became them against us. We agreed to table things and reconvene when more information was available.

There was no joy in Mudville that day.

LEE MACKLER BLUMER: John and Joel came back from the meeting and they were very disturbed. I guess that's when John's father said he was going to bail him out. Later he would say they could never use the logo or call anything Woodstock again. John Roberts promised he would never give anybody the license while his father was alive. His father thought it sullied the family's name. I think John's brother finally came around, realizing that it was a cultural phenomenon and that he had so much to do with it. But I don't think his father ever really forgave John for Woodstock.

I needed to get some sleep before heading back to White Lake to follow up on the situation there. I checked into the Chelsea Hotel and slept for eighteen hours. On my way out, about two o'clock the next day, I saw Janis Joplin, feathers and all, in the lobby. She and her band had been staying there too. "It's *you!*" she screamed. As I looked around to see who she was yelling at, she jumped all over me.

Public opinion was doing a complete turnaround over the festival. On Tuesday, the *New York Times* published yet another editorial, this time more positive and titled MORNING AFTER AT BETHEL. The *Boston Globe* compared Woodstock to the march on Washington, writing:

> The Woodstock Music and Art Festival will surely go down in history as a mass event of great and positive significance in the life of the country . . . That this many young people could assemble so peaceably and with such good humor in a mile-square area . . . speaks volumes about their dedication to the ideal of respect for the dignity of the individual . . . In a nation beset with a crescendo of violence, this is a vibrantly hopeful sign. If violence is infectious, so, happily, is nonviolence. The benign character of the young people gathered at Bethel communicated itself to many of their elders, including policemen, and the generation gap was successfully bridged in countless cases. Any event which can do this is touched with greatness.

There was one gap, though, that we weren't bridging.

Al Aronowitz concluded his daily coverage in the *New York Post* with an article on August 19 titled AFTERMATH AT BETHEL: GARBAGE & CREDITORS. In it he asked:

> You wonder where the four kids who promoted this thing are going to get the money [to pay off their debts], and Mike Lang smiles and tells you how happy he is. Meanwhile back in New York, his partner, 24-year-old John Roberts, is busy transferring several hundred thousand dollars from one account to another. It was Roberts' personal fortune that was used to underwrite the venture, with the liability divided four ways. "John," says Mike Lang, wearing the same Indian leather vest he has worn all week, "is very happy with the success of this thing," and he tells you how the town and the county and Max Yasgur . . . have asked the festival to return next year . . . You ask why you haven't seen John Roberts all weekend. "Oh," says Mike, "John didn't come. He was too nervous."

On Monday morning, when questioned by Aronowitz, I had been optimistic about the future of Woodstock Ventures. And I didn't really have a good answer as to why John or Joel couldn't find thirty minutes to come to the field.

I spent all day Wednesday in White Lake to make sure the cleanup was proceeding and to let the staff know what was up. John had promised that everyone would be paid. I borrowed a pickup truck and drove the fields and back roads to get a sense of the job ahead. It was extensive. We were missing about forty rental vehicles; more than twenty were never found. Some wound up in lakes and ponds.

That evening I headed back to the city. Joel and John had asked me to come to a meeting at their apartment so the three of us could talk. Before leaving Sullivan County, I thought to stop by the El Monaco and say hello to Elliot Tiber and see how he had made out. We caught up, and as I was leaving, he said, "Wait a minute! I have something for you." He went to the office and came out with $31,000 in a paper bag. "Here," he said. "We sold every ticket we had by the morning of the first day."

All the ticket outlets eventually yielded an additional $600,000. It was indicative of our paralyzed thinking in those first postfestival days that it took Elliot to remind us of the outlets.

I stashed the money under the spare tire in the trunk (actually, under the hood) of my Porsche and took off for the city. I arrived at about eight at their Upper East Side apartment building and parked out front. I was a bit nervous, not knowing quite what to expect. We had all been through a major ordeal together and had been blown apart when it ended. What now? Since the unpleasant meeting at the bank, communication between the four of us had been reduced to zero. When Ripp and Grossman had appeared at the bank that day, I honestly felt repulsed, finding myself cast with strangers against my partners. I thought to myself, "It's only the specter of John's family that keeps me on this side of the table." Artie's feelings were much less ambivalent. He wanted nothing more to do with John and Joel.

I rang the bell at apartment 32C, and John opened the door looking a decade older than his twenty-four years. Joel looked haggard as well. We sat down and tried to assess things. They wanted to know my plans. I really didn't have any plans beyond getting through the wrap-up of the festival and dealing with the odd situation our business was in.

John asked if I would be willing to stay with them in Woodstock Ventures, which they assumed they would keep. I had grown to like and respect John, and although I still had trouble relating to Joel, I thought his heart—if not his head—was in the right place, especially when it came to John. Should I choose to stay on, though, it was clear that Artie would not be with us going forward. While remaining their partner was probably the right move on several levels, abandoning Artie was not something I was prepared to do.

Joel and John were incredulous. They just couldn't understand my choice. I felt I didn't have a choice.

As I prepared to leave, I remembered the money I had stashed in the Porsche. "I almost forgot!" I said. "I stopped by the El Monaco and picked up the ticket receipts. After commissions, it came to thirty-one thousand. Would you like me to deposit it, or do you want to come downstairs with me and take—" Before I could finish my sentence, Joel was escorting me to the car.

Over the next several weeks, the four of us began to discuss the dissolution of Woodstock Ventures. It was determined that Woodstock Ventures was $1.4 million in the hole. Joe Vigoda, a music-business lawyer, represented Artie and me. We proceeded on the basis that either they would buy out our shares or we would buy out theirs. My interest was not in getting out of the partnership but in getting Woodstock out of debt. We made an offer that left John and Joel with the debt until we had the money in place to pay them back; John was outraged by this idea. Everyone was screaming at one another—nothing was resolved.

I'd always been pretty good at bringing disparate elements together, but with family pressures and distrust on one side, and the impossibility of a reconciliation with Artie on the other, I could see no way forward together unless we found some immediate relief from our financial problems.

Artie and I went to meet with Freddy Weintraub at Warner Bros. We asked for an advance of $500,000 against our share of the future profits of the film, so that we could take the corporation out of its immediate problems and pay off some debts. Weintraub said no, claiming that the film's profitability was in doubt. I thought that was bullshit. Ted Ashley and Warner Bros. execs knew what they had. They were happy to have us in a vulnerable position because that would make their own buyout offer more attractive.

I took the weekend off and flew to England for the Isle of Wight festival, slated for August 29 to 31. I went over with Albert Grossman and the Band, who were backing Dylan. I wanted to see if the spirit of Woodstock had crossed the pond. Should our company survive, this might have some effect on our future plans. The show was a bit of a letdown: As beautiful as the Isle of Wight was, it was missing the magic of Woodstock—at least for me.

Joel saw it this way: "When it was all over, Mike Lang and Artie Kornfeld went off somewhere, to the Isle of Wight, or onto TV shows and said, 'We're on to the next thing. Woodstock is history.' Their two ex-partners stayed there and cleaned up the land and paid the vendors."

Back in New York, the situation continued to deteriorate. At our next meeting, we sat down to discuss a settlement. This time, we offered to take Joel and John out of the picture by assuming all the debts and paying them $150,000, or they could take us out of debt and pay us $75,000. There must have been some basis for the disparity between those figures, but I no longer remember what it was. We needed an accounting of Woodstock Venture's financial status so we could present our position to prospective investors. In addition to Albert Grossman, Artie Ripp had found a few other possible backers, and it seemed possible we could raise the money we needed.

Ultimately, as it turned out, Artie and I had to sell our shares to Joel and John. The Roberts clan suddenly changed their tune, threatening the bankruptcy they had been so adamantly opposed to earlier in August, perhaps as a threat. By then I had had enough of the arguments, hassles, and resentments. Our offer to pay off the debts and take over the responsibilities had been sincere. I did not want our employees and vendors to suffer should the Roberts family go through with their threat of filing for bankruptcy. I was not in the Woodstock business, and I never looked at concert promotion as a career path. I had lived out my dream and gained much from its success. If we could not finish this well, I thought, then let's at least finish it.

So Artie and I agreed to leave the partnership. The split was reported in the *New York Times* on September 8. We relinquished our shares and any right to the Woodstock name. I retained the option to buy back the Tapooz property at cost. Though *Billboard* had run the article describing in detail the new studio to be operated by Woodstock Ventures, the project had languished since things had blown up in Wallkill.

Artie's and my buyout settlement was a whopping $31,750 each. In fact, our attorney made us sign a letter acknowledging that he was opposed to our accepting the deal.

JOYCE MITCHELL: I remember going to one meeting at the lawyer's; I could strangle him now. I didn't like the fact that they were buying Michael out. I thought that that was wrong—but I don't think he had a choice.

Shortly after we settled, Warner Bros. paid $1 million to Joel and John to buy out Woodstock Ventures' half of the film rights, along with a small percentage of the net. Artie and I would never have sold out our rights, and maybe Weintraub and others at Warners realized that. Artie and I later surmised that talks about a buyout were already in the works with the Roberts clan, unbeknownst to us, before we left Woodstock Ventures.

When *Woodstock* was released in March 1970, it became a tremendous success—and took the festival to people all over America and around the world. It won an Academy Award for best documentary and was nominated for an Oscar in several categories. In the film's first decade, Warner made over $50 million on it. In 1969, before the movie was released, Warner Bros. Pictures was the least profitable of the eight major Hollywood studios. By buying *Woodstock,* the studio had its first coup in many years. At the premiere, Warner Chairman Steve Ross came up to me and said, "You and Freddy Weintraub can do anything together!" Between the film and a pair of soundtrack albums, Warner's stock began to soar. The company was in the youth-culture business now. Artie and I never saw a dime from any of the proceeds from the film or soundtracks.

ARTIE KORNFELD: We probably lost, between us, about fifty million after we were forced out of the company.

Though we severed our ties with John and Joel, staff members who continued to work for Woodstock Ventures kept me in the loop on things connected to the festival. About six weeks after our split, a copy of a memo to John and Joel from our purchasing agent, Jim Mitchell, crossed my desk. It was in response to a far-fetched business proposition that Joel and John had become taken with: a sort of traveling Woodstock tour throughout the continent of Africa.

I found that pretty funny.

I had moved on, but Woodstock would be with me wherever I went—I didn't need a package tour for that.

November 10, 1969

TO: John Roberts
    Joel Rosenman

RE: African Tour

It is my feeling at this time that we should cancel,
at least temporarily, the proposed African tour.
Some of the reasons for this are:

 1. Lack of funding
 2. No talent
 3. Lack of information about the possible
    financial profit or loss from such a tour
 4. Lack of any real reason why this tour
    should take place
 5. No concrete information on how the mechanics
    of such a tour would be handled
 6. Lack of qualified personnel

I feel that a tour of this sort is a valid vehicle
for spreading Woodstock's fame. However, in this
particular instance, there are just too many loose
ends. I think that if we are to do an African tour,
it must be not just a single thing but should be part
of a greater over all plan. At this moment no such
plan exists.

Before we seriously commit ourselves to any tour,
especially in an area as unknown as Africa, I suggest
we send one of our own agents with Mr. Gibson to
thoroughly investigate the situation.

Thank you.

James. C. Mitchell

THE WOODSTOCK GROUP   47 W 57, NYC 10019   (212) 759-1525

EPILOGUE

It's two months after Woodstock, on one of those typically sunny October days in Los Angeles, and I'm driving my rental car down the Sunset Strip. I'd flown out from New York to meet with Columbia Pictures about a film idea. Rolling Stone, *with the headline* WOODSTOCK 450,000, *has hit the newsstands, along with* Life *magazine's special Woodstock edition. In a few months, the movie and soundtrack album of the festival will be released. I notice the driver of a blue convertible in the lane next to me slowing down and waving. I recognize the sandy hair, long sideburns, and chiseled face. It's Stephen Stills.*

"Hey, man, I can't believe I ran into you," he yells. "Follow me over to my house. There's something you've got to hear."

"Sure," I say, curious, and I follow him along the busy strip. I haven't seen Stills since he left Woodstock by helicopter early Monday the eighteenth. We turn right onto Laurel Canyon and drive up the hill until we pull into a driveway tucked behind a security gate. I park next to a Mercedes 600 with the hood up and follow Stills down some steps into a

basement music room, with amps and mics set up. Dallas Taylor is mess-
ing around on a drum kit as we walk in, and Stills tells him, "Let's play
Michael the song." He sits down behind a Hammond B-3 organ, starts to
play, and moves close to the mic:

> *I came upon a child of God*
> *He was walking along the road*
> *And I asked him, Tell me where are you going*
> *And this he told me*
> *He said, I'm going on down to Yasgur's farm*
> *Gonna join in a rock 'n' roll band*
> *I'm going to camp out on the land*
> *And get my soul free*
> *We are stardust*
> *We are golden*
> *And we've got to get ourselves*
> *Back to the garden . . .*

Stills sees the stunned look on my face, and breaks out into a gap-toothed
smile. "Right after we left the festival," he explains, "we went to see Joni
[Mitchell] on the set of The Dick Cavett Show. *We'd left her behind when*
we flew up to Bethel—[David] Geffen didn't think she could get back in
time to do the TV spot. She watched the festival coverage on television,
wrote this song at Geffen's apartment in New York, and gave us the tape
that night. We just recorded it for our next album."

I was completely overwhelmed. That feeling of hearing the song for
the first time that way has remained with me to this day.

W ithin weeks after the festival, people began calling with business
propositions. I was now in a position to become a national promoter. But booking typical concerts or tours held little appeal for me,

and I didn't pursue that kind of work. After experiencing Woodstock, I felt most music-business situations seemed mundane. And although I was nearly broke, I was still exploring and trying to understand who I was and where I really wanted to go.

Nevertheless, in December, I got a call from the Rolling Stones organization. Sam Cutler wanted help in the last-minute planning for a concert in northern California. The Stones were losing the Sears Point Raceway days before the free concert scheduled for December 6 and asked if I would fly out to help. It was a disaster in the making, but I agreed to give whatever assistance I could. The Stones and their staff had approached it with good intentions, but with almost no planning or infrastructure. The concert was moved to Altamont Raceway.

That day at Altamont was one of the worst experiences of my life. I truly got to see the dark side of the drug culture. People high on all kinds of exotic concoctions were just wandering through the crowd. There were beatings going on throughout the day, down front near the stage, and there was no one to stop them.

The Hells Angels, who were there to defend the stage and protect their bikes parked next to it, provided the only security. They beat up not only the audience members unlucky enough to have been pushed into their bikes, but also musicians like Marty Balin of the Airplane, who tried to intervene. A member of the audience, Meredith Hunter, was there with his girlfriend and got into a skirmish early in the afternoon. He left and returned later with a gun. When he pulled it out, he was stabbed to death by an Angel. Hunter's killing was captured on film by the Maysles brothers in their Altamont documentary, *Gimme Shelter.*

Only four months after Woodstock, people were saying that Altamont marked the end of an era. I didn't see it that way. What happened at Altamont was terrible and showed how awful things can get without foresight and proper preparation. Altamont should have been a great day of music for the Bay Area.

For me, the end came five months later when four students were shot and killed and nine others wounded by National Guardsmen at Kent State University. The image of unarmed American kids being gunned down on a college campus by other American kids in uniform brought home the insanity of how far out of control things had spun during the Nixon administration. Neil Young's immediate reaction, "Ohio," which Crosby, Stills, Nash and Young recorded within days, demonstrated again how music could reflect on the events of our time and help to point the way to turn things around.

In 1970, Artie and I formed a partnership and tried to build a new kind of entertainment business together. It didn't last long. While I loved Artie and Linda, being in business together just did not work. We separated within a year to pursue our own paths. We were such close friends that splitting up the business profoundly affected us personally. Artie felt that I was abandoning him; I felt that I couldn't stay. It strained our relationship for years.

In the early seventies, after turning down an offer from Gulf+ Western execs to run Paramount Records, I agreed to take on a production deal, which then became the label Just Sunshine. I made albums with people whose music I liked: a then-unknown Billy Joel, singer-songwriter Karen Dalton, the R & B vocalist Betty Davis, bluesman Mississippi Fred McDowell, and the gospel group the Voices of East Harlem, to name a few.

Like concert promotion, artist management didn't appeal to me, but I had managed Billy Joel on an interim basis while we looked for someone to work with him full-time. One day Billy and I were on our way to the airport and "You Are So Beautiful" by Joe Cocker came on the car radio. Billy looked over and said, "You know, no matter how many times they count this guy out, he always seems to get up again."

I became reacquainted with Joe Cocker in 1976. I knew he had destroyed his career by doing too many disastrous shows too drunk to stand up. Still, I was shocked by his physical condition and near incoherence. Remembering Billy's words, I agreed to work with him on a temporary basis to try and rebuild his health and his reputation. That association lasted for sixteen years. During that time I helped him to get control of his drinking, refocus on his incredible talent, and reestablish himself as a major star in Europe and around the world. (In a *Spinal Tap* moment in 1991, we would part company.)

While managing the careers of Joe and also Rickie Lee Jones, in 1987 I produced a festival with West German promoter Peter Rieger for 250,000 East German kids behind the wall in East Berlin. With Joe as the headliner, we added bands from East Germany, Russia, and West Germany. We followed that with another outdoor concert for 100,000 kids in Dresden. We were the first Westerners to play Dresden since World War II.

These events were to be the lead-up to a twentieth-anniversary Woodstock event in 1989. I hoped to have it take place on both sides of the Berlin Wall. I thought the spirit of Woodstock could create a bridge between East and West.

After an incredible two years of meetings and dozens of cloak-and-dagger interludes in East Germany, I finally attained tacit approval from the Honecker government to proceed. But in the end, the project was torpedoed by Warner Bros. and the Communist Party in Moscow. Strange bedfellows.

As it happened, on the day the wall fell in 1989, I was back in Berlin on a Cocker tour. With the mayor, we organized a spontaneous concert/celebration featuring bands from the East and the West. With millions of people in the streets of Berlin and more pouring "through" the wall, it was an amazing experience to be in the midst of history being made.

Though for years I would have bet against it, there would be two festivals celebrating Woodstock anniversaries: in 1994, on the twenty-fifth anniversary, and in 1999, for the thirtieth. John Roberts and I had always managed to stay in touch, and in the late eighties we began talking about Woodstock again. Eventually he, Joel, and I met to discuss the twenty-fifth anniversary.

In the winter of 1994, I managed to secure the 800-acre Winston Farm, the Schaller land near Saugerties we'd originally wanted for Woodstock. With three-fourths of Woodstock Ventures reunited, I brought in John Scher, then president of PolyGram, and together we produced what we all felt was a great festival for 350,000 very happy kids and, in many cases, their parents. Artie, whose wife Linda tragically died in 1988, came up from Florida to share the weekend of August 12, 13, and 14 with us.

Many of the original Woodstock performers returned, including Santana, Joe Cocker, and Crosby, Stills and Nash, as well as new artists Sheryl Crow, Green Day (whose manager had been in Sha Na Na in '69), Porno for Pyros (whose leader Perry Farrell started Lollapalooza, a kind of traveling Woodstock), the Red Hot Chili Peppers, and Metallica. The press criticized our getting corporate sponsorship (Pepsi), but that had become part of the concert business—even for Woodstock. And most people who came could have cared less. The realities of the festival's costs (over thirty million dollars) meant that the ticket prices for the weekend would have been substantially higher without sponsors. Though it was not my ideal scenario, I was basically okay with it as long as it didn't compromise our plans.

In true Woodstock style, the communal spirit lived, it rained like hell, Mud People abounded, and Woodstock '94 made money for everyone but us.

Five years later, on July 23–25, Woodstock '99 took place at Griffiss Air Force Base in upstate New York's Mohawk Valley, near Rome. John Scher (now at Ogden), Ossie Killkenny, and I produced the festival, with Woodstock Ventures serving as the licensor. We wanted to return to the bucolic Winston Farm, but the political balance of the Saugerties town board had changed and they could not reach a decision on moving forward with us. Griffiss was well suited should it rain, and the logistics there were fantastic: hundreds of buildings to house our crews and staff; hundreds of acres for parking, camping, and performances; and easy access to the site.

I again wanted a mix of classic acts, jam bands, and the less extreme side of the hard-edged music happening at the time. Going against my instincts, I went along with the consensus and so the lineup, an amazing amalgam of the biggest acts of the day, was darker and more aggressive than I would have liked. At one point during planning, I was talking to Prince about a Hendrix tribute, and he asked me, "Why are you having all those nasty bands?" I did not have a good answer. During the performances of acts like Limp Bizkit, Korn, and Rage Against the Machine, the mosh pit was a scary sight. The audience surfing got pretty aggressive, and we were horrified to later find out that incidents of women being molested had been reported.

The weather was brutally hot, with no rain for relief, and while there was plenty of free water on tap, concessions were selling it at $4 a bottle, as though it were Yankee Stadium. When I found out about the prices, I tried to get the concessionaires to reduce them to something sane, but I was told it was too late to change them. To balance this, I ordered several trailerloads of water to be distributed for the taking around the site. While the vast majority of the kids had a good time, the festival became more like a massive MTV spring-break party than a Woodstock.

At 7 P.M. on the final evening, the mayor of Rome and various county and state officials held a press conference to congratulate us on a terrific weekend and to invite us back. A few hours later, as the festival was ending with the Chili Peppers covering Hendrix's "Fire" (which had been so powerful in '69), some of the kids in the back of the audience began lighting bonfires. Soon a group of about fifty goons, bent on provoking the crowd, decided to torch a line of supply trucks; then they went through the concession stands, "liberating" whatever they could. When the melee grew to involve several hundred people, the police came in en masse. Kids were running everywhere, mostly to get out of the way. I waded out into the middle of it to make sure the cops were not overreacting. And to their credit, they showed great restraint in the mayhem.

In retrospect, I realized I had failed to heed the lesson I had so clearly learned in 1969 and many times since: trust my instincts.

In the years since Woodstock, I have put on many events in America and abroad and have pursued interests in music, film, and the arts. Along the way, I produced a short film by Wes Anderson called *Bottle Rocket*, which introduced Wes and the actors Luke and Owen Wilson to the world. While on a trip to Moscow and working with the Kremlin Museum, I acquired the film rights to the Russian classic *The Master and Margarita*, by Mikhail Bulgakov. It is now in development and projected to shoot in 2010.

In the past forty years, Woodstock has been the elephant in the room in my life. To keep it in perspective, I have made the room much bigger. It is full of family and friends and adventures lived and yet to come.

Many of Woodstock's artists look back to the festival in '69 as a turning point for all of us. As Carlos Santana recently said, "At Woodstock I saw a collective adventure representing something that still holds true today. When the Berlin Wall came down, Woodstock was there. When Mandela was liberated, Woodstock was there. When we celebrated the year 2000, Woodstock was there. Woodstock is still every day."

John Lennon once said, "Not many people are noticing all the good that came out of the last ten years—Woodstock is the biggest mass of people ever gathered together for anything other than war. Nobody had that big an army and didn't kill someone or have some kind of violent scene like the Romans or whatever, and even a Beatle concert was more violent than that."

And the late Abbie Hoffman never gave up on the newfound community he was part of that weekend in White Lake, which inspired him to write the book *Woodstock Nation*. Shortly before he died in 1989, he said, "Out of that sense of community, out of that vision, that Utopian vision, comes the energy to go out there and actually participate in the process so that social change occurs."

Fifteen years ago, the cultural critic Greil Marcus wrote of Jimi's performance of our national anthem as "his great NO to the war, to racism, to whatever you or he might think of and want gone. But then that discord shattered, and for more than four and a half long, complex minutes Hendrix pursued each invisible crack in a vessel that had once been whole, feeling out and exploring and testing himself and his music against anguish, rage, fear, hate, love offered, and love refused. When he finished, he had created an anthem that could never be summed up and that would never come to rest. In the end it was a great YES, both a threat and a beckoning, an invitation to America to match its danger, glamour, and freedom."

During a time of great challenges in America, a community grew out of Woodstock. Stemming from similar values and aspirations, a sense of possibility and hope was born and spread around the globe. It's taken forty years to see some of the changes that were first glimpsed during those three days in August. The spirit embraced at Woodstock continues to grow. You see it in the many green movements, in grassroots organizations like MoveOn, and in what some pundits have called a Woodstock moment, the election of our first African-American president. As Jimi Hendrix recast the national anthem that day in the mud, he gave voice to a future where a Barack Obama could bring change to America and hope to the world.

Forty years later, the *Wall Street Journal* would refer to Obama's inauguration as "Washington's Woodstock." Experiencing the joy in coming together with a million celebrants on the Mall in Washington, a blogger named Brian Hassett put it this way: "As it was happening, every single one of the people I met was beaming with joy. In terms of a crowd euphoric, the only thing I ever heard of that was like this was Woodstock in '69. That changed our country a lot, but this time Woodstock was in the seat of power. Jimi's 'Star-Spangled Banner' was the prelude, and a scant forty years later, here's that scorching soul of new thinking actually overtaking the reins of government."

The day after the inauguration, Gail Collins's column "Woodstock Without the Mud" appeared in the *New York Times*. "Having been lucky enough to attend two of the most memorable events in modern American history," she wrote, "I am able to report that Inauguration Day in Washington was very much like a cold-weather Woodstock. At both, there was a wonderful feeling of community."

In late 1969, Jimi Hendrix wrote a poem celebrating Woodstock, saying with words what his music had in August: "500,000 halos outshined the mud and history. We washed and drank in God's tears of joy. And for once, and for everyone, the truth was not still a mystery."

Jimi's words—and the spirit of Woodstock—reverberate even now.

ACKNOWLEDGMENTS

When I was asked to write this book, I thought about the many other stories that have been written about that weekend in August 1969. Some were funny, some cynical, but all were told by people who at best knew only part of the story and at worst made it up as they went along. There is an old saying that if you remember the sixties, you weren't really there. Working with Holly and doing the early interviews for this book convinced me that I was. Other than the stories I had been telling over the years, my memory of those times remained vague. I began searching for a way to reenter that part of my life. My friend Steven finally suggested that if this was to be my voice, I start by actually writing. A daunting proposition, but I jumped in. With the physical act of writing, the door swung wide open, and in flooded faces and places, sights and smells, and I was immersed in the adventure all over again. The relief was great, but I realized that much of what happened at Woodstock and the months leading up to it was the result of my own inner journey. That's something that is usually hard for me to reveal, but I now understand it is necessary if people reading this are going to understand why things happened the way they did. Holly and I found our groove, and I hope we succeeded.

Thanks to everyone who helped in this effort. To all the people who gave interviews and contributed their memories and insights: Ticia Bernuth Agri, Paula Batson, Dale Bell, Lee Mackler Blumer, Iris Brest, Stu Cook, David Crosby, Alan Douglas, Rona Elliot, Jane Friedman, Susan and Dick Goldman, Stan Goldstein, Jonathan Gould, Wavy Gravy, Don Keider, Rob Kennedy, Artie Kornfeld, Eddie Kramer, Lisa Law, Tom Law, Mel Lawrence, Gilles Malkine, Jocko Marcellino, Peter Max, Joyce Mitchell, Chip Monck, Graham Nash, Ric O'Barry, Christine Oliveira, Roz Payne, Artie Ripp, Gregg Rolie, Marsha Rubin, Carlos Santana, Michael Shrieve, Penny Stallings, Stephen Stills, Parry Teasdale, Bill Ward, Robert Warren, and Jeremy Wilber.

Thanks to Joel Makower for his generosity in sharing his interviews with those no longer with us. A special thanks to Steven Saporta, whose advice and guidance helped set me on the path when I was searching for the way to tell this story. Thanks to Dan Halpern at Ecco, whose enthusiasm convinced me this was a story worth telling, and to Abigail Holstein, who kept the book on track, to Suet Yee Chong for the book's design, and to Katharine Baker for her expertise. To Sarah Lazin for her calm assessments and great knowledge of the business: "Just put one foot in front of the other and you'll get there." Thanks to Lee Blumer and Penny Stallings for their stories and their encouragement. And especially to Holly George-Warren for her tenacity and humor, without which we might still be writing.

To Linda Kornfeld, whose love and support had much to do with why Artie and I carried through.

To John Roberts, who left too soon and whose character continues to give me something to aspire to.

To Tamara, Harry, and Laszlo for putting up with the late nights and early mornings of "I just need to finish this page."

A big thanks to the photographers who captured so many special moments and understood that the real magic was in the people. To Henry Diltz, who became a member of the team, to Jim Marshall, Lee Marshall, Ken Regan, and Baron Wolman, and to Ken Davidoff and Eddie Kramer for Miami Pop. Also thanks to others who helped: our transcriber Judy Whitfield, Damien Tavis Toman, Nicole Goldstein, KellyAnn Kwiatek, Bob Merlis, Bill Rush, Andy Zax, Charles Cross, and the Middletown *Times Herald-Record*.

And finally to all the people who worked, performed, attended, and endured—and changed our lives forever.

ML
Woodstock, New York
March 2009

WHERE ARE THEY NOW?

TICIA BERNUTH AGRI (*production aide and assistant to Michael Lang*) has worked for the past thirty years in the healing arts as a massage therapist, a Rolfer (structural integrationist), an Integrative Manual Therapist, and a plant spirit medicine therapist. She is currently studying and teaching shamanic healing for the School of Applied Spiritual Healing and the School of Empowerment.

DALE BELL (*associate producer of the film* Woodstock) continues to work in film and television, primarily for PBS, "trying to focus on aspirational and inspirational multimedia projects that reach global audiences."

LEE MACKLER BLUMER (*assistant to Wes Pomeroy*) rejoined Michael Lang and several Woodstock alumni to work on the twenty-fifth and thirtieth anniversary concerts. She is director of events for M2 Ultra Lounge and is aiding and abetting plans for the fortieth anniversary of Woodstock: "Woodstock is still my life."

JOE COCKER (*performer*) continues to record and perform around the world. His most recent album is *Hymn for My Soul* (2008).

DAVID CROSBY (*performer*) continues to perform and record with Stills, Nash, and sometimes Young.

RICK DANKO (*performer*) died of heart failure in 1999.

HENRY DILTZ (*photographer*) is based in Los Angeles and is cofounder of the Morrison Hotel Gallery (located in New York, Los Angeles, and La Jolla), which exhibits fine-art music photography.

ALAN DOUGLAS (*music executive*) lives in Paris and continues to work in film and music production.

RONA ELLIOT, a music journalist for television, print, radio, and the Web, was seen for a decade on NBC's *Today Show*. Today she serves on the Grammy Museum education committee.

JANE FRIEDMAN (*publicity*), who later managed such artists as Patti Smith, continues to work in public relations.

DON GANOUNG (*community relations*) died of a heart attack in 1973.

STAN GOLDSTEIN (*campsite coordinator and headhunter*) lives in Los Angeles, where he has recently begun mixing music again. He has two films in postproduction: a concert film with an R & B band called Reno Jones and a documentary on a settlement of squatters in Slab City, California. "The result of my most successful project are Tucker and Evelyn, the two wondrous grandchildren my son, Jess, and terrific daughter-in-law, Nicole, are raising and investing with all the positive attributes that went into making Woodstock a mythic success."

JONATHAN GOULD (*festivalgoer*) went on to study with the eminent jazz drummer Alan Dawson and spent many years working in bands and recording studios. He turned to writing in the nineties and is the author of *Can't Buy Me Love: The Beatles, Britain, and America*.

BILL GRAHAM (*concert impresario*) died in a helicopter accident in 1991.

ALBERT GROSSMAN (*music manager and executive*) died of a heart attack in 1987.

TIM HARDIN (*performer*) died of a heroin overdose in 1980.

RICHIE HAVENS (*performer*) continues to record and perform. His most recent album is *Nobody Left to Crown* (2008).

ABBIE HOFFMAN (*activist and writer*) committed suicide in 1989.

ROB KENNEDY (*festivalgoer*) cultivates medical marijuana and records and tours as front man extraordinaire with his Brazilian partner Uncle Butcher.

ARTIE KORNFELD (*Woodstock Ventures*) lives in Miami, where he runs his own entertainment company.

CHRIS LANGHART (*technical director and contributing designer*) lives in rural Pennsylvania.

LISA LAW (*Hog Farm*) is the author of *Flashing on the Sixties* and lives in Santa Fe.

TOM LAW (*Hog Farm*) divides his time between New York City and New Mexico. He and his wife, Caroline Faure-Gilly Law, operate a home design business.

MEL LAWRENCE (*chief of operations*) lives by the ocean in Venice, California, and works as a producer of action/reality shows for cable networks and documentaries "whenever I can get them financed."

GILLES MALKINE (*Tim Hardin's rhythm guitarist*) is a musician who lives outside Woodstock, New York, and performs and records in a duo with Mikhail Horowitz.

COUNTRY JOE McDONALD (*performer*) lives in Berkeley, California, and continues to record and perform.

JOYCE MITCHELL (*production administrator*) has retired to "exurb America, to the only county of the Hudson Valley that voted red in the '08 election." The last party she put together had one band and an audience of less than fifty people. "I wake up most mornings lightheaded with joy, surrounded by majestic trees, family, and friends; a world citizen, grandmother, spouse, grateful for all the moments of my life."

MITCH MITCHELL (*Jimi Hendrix Experience drummer*) died in Portland, Oregon, in November 2008 after completing a multicity tour celebrating the music of Jimi Hendrix.

E. H. BERESFORD "CHIP" MONCK (*production supervisor and stage lighting design*) lives in Australia, where he has continued his career as a lighting designer for the past twenty-two years, lighting retail with a theatrical flair. "There is never a day I'm not on a ladder. Why? I ask."

JOHN MORRIS (*director of production area*) lives in Santa Fe and works with Native American fine artists.

RIC O'BARRY (*Joint Productions partner*) founded the Original Dolphin Project and continues to advocate for the protection of dolphins and other marine mammals.

CHRISTINE OLIVEIRA (*festivalgoer*) founded and continues to oversee the School of the New Moon for children ages two to seven, outside Woodstock, New York.

ROZ PAYNE (*activist and festivalgoer*) teaches History of the Radical Sixties and Mycology at Burlington College in Vermont. She owns the Newsreel Films archive of sixties films, photographs, and paper documentation (www.newsreel.us).

WES POMEROY (*chief of security*) died in 1994.

NOEL REDDING (*Jimi Hendrix Experience bassist*) died in 2003.

ARTIE RIPP (*record executive*) is based in Los Angeles, where he runs Artie Ripp Productions.

JOHN ROBERTS (*Woodstock Ventures partner*) died of cancer in 2001.

JOEL ROSENMAN (*Woodstock Ventures partner*) is the president of JR Capital, a venture-capital firm based in New York City.

HUGH ROMNEY (*Hog Farm*), better known as Wavy Gravy, founded and runs Camp Winnarainbow for children in Northern California.

CARLOS SANTANA (*performer*) continues to record and perform.

JOHN SEBASTIAN (*performer*) lives in Woodstock, New York, and continues to perform and record.

PENNY STALLINGS (*assistant to Mel Lawrence*) splits her time between Los Angeles and New Orleans. She is currently creating apps from her books *Rock 'n' Roll Confidential* and *Flesh and Fantasy* for the Apple iPhone and iTouch.

PARRY TEASDALE (*festivalgoer and videographer*), following the festival, was a founder of Videofreex, a group of video artists and documentary filmmakers. He has since edited local newspapers in Woodstock and Chatham, New York.

TRAIN released one album, *Costumed Cuties,* on Vanguard in 1970. **Garland Jeffries,** who is based in New York, continues to perform and record as a solo artist. **Don Keider** has performed and recorded with a number of artists, including Rick James, and currently lives in North Carolina, where he plays vibes with a band called Pale Blue. **Bob Lenox** lives in Berlin, where he records and performs avant-garde music and performance art.

BILL WARD (*grounds designer*), now retired from the University of Miami art department, lives in Fort Pierce, Florida, where he chairs the art in public places committee in St. Lucie County. He ran his last sports car race in 2007 and now spends his time restoring a '58 Lotus 7 and making small wood and clay sculptures.

MAX YASGUR (*dairy farmer*) died of a heart attack in 1973.

MIRIAM YASGUR (*Max Yasgur's wife and partner*) lives in Florida.

THE MUSIC: WOODSTOCK'S COMPLETE SET LISTS

‐ ‐ ‐‐ ‐‐‐‐‐‐‐‐‐‐‐‐‐‐‐‐‐‐‐‐‐‐‐‐‐‐‐‐‐‐‐‐‐

Compiled by Andy Zax

DAY ONE: FRIDAY, AUGUST 15

RICHIE HAVENS

From the Prison > Get Together >
  From the Prison
I'm a Stranger Here
High Flying Bird
I Can't Make It Anymore
With a Little Help from My Friends
Handsome Johnny
Strawberry Fields Forever
Freedom (Motherless Child)
  and outro

SWEETWATER

Motherless Child
Look Out
For Pete's Sake

What's Wrong
Crystal Spider
Two Worlds
Why Oh Why
Let the Sunshine In
Oh Happy Day
Day Song

BERT SOMMER

Jennifer
The Road to Travel
I Wondered Where You'd Be
She's Gone
Things Are Going My Way
And When It's Over
Jeanette
America

A Note That Read

Smile

TIM HARDIN

How Can We Hang on to a Dream

Susan

If I Were a Carpenter

Reason to Believe

You Upset the Grace of Living When
  You Lie

Speak Like a Child

Snow White Lady

Blue on My Ceiling

Sing a Song of Freedom

Misty Roses

RAVI SHANKAR

Raga Puriya-Danashri/Gat in
  Sawaritai

Ravi talks

Tabla Solo in Jhaptal

Ravi talks

Raga Manj Kmahaj

MELANIE

Close to It All

Momma Momma

Beautiful People

Animal Crackers

Mr. Tambourine Man

Tuning My Guitar

Birthday of the Sun

ARLO GUTHRIE

Coming Into Los Angeles

Wheel of Fortune

Walking Down the Line

Arlo speech: Exodus

Oh Mary, Don't You Weep

Every Hand in the Land

Amazing Grace

JOAN BAEZ

Oh Happy Day

Last Thing on My Mind

Joe Hill

Sweet Sir Galahad

Hickory Wind

Drug Store Truck Drivin' Man

One Day at a Time

Why Was I Tempted to Roam

Let Me Wrap You in My Warm and
  Tender Love

Swing Low, Sweet Chariot

We Shall Overcome

DAY TWO: SATURDAY, AUGUST 16

QUILL

They Live the Life

That's How I Eat

Driftin'

Waiting for You

COUNTRY JOE McDONALD

Janis

Donovan's Reef

Heartaches by the Number

Ring of Fire

Tennessee Stud

Rocking All Over the World

Flying All the Way

Seen a Rocket

Fish Cheer/I Feel Like I'm Fixin' to
    Die Rag (encore)

SANTANA

Waiting

Evil Ways

You Just Don't Care

Savor

Jingo

Persuasion

Soul Sacrifice

Fried Neckbones

JOHN SEBASTIAN

How Have You Been

Rainbows All Over Your Blues

I Had a Dream

Darlin' Be Home Soon

Younger Generation

KEEF HARTLEY BAND

Spanish Fly

She's Gone

Too Much Thinkin'

Believe in You

Halfbreed Medley: Sinnin' for You
    (intro)/Leaving Trunk/Just to
    Cry/Sinnin' for You

INCREDIBLE STRING BAND

Invocation (spoken word)

The Letter

Gather 'Round

This Moment

Come with Me

When You Find Out Who You Are

CANNED HEAT

I'm Her Man

Going Up the Country

A Change Is Gonna Come/Leaving
    This Town

(I Know My Baby?)

Woodstock Boogie

On the Road Again

MOUNTAIN

Blood of the Sun

Stormy Monday

Theme from an Imaginary Western

Long Red

For Yasgur's Farm

Beside the Sea

Waiting to Take You Away

Dreams of Milk and Honey

Southbound Train

GRATEFUL DEAD

Saint Stephen

Mama Tried

Dark Star

High Time

Turn on Your Lovelight

**CREEDENCE CLEARWATER
REVIVAL**

Born on the Bayou

Green River

Ninety-Nine and a Half

Bootleg

Commotion

Bad Moon Rising

Proud Mary

I Put a Spell on You

Night Time Is the Right Time

Keep on Chooglin'

Suzie Q

JANIS JOPLIN

Raise Your Hand

As Good as You've Been to This
  World

To Love Somebody

Summertime

Try (Just a Little Bit Harder)

Cosmic Blues

I Can't Turn You Loose (Snooky
  Flowers)

Work Me Lord

Piece of My Heart

Ball and Chain

SLY AND THE FAMILY STONE

M'Lady

Sing a Simple Song

You Can Make It If You Try

Everyday People

Dance to the Music

Music Lover

I Want to Take You Higher

Love City

Stand

THE WHO

Heaven and Hell

I Can't Explain

It's a Boy

1921

Amazing Journey

Sparks

Eyesight to the Blind

Christmas

Tommy Can You Hear Me?

Acid Queen

Pinball Wizard

Do You Think It's Alright

Fiddle About

There's a Doctor I've Found

Go to the Mirror Boy

Smash the Mirror

I'm Free

Tommy's Holiday Camp

We're Not Gonna Take It

See Me, Feel Me

Listening to You

Summertime Blues

Shakin' All Over

My Generation

Naked Eye

JEFFERSON AIRPLANE

The Other Side of This Life

Somebody to Love

3/5ths of a Mile in 10 Seconds

Won't You Try/Saturday Afternoon

Eskimo Blue Day

Plastic Fantastic Lover

Wooden Ships

Uncle Sam's Blues
Volunteers
The Ballad of You and Me and Pooneil
Come Back Baby
White Rabbit
The House at Pooneil Corners

DAY THREE: SUNDAY, AUGUST 17

THE GREASE BAND (WITHOUT JOE COCKER)
jam
40,000 Headmen

JOE COCKER AND THE GREASE BAND
Dear Landlord
Something's Coming On
Do I Still Figure in Your Life
Feelin' Alright
Just Like a Woman
Let's Go Get Stoned
I Don't Need No Doctor
I Shall Be Released
Hitchcock Railway
Something to Say
With a Little Help from My Friends

COUNTRY JOE AND THE FISH
Rock and Soul Music
Love
Not So Sweet Martha Lorraine
Sing Sing Sing
Summer Dresses

Friend, Lover, Woman, Wife
Silver and Gold
Maria
The Love Machine
Ever Since You Told Me That You Love
  Me (I'm a Nut)
short jam
Crystal Blues
Rock and Soul Music (reprise)
The Fish Cheer
I Feel Like I'm Fixin' to Die Rag

TEN YEARS AFTER
Spoonful
Good Morning, Little Schoolgirl
Hobbit
I Just Can't Keep from Crying
  Sometimes
Help Me
I'm Goin' Home

THE BAND
Chest Fever
Don't Do It
Tears of Rage
We Can Talk About It Now
Long Black Veil
Don't You Tell Henry
Ain't No More Cane
This Wheel's On Fire
I Shall Be Released
The Weight
Loving You Is Sweeter Than Ever

JOHNNY WINTER

Talk to Your Daughter/Six Feet in the
  Ground
Leland Mississippi Blues
Mean Town Blues
Mean Mistreater
I Can't Stand It
Tobacco Road
Tell the Truth
Johnny B. Goode

BLOOD, SWEAT AND TEARS

More and More
Just One Smile
Something's Coming On
More Than You'll Ever Know
Spinning Wheel
Sometimes in Winter
Smiling Phases
God Bless the Child
And When I Die
You've Made Me So Very Happy

**CROSBY, STILLS, NASH AND
YOUNG**

Suite: Judy Blue Eyes
Blackbird
Helplessly Hoping
Guinnevere
Marrakesh Express
Four and Twenty
Mr. Soul
I'm Wonderin'
You Don't Have to Cry
Pre-Road Downs

Long Time Gone
Bluebird Revisited
Sea of Madness
Wooden Ships
Find the Cost of Freedom
49 Bye-Byes

PAUL BUTTERFIELD BLUES BAND

Born Under a Bad Sign
No Amount of Loving
Driftin' and Driftin'
Morning Sunrise
All in a Day
Love March
Everything's Gonna Be Alright

SHA NA NA

Get a Job
Come Go with Me
Silhouettes
Teen Angel
Her Latest Flame
Wipeout
Who Wrote the Book of Love
Little Darling
At the Hop
Duke of Earl
Get a Job (reprise)

JIMI HENDRIX

Message to Love
Hear My Train a Comin'
Spanish Castle Magic
Red House
Mastermind

Lover Man

Foxey Lady

Jam Back at the House

Izabella

Gypsy Woman

Fire

Voodoo Child (Slight Return)

The Star-Spangled Banner

Purple Haze

Woodstock Improvisation

Villanova Junction

Hey Joe

SOURCES

Michael Lang was the primary source of information for *The Road to Woodstock*. All additional sources for specific quotes are listed below, chronologically within each chapter for which the material was drawn. (Each source is abbreviated after first mention.)

2. THE GROVE

Holly George-Warren [HGW] interview with Don Keider [DK]; HGW interview with Stan Goldstein [SG]; Abbie Hoffman [AH] interviewed by Joel Makower for his book *Woodstock: The Oral History* (New York: Doubleday, 1989) © Joel Makower, all rights reserved for this and all Makower attributions; Henry Llach interview with Ric O'Barry; "Flower Children Strangely Mannerly: Reporter Rubs Elbows with Weirdos," *Fort Lauderdale News,* May 19, 1968; Mitch Mitchell, www.rockprophecy.com; Noel Redding and Carol Appleby, *Are You Experienced?: The Inside Story of the Jimi Hendrix Experience* (New York: Da Capo, 1996); Eddie Kramer, www.rockprophecy.com.

3. WOODSTOCK, NEW YORK

Alf Evers, *Woodstock: History of an American Town* (Woodstock, N.Y.: Overlook Press, 1987); Robert Shelton, *No Direction Home: The Life and Music of Bob Dylan* (New York: Beech Tree Books, 1986); HGW interview with Jeremy Wilber; HGW interview with Gilles Malkine [GM]; Barney Hoskyns, *Across the Great Divide: The Band and America* (New York: Hyperion, 1993); Sid Griffin, *Million Dollar Bash: Bob Dylan, the Band, and the Basement Tapes* (London: Jawbone, 2007); HGW interview with DK; HGW interview with Artie Kornfeld [AK]; Joel Makower interview with AK; Joel Rosenman, John Roberts, and Robert Pilpel, *Young Men with Unlimited Capital* [YMWUC] (New York: Harcourt Brace Jovanovich, 1974); Joel Makower interview with Joel Rosenman.

4. WALLKILL

"Woodstock Studios Set," *Billboard* magazine, July 5, 1969; HGW interview with SG; HGW interview with Mel Lawrence [ML]; HGW interview with Chip Monck [CM]; Joel Makower interview with Chris Langhart; HGW interview with Joyce Mitchell; *YMWUC*; HGW interview with Penny Stallings [PS]; HGW interview with Bill Ward [BW]; HGW interview with Ticia Bernuth Agri [TBA]; Joel Makower interview with Wes Pomeroy [WP].

5. NEW YORK CITY

HGW interview with ML; HGW interview with Joyce Mitchell; Joel Makower interview with John Morris; HGW interview with Lee Mackler Blumer [LMB]; HGW interview with Jane Friedman [JF].

6. DOWNTOWN

Joel Makower interview with AH; HGW interview with Roz Payne [RP]; HGW interview with TBA; "Public Notice and Statement of Intent," *Times Herald-Record* [THR], June 19, 1969; HGW interview with LMB; HGW interview with JF; HGW interview with SG; HGW interview with Hugh Romney [HR]; "Woodstock: Mud, Music, & Magic," reported by the *Record* staff, written by Mark Pittman with Stephen Israel, *Times Herald-Record* special publication [*THR*sp], August 12, 1989; HGW interview with AK; "Editorial," *THR*, June 27, 1969, used with permission.

7. YASGUR'S FARM

"Show Will Go On, Rock Fete Promoters Boast," *THR*, July 15, 1969; "Festival Seen Moving to Sullivan," *Kingston Freeman*, July 19, 1969; "Aquarian Expo Wins A-OK from Bethel Boards," *THR*, July 22, 1969; "Businessmen Throw Weight Behind Exposition," *THR*, July 31, 1969; "Rock at Woodstock," by Jane Stuart, Hackensack, N.J., *Record Call*, July 27, 1969; "Rock Fete Readies Bethel Site; Few Protest," *THR*, July 24, 1969; HGW interview with ML; HGW interview with SG; HGW interview with PS; HGW interview with TBA; Joel Makower interview with Miriam Yasgur [MY]; Joel Makower interview with John Roberts; Joel Makower interview with Joel Rosenman.

8. BETHEL

Joel Makower interview with WP; Joel Makower interview with John Roberts; Joel Makower interview with HR; "Members of the Hog Farm," *New York Post*, August 7, 1969; HGW interview with SG; Joel Makower interview with Lisa Law; "Woodstock . . . Well, Dylan Likes the Name," by Al Aronowitz, *New York Post*, August 11, 1969; HGW interview with Alan Douglas [AD]; HGW interview with Dale Bell [DB]; Henry Diltz quoted in Jack Curry, *Woodstock: The Summer of Our Lives* [WSOOL] (New York: Weidenfeld and Nicholson, 1989); HGW interview with PS; HGW interview with BW.

9. AUGUST 13–14, 1969

Joel Makower interview with WP; HGW interview with LMB; HGW interview with RP; HGW interview with CM; HGW interview with SG; Abbie Hoffman, *Woodstock Nation* [WN] (New York: Vintage Books, 1969); HGW interview with AK; HGW interview with Joyce Mitchell; HGW interview with DB; HGW interview with Parry Teasdale [PT]; HGW interview with Rob Kennedy [RK]; Bill Graham and Robert Greenfield, *Bill Graham Presents: My Life Inside Rock and Out* [BGP] (New York: Doubleday, 1992); "Thousands Rolling In for Woodstock Rock," *Washington Post*, August 14, 1969.

10. AUGUST 15, 1969

Richie Havens with Steve Davidowitz, *They Can't Hide Us Anymore* (New York: Spike, 1999); HGW interview with CM; HGW interview with Joyce Mitchell; Joel Makower interview with WP; HGW interview with RK; "The Woodstock Festival," by Greil Marcus, *Rolling Stone* [RS69], September 20, 1969; email from Jonathan Gould to HGW; HGW interview with PS; HGW interview with AK; Joel Makower interview with John Morris; *WSOOL*; HGW interview with Christine Oliveira [CO]; Joel Makower interview with AH; Rona Elliot [RE] interview with Alex del Zoppo; RE interview with Fred Herrera; Ellen Sander, *Trips: Rock Life in the Sixties* (New York: Charles Scribner's Sons, 1973); HGW interview with GM; "Rock Time in the Mountains," by Al Aronowitz, *New York Post*, August 16, 1969; "Woodstock Remembered," *Rolling Stone* [RS89], August 24, 1989; Joel Makower interview with John Morris.

11. AUGUST 16, 1969

HGW interview with ML; *WN*; Joel Makower interview with MY; *THRsp*; HGW interview with SG; "The Politics of Rock: Movement vs. Groovement," by Tom Smucker, *Fusion,* October 17, 1969; HGW interview with BW; HGW interview with GM; HGW interview with CO; Joel Makower interview with AH; HGW interview with PT; Joel Makower interview with HR; HGW interview with PS; HGW interview with RP; "300,000 at Folk-Rock Fair Camp Out in Sea of Mud," *New York Times*, August 17, 1969; *WSOOL*; HGW interview with JF; *BGP*; HGW interview with Gregg Rolie; HGW interview with Michael Shrieve; HGW interview with AD; Sander, *Trips*; Rock Scully with David Dalton, *Living with the Dead: Twenty Years on the Bus with Garcia and the Grateful Dead* (New York: Little, Brown, 1996); "Woodstock Remembered," *Rolling Stone*, August 24, 1989; Blair Jackson, *Garcia: An American Life* (New York: Viking, 1998); HGW interview with Stu Cook; HGW interview with Jocko Marcellino; *WSOOL*; Mark Wilkerson, *Who Are You: The Life of Pete Townshend* (London: Omnibus Press, 2008); *BGP*.

12. AUGUST 17, 1969

HGW interview with SG; Joel Makower interview with MY; *RS89*; HGW interview with BW; *RS69*; HGW interview with Joyce Mitchell; *WSOOL*; RE interview with Leo Lyons; *THRsp*; David Crosby and Carl Gottlieb, *Long Time Gone: The Autobiography of David Crosby* (New York: Doubleday, 1988); Payne: Charles Cross, *Room Full of Mirrors: A Biography of Jimi Hendrix* (New York: Hyperion, 2005); Joel Makower interview with Tom Law; HGW interview with ML.

13. THE AFTERMATH

HGW interview with PT; HGW interview with CO; HGW interview with ML; HGW interview with PS; *WSOOL*; "A 19-Hour Concert Brings Quiet Back to Max Yasgur's Cows," *New York Times*, August 18, 1969; HGW interview with SG; HGW interview with RP; "Nightmare in the Catskills," *New York Times*, August 19, 1969; "Woodstock Farmer Asks Another Fest," *Wayne* (N.J.) *Today*, August 19, 1969; HGW interview with Artie Ripp; HGW interview with AK; HGW interview with LMB; "Morning After at Bethel," *New York Times*; August 20, 1969; "Happening in Bethel," *Boston Globe*, August 19, 1969; "Aftermath at Bethel: Garbage & Creditors," by Al Aronowitz, *New York Post*, August 19, 1969; Joel Makower interview with Joel Rosenman; HGW interview with Joyce Mitchell.

EPILOGUE

"Carlos Santana," *Mojo*, November 2008; Joel Makower interview with AH; "Woodstock 25 Years Later" by Greil Marcus, *Interview*, August 1994; Brian Hassett blog, January 20, 2009; "Woodstock Without the Mud," by Gail Collins, *New York Times*, January 21, 2009.

INDEX

free kitchens, 98–101, 143–44, 155, 201, 204, 225–26. *See also* Hog Farm

free stage, 72, 98–101, 157–58, 186. *See also* Hog Farm

Friedman, Jane, 86–87, 97, 132, 205, 272

Ganoung, Don, 73–74, 96, 110–11, 125, 136, 151–52, 153, 163, 272

garbage removal, 129, 151, 195–198, 240–46, 249–51

Garcia, Jerry, 3, 25, 187–90, 195, 215. *See also* Grateful Dead

gate crashing, 71–72, 102, 175–76

Geffen, David, 55

Gimme Shelter film, 259

Glick, Jeff, 19

Goldmacher, Don, 202–3

Goldstein, Stanley, 28, 31–33, 49, 54, 56–57, 63, 65–68, 73–74, 98–101, 108, 110, 113, 115–17, 141–43, 161, 198, 206, 225–26, 242–43, 272

Goodrich, Peter, 70, 78–79, 112, 138, 154–55, 203

Gould, Jonathan, 179–80, 272

Graham, Bill, 43, 60–61, 76–78, 82, 83, 88, 104, 139, 168, 177, 214, 221, 273

Grant, Jim, 100–101

Grateful Dead, 24, 26–28, 83, 164, 190, 195–96, 212, 215–17

Grease Band, 103, 223, 226

Green Day, 262

Greenwich Village, New York, 13–14

Gross, Richard, 124

Grossman, Albert, 37, 46–47, 82, 83, 164, 229, 246–47, 253, 273

Gulfstream Race Track. *See* Miami Pop Festival

Guthrie, Arlo, 83, 191–92

hallucinogens. *See* acid; drugs; STP

Hanley, Bill, 61–62, 157–58, 175

Hardin, Tim, 38, 39, 82, 181, 186, 189, 273

Harris, David, 194

Harry, Debbie, 41

Hart, Malcolm, 146–47

Hartley, Keef, 131, 212

Hassett, Brian, 266

Havens, Richie, 6, 83, 164–65, 172–73, 181–83, 273

headliner system, 85

Head Shop South, 18–24

health issues, 53–54, 127, 197–98. *See also* medical issues; sanitation

helicopters, 29, 127, 138, 164, 173, 179–80, 187, 201–4, 232

Hells Angels, 259

Helm, Levon, 37–38. *See also* Band, The

Hendrix, Jimi, 1–2, 5, 27–30, 32–33, 40, 82, 84–85, 181, 237–39

Herrera, Fred, 187–90